Around Britain By Cake

Caroline Taggart worked in publishing for 30 years before being asked to write *I Used to Know That*, which became a *Sunday Times* bestseller. Her later books include *My Grammar and I (or should that be 'Me'?)*, *Her Ladyship's Guide to the Queen's English, The Book of English Place Names* and *The Book of London Place Names*. As a result, she has appeared frequently on BBC Breakfast and on national and regional radio, talking about such life-changing subjects as whether Druids Cross should have an apostrophe and, if so, where it should go.

Writing *Around Britain By Cake* has given her the opportunity to explore several other lifelong passions: travelling, talking to interesting people and eating self-indulgent things without feeling (too) guilty about it.

www.carolinetaggart.co.uk

@citaggart

AROUND BRITAIN BY CAKE

CAROLINE TAGGART

Published by AA Publishing, a trading name of AA Media Limited,
Fanum House, Basing View, Basingstoke, Hampshire, RG21 4EA, UK.
www.theAA.com

First published in 2014 under the title *A Slice of Britain*
This paperback edition published 2017

A CIP catalogue record for this book is available from the
British Library.

ISBN: 978-0-7495-7878-7

Editor: Donna Wood
Page layout: Tracey Freestone
Cake illustrations: Becca Thorne
Map illustration: David Wardle
Cover: May van Millingen

Printed and bound in the UK

A05523

Our books carrying the FSC label are printed on FSC
certified paper. FSC is the only forest certification scheme
endorsed by the leading environmental organisations.

Contents

GREAT BRITAIN

Aberdeen
Kirriemuir
Dundee
Cupar
EDINBURGH
Galashiels
Melrose
Selkirk
Ecclefechan
Keswick
Whitehaven
Grasmere
Helmsley
Whitby
Pickering
Kendal
Ripon
York
Chorley
Pontefract
Eccles
MANCHESTER
Hathersage
Conwy
Rhos-on-Sea
Bolsover
Bakewell
Wirksworth
Grantham
Aberffraw
Betws-y-Coed
Ashbourne
Melton Mowbray
Market Drayton
Oakham
Downham Market
Bosworth
Shrewsbury
Norwich
Ludlow
Coventry
Rothwell
Southwold
Banbury
Cambridge
Sandy
Lavenham
Clare
Long Melford
Witney
Harwich
Cardiff
LONDON
Orpington
Bath
Sandwich
Sherborne
Dover
Cattistock
Brighton
Folkestone
Newton Poppleford
Tavistock
Portreath
Truro
Redruth

For all my fellow members of Inebriate Tours –
in recognition of many years of friendship
and self-indulgence

A NOTE ON THE RECIPES

Most of the people I interviewed in the course of this book use recipes that are closely guarded secrets; unless I have specifically stated otherwise, the recipes I have given are *not* those used for the commercially available products mentioned. They come from a variety of sources that span a hundred years or more and have, where necessary, been adapted to suit the modern kitchen. Nonetheless, all should produce something acceptably authentic.

Some recipes give instructions for making shortcrust pastry, but ready-made pastry may be substituted in any of these recipes: 150g of pastry refers to the finished weight, produced from 100g of flour and 50g of fat. Many people prefer to use half butter and half lard for shortcrust pastry, as it gives a 'shorter', crumblier result; vegetarians and others who choose not to use lard may use vegetable fats or all butter.

When recipes ask you to grease a baking sheet or griddle, use a little extra butter or other fat: don't take it from the quantity specified in the ingredients.

Temperatures for fan ovens are usually 20°C lower than those for conventional ovens – check your manufacturer's instructions.

Introduction

There's a Caffè Nero five minutes' walk from where I live. I realise I am not alone in this – there's a Caffè Nero within five minutes' walk of almost everyone in London. But bear with me; it's relevant.

I spend more time in this café than I would if I had a proper job. I like it. It boasts the best espresso this side of Milan.

Those last two sentences are completely unconnected, because as it happens I don't drink coffee. It feels faintly wasteful to reject the exotic delights of an americano or a cappuccino, an espresso or a macchiato, but I don't care. I always have tea.

I usually have a *pain au raisin* too. If I felt like a change, I could have a croissant or a *pain au chocolat*. If I felt adventurous (or anti-French), I could go for a Belgian chocolate muffin or a Sicilian lemon cheesecake. I could cross the Atlantic into the realm of chocolate brownies, or cross the street to Patisserie Valerie and have a *tarte au citron*.

My options are almost limitless. But they aren't very British.

Don't get me wrong. I have nothing against the foreignness of any of these foods. I'm a consenting adult and I wouldn't eat them if I didn't like them. But their multi-nationalness set me to thinking about British cakes. After all, we invented tea – not the drink, obviously, but the meal – and we must once have had plenty of sweet things to go with it.

Five minutes' further thought made me realise that we had and we still do; also that they once differed a great deal from one part of the country to another. Nowadays, thanks to the growth of supermarkets and the use of preservatives, I could buy Eccles Cakes, Dundee Cake and Bath Buns in almost any town in Britain, but surely they must once have been local delicacies.

So that's where this book was born: in Caffè Nero in Pimlico. Why, I thought, shouldn't I travel round the country and sample some traditional British cakes – and buns and tarts and biscuits? I could talk to people who were making them and see if I could find out why they originated when and where they did, and why they were still important today – if, indeed, they are.

It would be particularly interesting for me, because it would tell me something about an aspect of British life that, given my hybrid background, was a bit of a mystery.

When people ask me where I come from I'm always tempted to ask, 'How long have you got?' My parents were Scottish but I was born in London and brought up in New Zealand. We moved back when I was 15; I finished my schooling in south London, went to university in Sheffield, then came back to the capital, where I have lived all my adult life. So now I'm a Londoner – through and through, and deeply proud of it – but for a long time I was more or less a foreigner wherever I went. My vocabulary, for example, was partly Scottish, partly Kiwi, partly Standard English, and certainly as a child I wasn't aware which was which. Didn't everyone carve a Sunday roast on an ashet? I have no trace of a Scottish accent – why should I? I've never lived there – except when I say the word Aberdeen. It was my parents' home city and I pronounce it the way they did. I know the names of lots of New Zealand birds, which comes in handy for Scrabble and really irritates opponents who don't know a weka from a takahe. And in recent years I have come to be seen as an expert on the English language, having written books about grammar and the so-called Queen's English. Hybrid, did I say? A cross between a mongrel and a muggle is more like it.

One of the things I missed out on in New Zealand was the regional and class divide over what you called meals. School dinners were unheard of – we took sandwiches to school and called it lunch. I had no idea that that was posh. When we got home from school we had a glass of milk and a biscuit or two, but that didn't have a name. In the evening it was dinner, but back in the 1960s that was meat and two veg, the same – I thought – as everyone else.

You'll notice that we never had tea.

The whole question of tea-the-meal is complicated. Mrs Beeton, the 19th century's most famous cookery writer, was probably being shrewder than she realised when she said, 'There is tea and tea.' She went on to differentiate between 'the substantial family repast in the house of the early diner' and 'the afternoon cosy, chatty affairs that the late diners have instituted'.

Tea itself – the drink – reached Europe in the 16th century but until the 1780s was so heavily taxed in Britain that only the richest could afford it. If you wanted a less extravagant drink to accompany your cake, it was likely to be a light wine such as Madeira (hence the Madeira Cake). By the mid-19th century, however, tea was widely available and affordable, and became the standard thing to drink in the late afternoon.

Afternoon tea is said to have been invented by Anna, Duchess of Bedford, a friend of Queen Victoria, to tide her over the long gap between a light luncheon and dinner served at half-past seven or eight o'clock. (Apparently she preferred Darjeeling, which would have been a novelty in her day and kept her a cut above the *nouveaux* tea drinkers.) She took to inviting friends to join her and started a trend for having a little refreshment around five o'clock.

The Duchess's meal consisted of a cup of tea and a few delicate sandwiches or cakes, but over the next half-century or so afternoon tea grew into a more substantial affair and might include several kinds of sandwiches, vol-au-vents, jellies and 'creams'. It even required a special, loose 'tea gown', presumably with the stays unlaced or removed underneath it, to give a bit of breathing space (literally and figuratively) before Madam had to be squeezed back into her corset and the tight-fitting dress she would wear for dinner.

In country houses, tea could be even more sustaining, served after the rigours of the day's huntin' and shootin', to hungry men who would have no trouble working up an appetite again when dinner was served a couple of hours later.

But whatever form it took, afternoon tea was a luxury. What farmers, factory workers and other less privileged persons ate was very different. Generally known as 'high tea', it might include bacon, sausages or cold meat, bread and cake, and it would be on the table as soon as the men came home from work.

In addition to serving different purposes, these two kinds of tea also involved two different types of cake: the delicate 'fancy' that was appropriate fare for a lady of quality; and something more solid that would keep a working man going – after all, a farmer coming in for his tea at five or six o'clock would, in the summertime at least, go out and do several more hours' work before it got dark. A few dainty sandwiches and a bit of feather-light sponge just wouldn't do.

The high tea could also be embellished for a special occasion. Arnold Bennett's novel *Anna of the Five Towns*, published in 1902, describes one, intended to celebrate a betrothal, as being 'of the last richness and excellence, exquisitely gracious to the palate, but ruthless in its demands on the stomach'. At one end of the table was a fowl, at the other 'a hot pork pie, islanded in liquor, which might have satisfied a regiment', and in between pikelets, crumpets, toast, sardines, ham and various sorts of bread and cake. While reeling at the sheer quantity of the food, I was impressed that in Arnold Bennett's Staffordshire there was a clear distinction between a pikelet and a crumpet. My investigations into this subject, which I'll tell you about later, had led me to believe that this was a very unclear area indeed.

The concept of little cakes or tarts as a treat for ladies goes back to Henry VIII's time (or it does if you believe the story about Richmond Maids of Honour); 'jumbles' were certainly popular at the court of Elizabeth I and we know that the Tudors used something we would recognise as puff pastry. But the more substantial kind of cake is older than that. In the days when housewives or village bakeries baked bread on a regular basis, 'cake' was no more than a spiced, sweetened bread, sometimes enlivened with the addition of dried fruits. This wouldn't have been an everyday thing – in poor households, any deviation from the path of strict necessity was reserved for special occasions. But it explains why recipes from medieval times tend to use the words bread and cake, or cakes and buns, or even cakes and biscuits, more or less interchangeably; and why so many regions have their own variation on the theme of fruit bread.

Nowadays the distinction between a bread and a cake is clearer: broadly speaking, bread uses yeast, cake doesn't. In the days before clean water (never mind tea) was readily available, many households brewed their own beer and the yeast or barm that this produced was the principal raising agent until baking powder came along in the 19th century. Beating eggs until you were blue in the face was another way of lightening a yeast-free mixture: an old recipe for an 8kg wedding cake, quoted by the pioneering cookery journalist Florence White in the 1930s, took four hours to put together, because of the amount of whisking recommended for the eggs. She reported that the result made it 'quite worth while', which in her day would have been more enthusiastic than it sounds now. As I was to discover, if eggs were in short supply you could also do great things with cider or vinegar.

As for the regional specialities, any local cuisine develops from the ingredients that are available and the equipment to hand. So, in Wales and other regions where few households had an oven, 'griddle cakes', cooked on a bakestone, emerged; in Scotland and the North of England, where the climate made it difficult to grow wheat, the grain that went into flour – and therefore into cakes – was oats. And, in the days when most people didn't travel much, if your ancestor took it into her head to make a pastry filled with dried fruit and form it into a boat shape, and my ancestor had the same idea 50km down the road but made a triangle, there would have been no cross-fertilisation of ideas: the boat and the triangle would have remained as regional specialities.

Of course some people did travel – and those who did brought back exotic ingredients. In the Middle Ages caraway, ginger and other spices were a way of making food tastier (and longer lasting) – as, in the centuries that followed, were sugar, rum and many other foodstuffs that weren't indigenous to this country. It was no different in principle from today's use of Belgian chocolate and Sicilian lemon (or Thai lemongrass, Japanese soy or Mexican chilli). Over a period of time these ingredients went from being exotic and unaffordable to a treat for high days and holidays to more or less commonplace; they were early, tentative steps towards the creation of an international cuisine.

If I'm in Caffè Nero first thing in the morning, I'm always amused by the number of people holding pre-meeting meetings. 'What are we going to say to this guy?' two colleagues ask each other over their cappuccinos at half-past eight, before confidently setting off to see their client at nine. It harks back to the original 18th-century coffee houses, where business was often done and which famously spawned the insurance brokers Lloyd's of London. But those coffee houses were strictly male preserves. It wasn't until 1864, when the Aerated Bread Company opened the first tea room, that it ceased to be shocking for women to eat out without a male escort. A late 19th-century tea room was a perfectly genteel place for a lady to go either alone or with a female friend. In the early 21st, my Caffè Nero is full of women on their own, often with laptops, quietly getting on with their work.

Some of these ideas were in my head when I set off on my travels; some were answers to questions that arose over the following months. I met a lot of fascinating people, many of them running businesses that their great-grandfathers had established and that they were hoping to pass on to their own children. Others were newcomers to the baking business who, for one reason or another, had decided to revive a local tradition. What they all had in common was their enthusiasm: they were passionate about their product, about using local and organic ingredients and about preserving something they saw as part of their local heritage. Even if some of them did then ship their products to London, Tokyo or Wellington.

When I embarked on this project everyone said, 'You'll put on a lot of weight.' I didn't, as it happened, because I was doing a lot of running around and skipped a lot of meals. I wouldn't have missed it for the world, but it wasn't a healthy few months and I really don't urge you to try it.

Because, when you get right down to it, however you attempt to justify it with thoughtful questions about history and provenance, writing a book about cake is an idea born of pure gluttony. I just like to think it was gluttony with an enquiring mind.

Prologue

Richmond Maids of Honour

WHERE BETTER TO START MY TRAVELS than somewhere close to my own doorstep? The Original Maids of Honour bakery and tea shop is a pleasant leafy walk from Kew Gardens Station, though it's easy to be sidetracked by the parade of shops as you come out of the Tube. The Kew Bookshop is the highlight and I allowed myself a few minutes of self-indulgence and expenditure. Then the window of the Spirited Wines shop suggested that I should defy Cognac and discover other cult brandies from France. Tempting. But it was 11 o'clock in the morning and I was on a mission to drink tea and eat cake, so I moved swiftly on …

Legend has it that Henry VIII, snaffling one of the little pastries that were being served to Anne Boleyn and her ladies-in-waiting, proclaimed that from that day forward they should be named in honour of those ladies. He also demanded that the recipe be handed over to him and kept under lock and key in Richmond Palace. One version of the story goes on to say that the maid who had done the baking was confined to the palace and ordered to make the cakes only for the king.

This illustration of Henry's high-handedness may have a ring of truth about it, but the rest of the story is surely pretty improbable: a maid of honour wouldn't have been rolling her sleeves up in the kitchen one minute and cavorting with the king's mistress the next. There's also no way that a man of Henry's known voraciousness would have been satisfied with only one of these delicacies: they're not much more than bite-sized.

Whatever its origins may be, the recipe has been a favourite in the area for hundreds of years. Richmond Palace was largely demolished under the command of Oliver Cromwell, so the pastry cook, looking for another job, may well have thrown his confidentiality agreement out of the window. Certainly by the early 18th century the Maids of Honour secret was in the hands of a baker in Richmond; shortly afterwards it came into the possession of a family called Newens, who were until recently proprietors of the present eponymous premises in Kew Road.

The first thing you see as you enter the shop is an array of goodies that makes you glad you had a meagre bowl of fruit for breakfast. Quiches and other pastry-clad savouries straight ahead; cakes to the left. Pear tarts, lemon tarts, a mini-plethora of chocolate and a perhaps less than traditional passion fruit cheesecake. Then, waiting modestly in the background, more Jane Seymour than Anne Boleyn, a large tray of Maids of Honour.

The tea shop (turn right as you go in) is a step back in time. On this grey February morning, the room looked as I imagine it must have looked for 50 years. The tables and chairs were slightly shabby dark wood, the light fittings wrought iron, the china blue and white Spode. It was a carefully cultivated image of down-at-heel gentility.

That said, the service was both prompt and friendly. My pot of tea was generous and came with separate hot water – I easily got four cups out of it, which satisfied even me. Sadly, I was so preoccupied with writing notes that I scoffed my Maid of Honour without taking any notice and had to have another. Scoffed is the wrong word, really. It was too small and delicate for that, about 5cm across and 3cm high, with soft, flaky puff pastry and a custardy filling. Served slightly warm, it was entirely delicious; it took considerable willpower not to order a third.

After all these years and all that passing from hand to hand, the exact recipe is a closely guarded secret, but here is something similar.

Maids of Honour

Makes about 12

250g puff pastry
icing sugar, to serve

For the filling
150g curd cheese, such as ricotta
30g candied lemon peel, finely chopped
juice and finely grated rind of 1 lemon
30g caster sugar
25g ground almonds
2 medium egg yolks, beaten

1. Preheat the oven to 200°C/400°F/gas mark 6. Grease and flour 12 patty tins.
2. On a lightly floured surface, roll out the pastry thinly and cut out 12 circles using an 8cm cutter. Line the patty tins with the pastry.
3. In a large bowl, thoroughly mix the curd cheese, lemon peel, juice and rind, caster sugar and ground almonds. Add the beaten egg yolks and mix until everything is well combined.
4. Place a dessertspoon of mixture in each pastry case. Place the tins in the preheated oven and bake for about 20 minutes until well risen and golden.
5. Turn the little tarts out on to a wire rack and leave to cool. Sprinkle with icing sugar before serving. They are best served very fresh, while they are still slightly warm.

It occurred to me that if I had to eat two – and resist the temptation to have three – of everything I was tasting in the course of the book, I could do myself serious damage. So, first lesson learned: pay attention while eating.

On the other hand, I'd made my first excursion and I was home in time – I was going to say for lunch, but I decided I should perhaps skip lunch just this once.

Let's say I was home in time to start planning a longer trip.

1

Cornwall

Saffron, Saints and the Odd Giant

After that outing to Kew I did some research, so that I wouldn't find myself wandering around the country at random. I made contact with a lot of people, most of whom were incredibly enthusiastic about the project and said they would be delighted to talk to me. Only then did I realise what a challenge I had taken on. There were just so many places to visit, so many cakes that I could try. I was excited, but a little bit daunted. Had I bitten off more than I could chew, before I'd sampled more than a couple of tiny custard tarts?

But I wasn't going to back out now. I began planning a route and decided that, although I wasn't intending to travel the entire distance from Land's End to John o' Groats, starting in deepest Cornwall and working north and east made a lot of sense. A few years before, I'd been to Newlyn, a pretty little artists' retreat that is also the most important fishing port in England. I hadn't realised then that this would be relevant to a book about cake, but that was before I started reading about pilchards.

The name of Cornish Heavy Cake does it no favours, because not many of us speak Cornish these days. *Heavy* in this context has nothing to do with weight; it comes from the cry *hevva,* meaning a shoal of fish. A lookout, known as the *huer*, used to give this cry when he spotted a dark red shadow under the water indicating the presence of pilchards. He also sounded a horn (setting up a *hue and cry*), then, by means of hand signals, directed the fishermen to the spot where they should cast their nets. There's still a former huer's hut on the cliff above Newquay: it's probably 700 years old, round and squat, with an external staircase and a square chimney described as 'typically Cornish late medieval', a style of architecture about which I can tell you very little.

The point about all this, as far as my cake investigations were concerned, was that, on hearing the cry, the womenfolk knew that their husbands would soon be home for their tea and quickly threw a *hevva* cake together. It was a simple recipe whose charm lay in the fact that it was decorated with a diamond criss-cross to represent the fishing net.

Cornish Heavy Cake

Makes 1 thin cake

175g plain flour
¼ tsp fine salt
1–2 tsp ground ginger, cinnamon or mace, or a combination, to taste (optional)
40g granulated sugar
40g each of unsalted butter and lard (or 80g butter, if you prefer)
75g currants
25–50g chopped mixed peel (optional)
about 2 tbsp milk or water

1. Preheat the oven to 190°C/375°F/gas mark 5. Lightly grease a baking sheet.
2. Mix the flour, salt, spices (if using) and sugar together. Rub in the fat until the mixture resembles fine breadcrumbs. Mix in the other ingredients, including just enough milk or water to make a stiff dough.

3 On a lightly floured surface, roll out the dough to about 1cm thick and in a rough oval shape. Carefully lift on to the baking sheet. Make a criss-cross pattern on the top with a sharp knife.

4 Bake in the preheated oven for about 25–30 minutes, until golden (it won't rise very much). Serve warm, or allow to cool, then store in an airtight container.

Another Cornish speciality I had read about was Saffron Cake, which is odd, as saffron was never widely grown in the county. Tradition has it that it was introduced by the Phoenicians, who traded it for Cornish tin well over 2,000 years ago. But Jane Grigson, perhaps Britain's leading cookery writer of the 1980s, stated firmly that this isn't so: the Phoenicians, renowned traders though they were, never made it to Cornwall. The legend persists, however, as legends do. In fact, although saffron was once grown in profusion around Saffron Walden and in other parts of East Anglia, imports from Spain have supplemented the home-grown variety for over 700 years. It has always been fantastically expensive – as many as 150,000 flowers may be needed to produce 1kg of spice – so it's just as well that a very little goes a long way. A word of warning, though, from all the experts: never buy saffron powder. It may be cheaper, but it's like drinking Lambrusco when you were expecting Laurent-Perrier. Splash out on the real thing, which comes in strands.

Saffron-flavoured cakes or buns, known variously as Cornish Tea Treats, Cornish Revels or Feasten Cakes, were traditionally served at wakes – not the funereal kind, but village festivals in honour of the saint to whom the local church was dedicated. It's said that there are more saints in Cornwall than there are in heaven, so you could make these cakes pretty well any time you liked and find a saint whose feast day it was. There are many recipes for baked goods using saffron, but I particularly liked this one because it contained another Cornish speciality, clotted cream.

Cornish Feasten Cakes

Makes about 15

a large pinch of saffron strands
150ml warm milk
450g plain flour
1 tsp ground cinnamon
1 x 7g sachet fast-action dried yeast
100g unsalted butter
175ml clotted cream
1 medium egg, beaten
50g granulated sugar
100g currants
milk and sugar, to glaze

1. Crumble the saffron into the warm milk and leave to infuse for about 30 minutes. Meanwhile sift the flour and cinnamon into a large bowl, add the yeast and rub in the butter until the mixture resembles coarse breadcrumbs.
2. Strain the saffron milk into a bowl, and beat the cream into it. Mix in the beaten egg, then add this mixture to the flour. Add the sugar and currants and mix well to form a moist dough.
3. Cover the bowl with a tea-towel and leave to double in size (about 1–1½ hours).
4. Knead the dough briefly, then shape into small buns and place on a greased baking sheet. Leave to prove for half an hour.
5. Meanwhile, heat the oven to 190°C/375°F/gas mark 5.
6. Brush the buns with milk and sprinkle a little sugar over the top. Bake in the preheated oven for about 25 minutes, until golden, then cool on a wire rack. Eat fresh or store in an airtight tin for a few days.

I'd read about all this before I left home, but my reason for going to Cornwall was to talk to people. When I discovered that Marion Symonds thought her Portreath Bakery was the only one in Cornwall making Saffron Heavy Cake – two local traditions in one cake – I knew I had to visit her. Her response to my email had been warm and enthusiastic, but where on earth was Portreath?

I'd initially planned to hire a car in Exeter and drive round the Southwest. That was before I discovered how good the public transport was down there. I could catch a train direct from Paddington to Redruth, centre of the UNESCO World Heritage site known as the Cornwall and West Devon Mining Landscape, and from there a bus would get me to Portreath in half an hour.

Portreath is only about 5km from Redruth by the main road, but before the bus left Redruth it wound through residential areas like a school bus or one that collects elderly people to take them to a day centre. It was so unlike the bus routes I was used to in London that I was surprised we didn't stop to ring doorbells and lend supporting arms to old ladies with Zimmer frames. Then we got out of town and started to speed along, stopping every now and again to let people on and off. There were never more than eight people on the bus, but it was never the same eight for long. People were using this amenity in the middle of nowhere (and in the middle of the morning in the middle of the week) – and they all said hello. Not specifically to me, but to everyone. It was lovely, and so was Portreath. It's a gentle, unspoilt fishing-cum-tourist village and as I sat outside the bakery with Marion and her husband Pete, half the village stopped by to say hello, to tease my hosts about the hard life they seemed to be leading that morning and to sample the cake that had been made for me.

In real life Marion was as vivacious as she'd sounded in her email – and the fact that she was wearing a saffron-coloured jacket seemed to emphasise her passion for all things Cornish. I'd timed my visit well, because Pete's great-uncle, retired Captain Gordon Greenslade, had turned 101 the previous day and they were full of enthusiasm for his story and the way it linked to Heavy Cake. Uncle Gordon wasn't a fisherman, but he was a seaman and his mother's home-made Heavy Cake always went with him on his voyages. At the outbreak of World War II he was skipper of a coasting vessel called the SS *Islesman*; it dealt in coal and ore with the ports of South Wales and Northwest England and was the only Portreath ship to survive the war. Marion told me that Heavy Cake was as valuable on the colliery ships as it was to the fishing fleet.

'It was really nutritious, really calorific,' she said. 'It had both butter and lard in it. People forget that lard is fantastic for cooking with: the salt comes out and gives a really nice taste. When Uncle Gordon was coming up for 100, we made Saffron Heavy Cake for a TV programme we were on called *Britain's Best Bakery*. I invited him to come along and taste it. He loved it: it brought back so many memories, it was quite emotional.'

The fat has keeping qualities, but so do the sugar and the fruit, important for sailors who were often away from home for six weeks at a time. 'They couldn't get fresh produce, but the cake would stay fresh. It's quite dense in texture but has a really fine crumb and an absolutely delicious flavour.'

Traditional Heavy Cake doesn't have saffron in it, so Marion makes a plain version too. But she's a great one for giving recipes a little twist, and Saffron Heavy Cake is her own invention. She was cagey about the details, but had advice on using saffron that ran contrary to what many other people say: 'The best way is to pour boiling water on it. Some people suggest using warm milk, to keep the texture of the saffron, but actually the fat in the milk stops the flavour coming out. The other thing we do is soak the currants in green tea, which really complements the saffron flavour. Even if you're using saffron in a savoury dish – say you're making paella at home – wash the rice in green tea and you'll taste the saffron better.'

With Saffron Heavy Cake, after soaking the fruit, Marion advised laying it out to 'rest' for a while. Otherwise, because the batter is quite thick, you risk breaking the fruit up as you mix it in. Looking at her version, I could see that the currants were completely intact, sitting separately amid the clearly delineated yellow crumbs. It wasn't densely fruity, like a fruit cake. It was a cake with fruit in it. She'd done away with the diamond criss-cross: her version was topped with granulated sugar. Not too saffrony, not too sweet; a lovely, delicate flavour. She wouldn't let me in on any more secrets, but told me she had devised a cake mix, the Cornish Luxury Saffron Cake™ – available in the MadeMarion range through her website and other outlets across the country – that would allow me to make my own by adding only butter and milk.

Marion is a great advocate for Cornish food: her television show *Made with Marion* is broadcast on a local channel and features local produce; she's campaigning for a bakery school to be established in Cornwall and in the meantime trains local youngsters in her own bakery. She's also involved with Real del Monte in Mexico, a mining town twinned with Redruth. Cornish miners took mining equipment and pasties there in the 19th century, with the result that Real del Monte now has the world's first pasty museum.

Would you believe it? There's a pasty museum in Mexico, but not in Cornwall. That's another thing Marion is working on. ('And she'll get it,' Pete said, with the air of a man who had been watching his wife working on things for some time.) There is, however, an annual Mining and Pasty Festival in Redruth in early September, with a delegation from Real del Monte giving away Mexican-style pasties at the closing concert on the Sunday night.

Marion's bakery was making pasties the morning I was there, so I was privileged to watch some expert crimping in action. That's the technical term for making the decorative twists on the sealed edge of the pastry. The Cornish Pasty has European Protected Geographical Indication status, which means it has to be made in Cornwall and also that its ingredients are strictly defined: steak, potato, swede and onion, yes, but there mustn't be a carrot or a pea in sight. Pasties didn't really count as the sort of teatime treat I was investigating so, hoping to move them out of the 'entirely savoury' category, I asked about the tradition of having meat at one end and fruit at the other, a full two-course meal in one pastry casing. Two or three of the bakers smiled in a slightly pitying way, as if they were wise uncles and I a foolish child who'd been taken in by some well-worn tourist scam. 'They say that,' Marion explained, 'but we've traced it back with the World Heritage people and there's no evidence.' I would have to wait until I got to Bedfordshire to find out about that.

Saffron Cake is different from Heavy Cake, even if it's Saffron Heavy Cake: Marion's Saffron Cake is made from an enriched dough, containing yeast. She uses the same dough to make Saffron Buns, but dividing it into buns, as opposed to baking it as a single cake, produces a different texture. It's to do with the way you mould them, apparently. 'They rise differently, prove differently, bake differently,' she said. My grasp of chemistry wasn't up to taking in the details; however, sitting with a Saffron Bun alongside a piece of Heavy Cake, I could see a clear difference: the cake was crumbly, the bun squashy and malleable. 'In its raw state,' Marion said, 'it feels like Play-Doh.' It was also a wonderful DayGlo colour. As with the Saffron Heavy Cake, the fruit benefited from being washed in green tea.

You could contemplate eating one of Marion's Saffron Buns on your own, but she continues an old Cornish tradition of making them in different sizes for different purposes. Her Tea Treat Buns, twice the size of a normal bun, are for sharing on special occasions – they're associated with Sunday School outings or family activities. When the need arises, she still does a half-sized Saffron Bun (accompanied by a cocktail-sized pasty) for funerals.

Back in Redruth later in the day, I bought a Saffron Cake made by Simply Cornish of Penzance, a brand produced by Cornwall's oldest commercial bakery, Warrens'. It was larger and flatter than Marion's Saffron Buns – roughly circular and about 12cm in diameter. I was staying the night in a friend's holiday home, so was able to contemplate it in my solitary state the following morning. It suggested (on the packet, I mean; I wasn't yet at the stage where I thought a cake was talking to me): 'Why not toast me and cover me in butter.' There was no question mark, so I took it as more or less a command, especially as it was just the right depth that if you split it, it fitted neatly in the toaster. Hot and buttered, it was *very* good. It tasted surprisingly undoughy, with plenty of raisins, sultanas and citrus flavours. It was also a lovely saffron yellow colour.

What was lacking, though, was the distinctive *taste* of the saffron. If it hadn't been for the label telling me it was a Saffron Cake, I'd have thought it was a delicious fruity teacake. As it is, I have to record a little disappointment. Analogy: many years ago I went to Ranthambore National Park in India in the hope of seeing tigers, but there were none to be seen. Ranthambore is one of the most beautiful places on earth, we went in the early morning, the light was simply magical and the photographers in the group were falling over themselves with excitement. If nobody had mentioned tigers in the first place, we would all have been ecstatic.

As with tigers, so with saffron, if you see what I mean.

Anyway, because of the citrusness, and because it was breakfast time, I added marmalade to my second slice. I was immediately reminded of Jim Carrey in one of the *Batman* films: 'Was that over the top? I can never tell.'

Half an hour later, head buzzing slightly, I decided it probably was.

In addition to its mining claims to fame, Redruth has plenty of charms. Wandering around to allow the Saffron-Cake-and-marmalade buzz to calm down, I discovered St Rumon's Gardens. This haven was surrounded by the ruins of the Druid's Hall, a Victorian precursor of the cinema, and was just the sort of peaceful garden you might find in the City of London amid the bombed-out shell of a Wren church. The differences were that, this being Cornwall, the garden's centrepiece was a palm tree, and it was dedicated to a saint I'd never heard of.

There was also a lovely needlework shop called The Sewing Studio, which had a brilliantly coloured patchwork quilt in the window. A notice told me that 'this quilt uses 2 x layer cakes plus 3 x ½ metre of three contrasting or toning fabrics'. I had absolutely no idea what a layer cake meant in this context, but I made a note of it in case it was another local speciality.

It turned out not to be. It was a collection of 25 x 25cm squares of patchwork, normally sold in a packet of 42. Who knew?

But the cutest thing was a piece of public art in Fore Street. It was a collection of bronzes of old miners' boots that had been sculpted to look like dogs. The dogs' legs were all boots, a boot formed each one's back, with the toe curling up to make a tail, and boots had been used to make the heads and the ears. It made me smile as I walked past and mentally poked my tongue out at people who say this sort of thing is a waste of money.

Just beside the bronze was a promising-looking greengrocer-cum-grocery. Promising in the sense that it might sell me Redruth's other local speciality: Original Cornish Fairings™. I went in and sure enough there they were, in pretty boxes adorned with a map of Cornwall and a photograph of St Michael's Mount.

Fairing was originally a name given to anything sold at fairs – trinkets as well as edible treats. By the 18th century the word had come to be applied specifically to a sort of ginger biscuit and, according to Marion Symonds the previous day, Fairings were the subject of heated rivalry at fairs: competitive housewives of the day would bring their biscuits to be judged against those of their neighbours, just as later generations did with a Victoria Sponge. The benchmark was how well you achieved the distinctive cracking on the top. Nowadays, Marion had said, you put lots of baking powder in the mixture, so that the biscuits puff up in the oven, then turn the heat down part way through the cooking to make the tops crack.

Cornish Fairings

Makes about 12

200g plain flour
½ tsp fine salt
2 level tsp each of baking powder and bicarbonate of soda
2 level tsp each of ground ginger, cinnamon and mixed spice
100g unsalted butter or margarine
100g granulated sugar
6 tbsp golden syrup

1. Preheat the oven to 180°C/350°F/gas mark 4. Grease a large baking sheet.
2. In a large bowl, mix together the flour, salt, baking powder, bicarbonate of soda and spices. Rub in the fat until the mixture resembles fine breadcrumbs, then mix in the sugar.
3. Heat the golden syrup in a small pan until it becomes runny, then add to the mixture. Mix well to a dough texture.
4. Roll the mixture into balls the size of a walnut and place on the baking sheet. Place in the preheated oven, on the top shelf. When the biscuits begin to colour (after about 10 minutes), turn the oven down to 150°C/300°F/gas mark 2 and continue to bake for a further 5 minutes. The biscuits should flop and crack.

5 **Remove the baking sheet from the oven and transfer the biscuits to a wire rack to cool, using a palette knife. They will still be soft, but will firm up as they cool.**

Furniss – the only people who produce Fairings commercially – make several varieties: Stem Ginger & Honey Crunchy Biscuits come nearest to the tradition but the shop I was in also offered Orange & Lemon, Apple & Cinnamon and Spiced. I knew I was going to be eating a lot of ginger in the course of my travels, so I opted for Orange & Lemon. They were nice enough but, despite the quantities of lemon peel and orange peel detailed in the small print, I found them disappointingly uncitrussy. Perhaps I should have opted for ginger after all.

On sale in the same shop – and too decadent to resist – was Rodda's Classic Cornish Clotted Cream Shortbread, in a pretty tub done up to look like a cream churn. I remarked to the lady in the shop that I'd not come across this before. I meant that I didn't know the name Rodda, but I obviously hadn't made myself clear.

'Haven't you been to Cornwall before?' she asked.

Yes, I said, I'd just never heard of Rodda's.

I might have been speaking Klingon. The lady was friendly and helpful but baffled. How could I have been in Cornwall and not come across Rodda's?

By the time I'd been in three more shops I could understand her confusion. Rodda's brand name was everywhere and their cream extraordinarily good. The shortbread – which contained butter as well as clotted cream – was softer, less crumbly than the more conventional all-butter shortbread, but not to be despised for that. I later took it on a picnic and served it with raspberries, blackberries and (just a very little) clotted cream. I can vouch for that being a fine combination.

When I was ready to leave Redruth, I found I had an hour to wait for a train to Truro. The train journey took 11 minutes, but I reckoned that if a bus came along soon it'd be quicker to catch it.

It did and I did and it was another wonderfully wiggly journey like the one to Portreath. Redruth is 17.5km from Truro and the AA Route Planner suggested it would take 19 minutes. Not on the bus it didn't. Every time we reached a crossroads with a sign pointing to Truro (which was remarkably often once I started looking out for them), we turned the other way. We went through a place called Vogue and another called St Day, one called Carharrack and another called Gwennap, one called Frogpool and another called Perranwell, but we were still, at every junction, always 8km from Truro. But it didn't matter in the slightest: it was a lovely morning, the countryside was glorious, the bus driver called me 'Miss', which doesn't happen to me very often in the normal course of events, and people got on and off and said hello and goodbye and I could have done this all day if I hadn't had a cream tea to eat.

Although my plan was to spend the night in Tavistock, the Devon town which claims to have invented the cream tea, I felt duty bound to have one in Cornwall first. Charlotte's Tea House in Truro came highly recommended, so that was where I was going. In the meantime, and in between checking out the signposts, I read a useful book by Carolyn Martin that I'd picked up in Redruth. It was called, with a pleasing lack of whimsy, *Clotted Cream*.

In the days before modern transport reached remote areas, I learned, making clotted cream was a way of using up surplus milk. *Clotted* derives from *clout*, meaning a patch and referring to the way a thick, blister-marked crust forms on the top of the cream.

It required, of course, full cream milk, which would be left in a cool place overnight for the cream to rise, heated to near boiling point and kept at that heat until the desired crust formed. Then it would be left to stand again (for as much as 36 hours, depending on the temperature of the room) and the cream skimmed off. On no account should it be allowed to boil, as that would result in a milky skin rather than a creamy crust.

The rivalry between Cornwall and Devon on the subject of cream teas is well known, but Carolyn Martin enlightened me about the Cornish claim. According to legend, Giant Blunderbus from Dartmoor (which is firmly in Devon) exiled his favourite wife Jennie to Cornwall because she could not cook as well as his other three wives. She went to live in a cave on the Cornish cliffs, from which one day she spotted a Phoenician ship that was about to be set upon by wreckers. She lit a bonfire to warn the sailors and, as a reward, the Phoenician captain taught her the art of making clotted cream. 'This so delighted Giant Blunderbus,' Carolyn concluded, 'that he restored her to his home in Devon, where she taught the secret of this new food to all who came flocking to her door.'

Glossing lightly over Jane Grigson's assertion that the Phoenicians never made it to Cornwall, it would have been a shame to come all this way and not find a legend about giants. There are, after all, nearly as many giants in Cornwall as there are saints.

Less fanciful were some early travellers' tales: in the 1540s a physician named Andrew Boorde wrote that 'clotted cream is eaten more for a sensual appetite than for any good nourishment'. It may be relevant to note that Andrew Boorde gave up the opportunity to be a bishop because he couldn't endure the *rugorosite* of the religious life. That wonderful word means rigorousness or severity, so presumably Andrew had his views on the sensual appetite. Whether he indulged it in Devon or in Cornwall is not recorded.

Charlotte's Tea House is situated on the upper level of the old Coinage Hall in the centre of Truro. The hall was built in 1848, but is on the site of an older building; it dated back to 1802, described on a plaque outside as 'the halcyon days of Cornish tin mining'. The Tea House, though, is deliberately Victorian, with dark wood, ornate mirrors and waitresses in pinnies and little white caps. The one who served me called me 'my love' – something else that doesn't happen often. There was a sign on the wall asking that, out of consideration for other customers, we didn't use our mobile phones and – such was the atmosphere of the place or perhaps the good manners of the customers – nobody did. A far cry from the businesslike conversations in Caffè Nero.

I sat looking out of the window on to the cobbled high street and saw everything from a dust cart to a double-decker bus pass by. Truro is an odd combination of the old and the new. Its cathedral was completed as recently as 1910, but the town (as it then was) was an important port and mining centre 600 years before that. Despite the cobbles, the high street has such modern features as a Waterstones, a BHS and a River Island. And its deliberately olde worlde tea room is upstairs from a branch of Pizza Express. Which probably doesn't prove anything, but I had to think about something while I was waiting for my tea.

Charlotte's menu illustrated a cream tea in the Cornish style, with the jam on first and the cream on top. One suggested reason for this is that the substrate was originally a Cornish Split, more like a bread roll than a scone, served warm. Presumably if you put cream directly on to this it would melt or separate in some undesirable way, so the roll was spread with jam and the cream dolloped on top. But it is the subject of a great deal of controversy – the Devonians do it the other way round, for reasons I hoped to discover in Tavistock. In the meantime my tea had arrived and I needed to do it justice.

'Doing it justice' is perhaps a rather clinical way of putting it – it sounds as if I was eating out of a sense of duty. But there have been few occasions in my life when duty and pleasure overlapped so completely. The scone was soft and crumbly – 'short' in the pastry sense and also short in the length of time it spent on my plate. The strawberry jam was perfectly smooth and just right, not too sweet; the cream passed every visual test: it was a pale buttery colour and even smoother than the jam.

Once I'd eaten the scone I tried a little cream on its own on the tip of my teaspoon. It was flawless. But to all intents and purposes it had no taste at all.

This isn't a criticism. Far from it. It simply raises a point to which I would revert more than once in the course of my cake-eating: that texture can be as important as taste when it comes to food.

The other test that needs to be applied to a cream tea is this: do they give you so much cream and jam that you can't possibly fit them on to the available scone space, no matter how high you pile them? Charlotte's passed that with merit.

As I was paying the bill, I scrutinised the trolley on which the afternoon's offerings of cakes were displayed. They included quite the tallest Victoria Sponge I'd ever seen: probably 5cm of cake and a full 3cm of cream topped by another 5cm of cake. I thought of those snakes you see in wildlife programmes that can dislocate their jaw in order to get their mouths round improbably large prey. It's a trick that would come in handy here. There was also something that looked like a custard tart but, wondering if it was a local speciality I'd missed, I asked the waitress what it was.

'Egg custard,' she assured me. 'Lots of people think it's a cheesecake, but it's an egg custard, just like mother used to make.'

I'm not sure about my mother – she was more a Betty Crocker sort of girl – but I took her point.

2

Devon

Cream and Jam

I LEFT TRURO EARLY THAT AFTERNOON – skipping lunch was already becoming a habit – and took the train to Plymouth, crossing the magnificent Brunel bridge that takes you over the Tamar, out of Cornwall and into the Rest of the World. From Plymouth Station I caught a bus to Tavistock. Earlier in the day, crossing the Cornish peninsula by bus had felt both adventurous and fun, but coming out of Plymouth at four in the afternoon was frankly boring. We'd been going 15 minutes when we passed a shopping centre containing a KFC, an M&S Simply Food and a Pizza Hut. I live in the centre of London: I can sit in traffic any time I like. This wasn't why I'd come to Devon.

I amused myself by looking up statistics on my iPad and the conclusion I came to was, 'Well, what did you expect?' At around the 250,000 mark, Plymouth's population is almost half that of the entire county of Cornwall and nearly ten times that of any single Cornish town. It's twice the size of Exeter and far and away the biggest place this side of Bristol. It's so big that the bus I was on was full and no one talked to anyone. If I was going to find a traffic jam in the Southwest, this is where it would be.

However, once we were out of town our rate of progress improved and I found that rural Devon shared one characteristic at least with rural Cornwall: there were bus stops in the middle of nowhere where people got on and off buses. We passed along the fringes of

Dartmoor National Park and saw things I like to think were Dartmoor ponies but might just have been horses for all I know. And, all credit to the First Devon & Cornwall bus service, they must have known about the traffic because we arrived in Tavistock bang on time.

As I mentioned earlier, it's Tavistock that claims to be the home of the cream tea. Or perhaps I should specify the *Devon* cream tea, given what the Cornish have to say about the Phoenicians and Giant Blunderbus.

I was staying in the Bedford Hotel, which turned out to be bang in the centre of town, historic, charming and efficient. As I checked in the receptionist told me perkily that they'd given me a free upgrade to a double room.

'Oh, good,' I said. 'I'll tell my lover he doesn't have to doss in the bus station after all.'

No I didn't. I said something anodyne like 'How nice', and went and spread my belongings over the (marginally) larger space than I'd been expecting.

Tavistock took me by surprise. A friend who lives in Exeter had described it as the Aberdeen of the Southwest, because much of it is built in granite. It's situated on the banks of the River Tavy and in the early evening the riverside walk was a delight, even though the promised kingfishers didn't appear. (Perhaps 'promised' is overstating it: 'If you're lucky you might' were the words on the sign.) There are ruins of a Benedictine abbey dating back to 974, and splendid Victorian buildings erected under the auspices of the 7th Duke of Bedford, whose family has owned large tracts of land here since Henry VIII's time. Tavistock is also the birthplace of Sir Francis Drake and he was probably baptised in the very font that still stands in the 14th-century church. We can't be sure, because church records go back only to 1615, whereas both the font (15th century) and Sir Francis (born *c.*1540) are older than that, but he had to be baptised somewhere and the odds are that it was here.

So far, so charming. But there were lots of chain shops – a Dorothy Perkins, a WH Smith, an M&Co and even a Fat Face – which sat oddly in this environment. More to the point as far as I was concerned, why didn't it say 'Home of the Devon cream tea' all over the place? Why weren't there lots of old-style tea shops? There were coffee shops aplenty, but most of them offered a cream tea as an afterthought: on one menu it came further down the list than chilli with nachos, jacket potatoes and sandwiches; and the one café that illustrated its menu with a photo of a scone with cream and jam had it in the Cornish way, with the cream on top. The tourist leaflet I picked up in my hotel devoted a mere three lines to the cream tea and the woman on the cake stall in the market next morning said that yes, she'd read somewhere that it might have been developed in Tavistock. But that was as far as it went until I got to the Tourist Information Centre.

There, the lady was extremely enthusiastic. Yes, she could tell me all about it and indeed there was an information board in her office that went into some detail. Apparently, after Tavistock Abbey was plundered and badly damaged by marauding Vikings in AD 997, restoration was undertaken by Ordulph, Earl of Devon. He employed lots of local workers, whom the monks rewarded with bread, clotted cream and strawberry preserves. 'So the Devonshire cream tea was born,' the board concluded triumphantly. 'Cream teas were so popular that the monks continued to serve them to passing pilgrims and travellers.'

It also had a picture with the cream on first, which, my new-found friend told me, was the only way that made sense: 'Even if you have butter, you still want the cream to soak into the bits of scone that the butter's missed.'*

* I mentioned earlier that the book on clotted cream was refreshingly lacking in whimsy. Carolyn Martin, for all that she is based in Redruth, expresses the down-to-earth but decidedly pro-Devonian view, 'I find that you can get more cream on to the scone by putting it on first.' So perhaps doing it this way is simply to do with gluttony. Or, as Andrew Boorde put it, the sensual appetite.

She then led me out of the office into the passageway known as Court Gate, which once opened into the Great Court of the Abbey. There, closed up but still very much visible, was an ancient archway like a serving hatch through which, apparently, the cream teas were served to those tenth-century workers.

Perhaps the reason why this information isn't more widely known is that it's fairly recent: it seems to be based on a discovery that local historians made in 2004. Perhaps it simply isn't true. Or perhaps my Exeter friend hit the mark. When I mentioned that the Cornish disputed this story, she suggested that Tavistock was keeping a low profile because it didn't want to start a civil war.

Whatever the truth, I was going that afternoon on a nostalgic trip to sample a Devon cream tea. Newton Poppleford (half an hour by bus out of Exeter on the Sidmouth road) turned out to be a funny village, very long and thin, and surprisingly uncharming, given its wonderful name. There were a few thatched cottages, including Ye Olde Tolle House, which looked as if it might well have been there since 1758, as its plaque claimed. But only a few. It was also a difficult place to be a pedestrian, because the pavement kept disappearing, a bit of a hazard on this busy road. One redeeming feature: it boasted an exotic style of layabout – the empty bottle under the bench by the bus stop was Amaretto. But basically, the only reason for coming to Newton Poppleford is to sit in the lovely walled garden at the Southern Cross and have a cream tea. I used to come here 30 years ago when it was – I was going to say notorious, but perhaps fabled is a better word – as the place that put the 'Does it give you more cream and jam than you could possibly need in your wildest dreams?' test on the map. Miss McKenna, who ran it for many years, has retired now, but the current owners were working hard to maintain the reputation that once won her a mention in the *New York Times*.

I'd foolishly planned to go out for dinner, so I opted for the 'half' cream tea – just the one scone. It was enormous and still warm from the oven. I also suspected that there was only one size of cream and jam bowl and that I was getting the same quantity I would have been given if I'd ordered the full monty. I did my best but I managed about a third of it; across the garden I noticed an older couple reeling back to their car, obviously sated but leaving their jam and cream almost untouched. Behind me, a group of youngsters giggled with disbelief at the quantity and took photos as evidence. Two of them were American and asked how you pronounced the name of what they described as 'this pastry'. Fortunately, their English companion rhymed *scone* with *gone* rather than *bone*, so I didn't feel obliged to intervene. (I've always pronounced it to rhyme with *gone* and was delighted, when I was researching my book about the Queen's English, to discover that I was right and that rhyming it with *bone* was very non-U.) Then they started talking about *Pride and Prejudice and Zombies*, so I stopped eavesdropping and returned to my own tea.

Scone, as I said, sumptuous, with a nice bit of crustiness about it. Cream, sourced from a herd of Devon-based Guernseys, also had bits of crust, as if what had formed on the top had been stirred in; it was a richer colour and had more taste of its own than the Cornish version I had had the day before. Jam, strawberry of course, with a few pips in. Generally more emphasis on character, less on perfection.

The Southern Cross is an 18th-century Devon cob cottage, with bedrooms accessed by one of those steep, narrow, 'mind your head' staircases that B&Bs love. The website invited you to 'savour an intriguing mix of the rustic and the elegant in the charming, low-beamed tea room, with its hotch-potch of antique tables'. The cottage garden had that beautifully informal look that takes a lot of work to maintain. So, just as the Victorian fastidiousness of the Charlotte's tea was entirely in keeping with its surroundings, so the less 'refained' Southern Cross version suited its less formal setting.

I'd eaten a grand total of one cream tea in Cornwall and another in Devon and I'm not going to pronounce on which is better – though

I will stick my neck out and agree with the woman in the Tavistock Tourist Information Centre that it makes more sense to put the cream on first. I'll also return one last time to Carolyn Martin's book. She quotes the Reverend Richard Warner of Bath, who toured Cornwall in 1808 and wrote on the subject of clotted cream:

> *Devonshire had regaled us with this delicious article, before we reached Cornwall, but as soon as we had tasted the clouted cream of the latter … we acknowledged it was only here that this production could be had in perfection.*

Funny that a man of the cloth should be so unconcerned about starting a civil war.

3

Bath

A Tale of Two Buns

MY NEXT STOP was the home of two of England's most famous buns – the Bath Bun and the Sally Lunn. I realised, as I sat on the train from Exeter to Bath, that I was ignoring considerable tracts of apple and cider country, but I had plans to take in (as it were) Apple Cakes and Cider Cakes later.

Having made the reservation in a bit of a panic – I was committed to going that weekend and lots of places were full – I discovered that I had booked myself into a temperance hotel. I didn't know they still existed and I frittered away a certain amount of time on my train journey wondering what it would be like.

Imposing temperance is surely like imposing any other strongly held opinion on other people: it takes no account of what might make them feel comfortable. I imagined the hotel as having exclusively single beds, providing hot water for only a couple of hours morning and evening, and charging 5 shillings extra if you wanted a bath. I say 5 shillings because in my mind I was going back a bit: my hotel was in black and white and the proprietrix (for that was her title) was played by Joyce Grenfell. Or possibly Joyce Carey, who on her day off ran the station buffet in *Brief Encounter*.

And what about the other guests? Perhaps they smuggled whisky into their rooms for consolation in the middle of the afternoon. No tell-tale rattle if you wrapped the bottles in a jumper or two.

But imagine the embarrassment if – in a quantum leap of technological sophistication from my cold-water-and-single-beds fantasy – they X-rayed the luggage with this in mind.

Needless to say, all this turned out to be nonsense. The Carfax was comfortable and pleasant, converted from three Georgian houses and featuring handsome fireplaces and steep staircases. The bed was perhaps a bit celibate, but as I wasn't inviting anyone to join me in it, it was a small complaint.

To the buns. Bath is a UNESCO World Heritage Site and the centre, with its truly gorgeous abbey, cobbled streets and carefully preserved Georgian houses, felt rather like a living museum. It was odd that such a genteel place should have two versions of an original local bun and that there should be rivalry between them.

What most of us think of as a Bath Bun is a generous-sized sweet bun with a sprinkling of currants on the top and a crystallised slab of sugar called a comfit inside. There was a time when this would have been caraway flavoured, comfits being, to quote Elizabeth David, 'tiny, sugar-coated sweets, enclosing the [caraway] seed'. She goes on to say that the use of comfits in cakes and buns, which was common in the 17th and 18th centuries, must have been an interesting way of introducing sugar into the dough, giving a crunchy effect.

Caraway may be the oldest cultivated spice plant in Europe – it was certainly known to the Romans and was once used for sweetening the breath. I've even seen a 19th-century recipe that puts it in gingerbread, which smacks of overkill. It has rather gone out of fashion, now that we have other spices to choose from and other seeds to put in seedy bread. Today, sugar on its own serves the purpose in a Bath Bun.

Laurence Swan, owner of The Bath Bun and The Georgian Tearooms (formerly Hands), filled me in on some background. Legend has it that the Bath Bun was the creation of one William Oliver, a Cornish doctor who moved to Bath in 1728 and made a reputation – and a handsome fortune – by using the local mineral waters to treat rheumatics. Why he thought that a sugary bun would be helpful in this respect I don't know; but his invention coincided with a huge boom in the importing of sugar from the West Indies. Sugar would have reached bakeries and consumers in a rawer form than it does today, so it would have packed quite a punch. It was also still a novelty: according to Laurence, to say you'd eaten sugar would have been a bit like slipping Beluga caviar into a modern-day conversation. It's easy to imagine Dr Oliver's patients being excited by their new prescription, finding themselves permanently on a bit of a high and, regardless of the state of their rheumatics, congratulating Dr Oliver on making them feel better. However, they would soon also have discovered that they were putting on weight: no one had realised how fattening sugar was if you stuffed your face with it all day long. So Dr Oliver came up with something less sugary – the Bath Oliver biscuit.

There seem to me to be two fatal flaws in this story. I am partial to a Bath Oliver or two, but surely you have to have them with cheese. And, unless it's a particularly creamy cheese, preferably butter as well. So your calorie count is not much reduced. Also – call me weak-willed – if I were a sugar junkie and you were trying to wean me off Bath Buns, I wouldn't see much difference between a cheeseless Bath Oliver and, say, a cold turkey.

However, this is another of those legends that persist in the face of a complete lack of evidence to support them. Before I move on, though: the Pump Room, where the fashionable once came to promenade and hypochondriacs 'took the waters', is now an elegant tea room. Here, for the princely sum of 50p (or for nothing if you have a ticket to the Roman Baths), you can taste the water for yourself. I was, frankly, disappointed: I was expecting it to be considerably more disgusting than it was.

Legend Two – for there are two – puts the invention of the Bath Bun about 100 years later: 1851, to be precise, the time of the Great Exhibition in Hyde Park. The bun was Bath's contribution to the exhibition and some 934,691 were sold during the five and a half months that it ran, more than any other single foodstuff. Plain buns clocked up a mere 870,027 and Banbury Cakes, the only other place-named offering, a meagre 34,070. The only things to outsell the Bath Bun were Schweppes soft drinks: 1,092,337 bottles of soda water, lemonade and ginger beer were purchased, which may not be unconnected with the high price of tea and the total absence of alcohol available on the site.

Again, I have to express a reservation about this story: why would Bath *invent* a bun to contribute to an international expo of unprecedented magnitude? Surely it's more likely that the bun already existed and the local bakers, whoever they were, chose to *showcase* it at the Exhibition. No matter: there is no doubting that the Great Exhibition brought the Bath Bun to the attention of a great many people. Sadly, this wasn't entirely good news: the mass production required to satisfy the appetites of almost a million sweet-toothed punters meant that standards had to be lowered. Lard seems to have been used instead of butter, for one thing, and the result actually gave rise to the term 'cheap Bath Bun' or 'London Bath Bun' – a widely despised poor relation.

This bad reputation persisted for at least half a century: a West Midlands headmaster named Frederick Hackwood, who wrote more books about his home town of Wednesbury than you would have thought the world needed, clearly shared the opinion of many of those who had criticised the Great Exhibition's product. In his book *Good Cheer: the romance of food and feasting* (1911), he remarked:

> *The comestible known as the Bath Bun and now sold everywhere throughout the kingdom … is a sweet bun of a somewhat stodgy type, and is popularly supposed to constitute, with a little milk, the average form of luncheon taken by mild curates.*

I had never heard of Frederick Hackwood and I doubt if I shall ever read a book about Wednesbury, but that use of the word 'mild' is surely sublime.

Happily, the bun that Laurence served was rather more tasty than whatever Mr Hackwood had eaten, although it did have to be eaten or frozen on the day it was baked: the high butter content, he told me, made it feel a bit rigid if it wasn't 100 per cent fresh. Laurence's baker doesn't work on Sundays, so he freezes about 80 buns (more than double that number during the Christmas markets) first thing on a Saturday morning and takes them out first thing on Sunday to ensure that Sunday customers are as contented as everyone else.

This recipe is similar to the one displayed on the wall of the upstairs tea room at The Bath Bun. It makes a very decent bun, whether or not you have a mild curate to feed it to.

Bath Buns

Makes 12

450g plain flour
2 x 7g sachets fast-action dried yeast
225g unsalted butter
150ml milk
3 medium eggs
175g caster sugar
50g currants, plus a few extra for topping
50g candied citrus peel
a few crushed sugar cubes, to sprinkle

1. Place the flour in a large bowl, and add the yeast, then rub the butter in until the mixture resembles coarse breadcrumbs. Make a hollow in the centre and pour in the milk.

2. In a separate bowl, beat the eggs and pour nearly all of them into the hollow in the flour mixture, keeping back a little to brush over the top of the buns. Mix the flour into the liquid gradually, until you have a soft, smooth dough. Cover the

basin with a tea-towel and stand in a warm place for 1 hour for the dough to rise.

3 Meanwhile, grease 2 baking sheets. Beat the caster sugar, currants and chopped peel into the risen dough. Knead the dough with floured hands for a few minutes, then form it into 12 buns. Place these on the greased baking sheets, leaving room for them to rise and expand. Let them prove in a warm place for 30 minutes.

4 Preheat the oven to 190°C/375°F/gas mark 5.

5 Brush the tops of the buns with the remaining egg and sprinkle with crushed sugar cubes and a few currants. Bake in the preheated oven for 20–30 minutes. Remove and leave to cool a little on the sheets before transferring to a wire rack to cool completely.

Bath's other claim to teatime fame, the Sally Lunn, is, um, a different kettle of fish. It's housed in one of the oldest buildings in Bath (1482 is the date above the door), but Sally herself arrived in about 1680. A Huguenot refugee from France, she wouldn't have been a master baker (women weren't in those days), but may have worked as something lowlier in an existing bakery. One version of the story gives her name as Solange Luyon, which could easily have been garbled into Sally Lunn; it's also possible that because of the bun's toasted top and paler underside it was described as 'sun and moon'. Sally may well have walked the streets of Bath calling out the name of her wares in her native tongue; and turning '*soleil et lune*' into 'Sally Lunn' is less of a stretch than is required by many similar tales.

Sally Lunn's buns never claimed to have the medicinal properties ascribed to Dr Oliver's creation. But they did find favour with the gentry when Bath was at the peak of its fashionableness in Georgian times, being served at elegant public breakfasts.

One thing that the Bath Bun and the Sally Lunn have in common is the olde worldiness of their shops and cafés. Both occupy several floors, linked by narrow and uneven staircases, with not a right angle to be seen in any of the rooms. Sally Lunn's is on four floors if you include the shop/museum in the basement – the manager, Dale Ingram, does a lot of running up and down and admitted to losing 6kg in his first six months in the job. The usual health and safety regulations don't apply in this listed building, but customer service does its best to make up. Arlene, the bubbly lady who presides over the museum and shop, expends almost as much energy warning people to mind their heads as she does explaining about the old oven on display.

The museum consists of two tiny rooms, one showing Roman remains excavated in the 1980s and the other featuring the faggot oven in which the original buns were baked. Faggots – bundles of sticks – were set alight in the oven's stone chamber; once they had burned down, the ashes were cleared out and the residual heat of the stone was sufficient to bake the day's bread. Dale told me he hoped to get it up and running again some time, but I couldn't help wondering if it would present a fire hazard that even the building's listed status wouldn't let it get away with. For the moment Sally Lunns are baked in Corsham, a few kilometres out of Bath. It happens to be where Arlene lives and she rebuked Dale when he called it a village. 'We've got a town hall,' she said firmly, 'so we're a town.'

The recipe for the Sally Lunn is another closely guarded secret. 'You wouldn't believe what I've had to sign,' Dale said with a rueful grin. Lost for some time after its Georgian heyday, the recipe was, he told me, rediscovered in the 1930s in a cupboard over a fireplace and is now passed on with the deeds of the house. It's a brioche-like product of great versatility, rich with butter and eggs and remarkably light. (If you want to test how light it is, go downstairs again and talk to Arlene: she keeps a sample bun on the counter and visitors are encouraged to press gently on the top to watch it bounce back.) Dale told me he had spent his entire working life as a chef and never come across anything quite like it: although versions exist in Australia, New Zealand, the US and one or two other places in Britain, they are all very different. It must have been quite a novelty in the 17th century – large, white and fluffy, when people were used to buns made with darker, coarser flour. It was traditionally served warm with cream, but Sally Lunn's now top it with anything from Welsh rarebit to their home-made cinnamon butter, and use it as the basis of their bread-and-butter pudding and treacle tart.

The truly surprising thing about it is its size: fully 15cm in diameter and 7cm high. With a salad garnish (if you're having it with, say, rarebit, smoked salmon or crunchy nut pâté) or a pot of clotted cream (if you go for cinnamon butter, lemon curd or coffee and walnut butter), it fills the sort of plate you'd have expected if you'd ordered an omelette and chips. Your first reaction – my first reaction – was 'Good grief! Am I supposed to eat all that?', but it really was as light as it felt and the savoury version left an unexpected amount of room for pudding.

Dale had been experimenting with older versions of the Sally Lunn: for a recent Bath Food Festival he re-created a recipe from way back that contained caraway comfit. There may come a time when this and other variations find their way on to the menu, but until then lots of people were very happy with what was already on offer.

And lest you think that Arlene might be lonely down in her basement, fear not: she has company. Carved into the wall at the bottom of the stairs just before you enter the museum is a tiny grotesque discovered at the time of the 1980s excavations. Not a gargoyle, those who know about these things will tell you, because he has no water supply, but a funny little stone man who likes to have his head patted. He's called Cedric. I didn't ask why – I expect he just looked like a Cedric.

In addition to everything else it has to boast about, Bath is justifiably proud to have the UK's oldest farmers' market. This is held on Saturday mornings in a disused railway station called Green Park. Not quite on a par with the Musée d'Orsay, but still not a bad way to use a station that is surplus to train requirements. On the day I visited, it was selling lots of local meat, veg and other produce, as well as handbags, small suitcases billed as Ryanair friendly, stylish antique furniture and curtain poles hand forged in Bath (that struck me as a worrying claim; I hoped the ironmonger wore extra-thick gloves).

I could find only one stall selling Bath Buns – a family concern called Bakers of Bath, whose family name really was Baker and whose traditions and recipes went back to the current generation's great-grandfather. Very tasty it was, too, and not bad value at 75p. If I'd wanted to satiate my sweet tooth I could have bought – in ascending order of distance from home – any number of Bakewell Tarts, an Eccles Cake, a *pastel de nata* (Portuguese custard tart) and several Mississippi Mud Pies. But I resisted: I was at an early stage in my journey and my sugar high was already worrying enough.

Instead I went back to the hotel, whose temperate nature didn't stop an American couple of a certain age bickering in the lounge. How stupid could she be, he wondered at full volume, wanting to stay three whole days in this ridiculous place? That Royal Circus, or whatever they called it, was just a road round some houses.

He was expecting acrobats and flaming hoops, perhaps?

4

Wales

Griddle Cakes Galore

From Bath Buns to Welsh Cakes was, geographically, a small step, so I'd invited myself to stay with friends just outside Chepstow. Where they live is in England, but if we went into town to Waitrose, we'd be in Wales. To a lot of people this is important; to me it meant I could stop messing about on buses for a while and scrounge a lift into Cardiff.

I remember Cardiff Bay when it was in its infancy as a docklands development. Environmentalists were arguing about whether or not a barrage should be allowed to enclose what always seemed to me a rather birdless stretch of mudflats, and interested parties were fighting over the design of the proposed new opera house. A few pioneering shops and cafés had opened, but you had to use a lot of imagination to visualise the shape of things to come.

The opera house never made it – they built the rather funky Wales Millennium Centre instead – and ten years since my last visit the area had changed beyond recognition. Look out across the bay and the stark white of the cosy little Norwegian church, dating from the 19th century, still leaps out at you on a dull day; turn a little to your left and there's the gloriously Gothic Pierhead building, the former customs house. But most of the rest is modern, dominated by Richard Rogers' Senedd, home of the Welsh National Assembly and, across the water, in a bizarre juxtaposition with the church, the extended polytunnel that, for the next few years at least, will house the Doctor Who Experience.

Turn your back on the water, head up the narrow pedestrianised stretch of Bute Street and you'll find an alluring little gift shop called Fabulous Welshcakes. Its owner, Jo Roberts, had told me over the phone that everything she sold was craft-based, quite up-market: 'not inflatable daffodils' was how she phrased it. Jewellery, cards, soap, ornamental sheep, honey and lavender jelly were all Welsh-made, as was a splendid range of mugs in the style of the familiar Penguin Books ones. These offered titles such as *Apocalypse Now in a Minute*, *Last Tango in Powys* and – my favourite, because it was inspired by my favourite Cardiff suburb – *Some Like It Splott*. Ever since I got to know Cardiff a generation ago I've felt that every city should have a suburb called Splott.

To the casual observer, Fabulous Welshcakes would have been quite like a hundred other imaginative gift shops up and down the country were it not for two things. One was the warm, homely aroma of baking that struck us the moment we walked in; the other was the presence, just inside the door, of a large griddle on which Welsh Cakes were being cooked before our very eyes.

If you've never come across one, it's hard to describe exactly what a Welsh Cake is – not quite a scone, not quite a cake, not quite a North of England pikelet or Scottish pancake. It's made from a simple dough, fat rubbed into flour and bound with eggs, not milk; like all griddle cakes, it was once a substitute for bread in homes that had no oven. It's not kneaded, just pulled together, rolled out into a circle about 5cm in diameter and 1cm deep and baked on a bakestone or in a heavy frying pan for a few minutes on each side. The less handling the better; the more you work the dough, the heavier the cake will be. In Jo's production kitchen (a converted garage at her home up the coast in Penarth), everything except the rubbing in of the butter is done by hand: a food processor bashing the ingredients about wouldn't do the dough any good at all.

What you put into the dough, of course, makes all the difference. Jo swears by self-raising flour, which avoids the aftertaste of soda that is always a risk with plain flour and baking powder; it also helps with the lightness. She uses butter, not lard or margarine: when she was recipe testing in the early days she thought lard would make the cakes 'short' and crumbly, but it just made them hard. Butter also gives a much better taste, she told us. It has to be salted, though. The experiment with unsalted butter was a disaster – the cakes turned out very pale and, even though she had added extra salt to compensate, they'd lost out on flavour too. She prefers sultanas to the traditional currants because they are plumper and moister. One recipe I'd looked at before I came used half a teaspoon of mixed spice, another had mixed spice or nutmeg; Jo goes for a combination of cinnamon and nutmeg. 'I don't really like cinnamon,' she said, 'but I've tried it with just nutmeg and it isn't right. You notice the cinnamon is missing.'

It occurred to me as I listened that Jo had changed every one of the principal ingredients in the traditional recipe. Purists would be throwing up their hands in horror, but they'd be missing out on a treat. And anyway, throwing up their hands in horror is what purists do – let them get on with it.

Jo used to work for the Welsh Development Agency, promoting Welsh food and drink. For one event she wanted square Welsh Cakes in different flavours – square so that they would stack neatly and different flavours just for the heck of it – and couldn't find an artisan baker who could supply them. Perhaps 99 per cent of a classic baker's output goes in the oven, she told us, so a griddle, which takes up a lot of surface area, is a waste of space for a small business. Although Welsh Cakes were available commercially and lots of people still baked them at home, this set Jo thinking about a gap in the market. Why not go into business producing *only* Welsh Cakes, but home-made, using the best possible ingredients, on an artisan scale and coming up with something truly excellent? Or, as it turned out, Fabulous?

Four years of research later, she opened her shop. 'I was trying to reinvent the Welsh Cake,' she explained. 'I wanted to get away from the "granny's kitchen" imagery of flowery cloth on top of jams and chutneys, or labels with pictures of women in tall black hats.' Inspired by other trail-blazing Welsh companies such as Rachel's Organic, she wanted to do something that was recognisably Welsh, but had a modern look and a wider, younger appeal. After all, if you are going to make only one thing, you have to tap into as many markets as possible. She now makes corporate gifts and supplies local hotels with mini-Welsh Cakes to be placed in the saucer of every cup of tea or coffee. She also offers mini-cakes for wedding favours: as we were talking in her shop, a customer came in to collect an order of heart-shaped cakes, beautifully packaged in threes and tied up with ribbon to be used as part of the wedding table setting.

Jo also sells the cakes online, taking advantage of the fact that they have a two-week shelf life. That isn't enough for her to supply supermarkets – they'd need more like six weeks, which you simply can't get using all butter – but is fine for customers whose needs are shorter term.

As for reinventing the Welsh Cake itself, she's certainly succeeded, offering not only round and heart shapes, but squares, stars, butterflies, teddy bears and rugby balls; gluten-free and diabetes-friendly variations; and upwards of 20 flavours. On any given day there are three flavours available freshly baked in the shop: the traditional version, a chocolate one and, on the day of our visit, lemon. The range includes white, dark and milk chocolate – with or without lemon, cranberry, vanilla or orange – plus pistachio and lemon, coconut and lime, cherry and more. Traditional cakes and milk chocolate ones are available in boxes of six to take home and savour, but you can buy today's flavours either individually, or in a bag of 12 for £4.50.

Welsh Cakes seem to appeal to everyone, young and old, lads on skateboards and elderly couples. Maybe it's because griddle cooking is rare nowadays, but they have a considerable nostalgia value too:

people in their forties come into the shop and say, 'Ooh, it's like my nana's kitchen.' Not 'my mum's', you notice – the concept of home baking seems to have skipped a generation. The only resistance Jo has encountered is from ladies of a certain generation, ladies who bake and say, '£4.50? I could make 50 at home for that!' To which the answer is, 'Fair enough, if you can be bothered. They'll probably be excellent. But if you can't be bothered and if you want them right here and now, treat yourself.' She probably doesn't say that in so many words.

Her view is that people wouldn't buy them if they weren't delicious. (My friend and I can vouch for this. Our sample pack of 12, four each of the three flavours, disappeared in no time flat when we got it home. And we can't blame her husband, whom we felt obliged to admit to our tasting session; it was largely because the two of us couldn't decide which was the yummiest and had to keep sampling.)

Welsh Cakes date back to the days when people cooked with a cauldron over an open fire. They were once popular in miners' lunch boxes: with their high fat and high sugar content they are a great energy booster and helped to keep the men going during a gruelling 12-hour shift. Nowadays professional athletes feel the same way – Jo's list of customers includes competitors in the Tour de France.

There are those who say that Welsh Cakes are a South Wales invention, but this may be because they are saying it in Welsh. Some confusion arises from there being different names for the same thing – *pice âr y maen* in the south, *cacen gri* in the north – but in fact they are a pan-Welsh delicacy, with regional variations. A friend of Jo's, Welsh food consultant Siân Roberts, later filled me in on this: 'up the valleys', she told me, they made a slightly thicker version, without fruit, which they split down the middle and served with jam. A delegate at one of Siân's courses once remarked that she had never seen Welsh Cakes with fruit until she came to Cardiff – and she was from Aberdare, a former mining town not 35km away. Fruit rather than heavy spicing is favoured in some parts of Mid Wales, while a buttery version containing a few currants but no spice also appears in a book called *Lloyd George's Favourite Recipes*, compiled by the Criccieth Women's Institute, which is very much in the north.

If you fancy trying your hand at Welsh Cakes, a bakestone about the size of a dinner plate is ideal. Cast-iron ones are hard to come by these days; you may have to make do with steel or, if the worst comes to the worst, a cast-iron frying pan.

Not Entirely Traditional Welsh Cakes

Makes 20–25

175g self-raising flour
a small pinch of fine salt
½ tsp mixed spice (or ¼ tsp each of ground cinnamon and freshly grated nutmeg)
75g salted butter
50g granulated sugar
55g sultanas
1 medium egg, beaten

1. Lightly grease a griddle or heavy-based frying pan and heat it until it sizzles.
2. Sift the dry ingredients into a large bowl, then rub in the butter until the mixture resembles fine breadcrumbs. Add the sugar, sultanas and egg, and mix to a soft dough.
3. On a lightly floured surface, roll out the dough to about 5mm thick. Cut into 5cm circles – or triangles, heart shapes or anything else you fancy.

4 Place the cakes on the heated griddle or frying pan and 'bake' for just a couple of minutes on each side until lightly browned. Serve hot or cold, on their own or with Welsh butter.

Note: For an even less traditional version, replace the sultanas with 55g chocolate chips. And possibly – just possibly – forego serving them with extra butter...

Having started the morning talking about scones and pikelets made me think that between the three of us – Jo, who had a Lancastrian mother and grandparents from Newcastle but was raised in the Midlands and had been in Wales for 20 years; my companion of the day, who was from Yorkshire; and me, brought up in New Zealand by Scottish parents – we covered a broad spectrum of conflicting regional vocabulary. I think of a pikelet as a small, fat pancake, made with a slightly thicker batter than usual, cooked on a griddle and served warm at teatime with butter and jam. My mother used to make them like that and I'd always assumed they were Scottish; later research told me they were Antipodean. I also found I could have been describing a Welsh *crempog*, which is a word that looks remarkably like crumpet but is usually translated as pancake. Elizabeth David's comprehensive-to-a-fault *English Bread and Yeast Cookery* devotes an entire chapter to crumpets and muffins, largely a collage of conflicting descriptions and advice about what these are and how they should be made. I even read somewhere (*not* in Elizabeth David, I hasten to add) the not madly helpful remark that a pikelet could be a regional type of crumpet.

There's one thing we can be clear about, whichever part of Britain (or the Colonies) we come from: a traditional English muffin is nothing like the chocolate chip and blueberry confections now ubiquitous in our chain coffee shops. Those are American muffins and, while anything with chocolate chips in it will always have a passing claim on my attention, they have no place here.

According to Elizabeth David, the mid-18th-century cookery writer Hannah Glasse made muffins from a light yeasty dough and advised, 'Toast them with a Fork crisp on both Sides then with your Hand pull them open, and they will be like a Honeycomb.' Hannah, for what it is worth, was born in London but had a Northumbrian father. Elizabeth Raffald in *The Experienced English Housekeeper* (1769) put eggs in her dough. Maria Rundell's *A New System of Domestic Cookery* (1841 edition) gave two similar-sounding recipes for crumpets and muffins; both contained yeast but the muffins were left to rise, while the crumpet batter was cooked straight away. A Lady Clark of Tillypronie, Aberdeenshire, who kept cookery notebooks from 1850 to 1900, made what she called Scotch crumpets from a batter containing a little fresh yeast; Elizabeth David observed that this produced something more like what a Southerner would call a drop scone than a 'thick honeycombed crumpet'.

It goes on. There are Scarborough Muffins, Lancashire Muffins, Leicestershire Pikelets and Staffordshire Pikelets. With reference to the last, the same Lady Clark has this to say:

> *Orthodox pikelets come up as thick only as pancakes, piled up and buttered while hot on both sides; but they can be made as thick as a muffin, split, and buttered inside; they can also be served thin as toast, in a silver rack.*

Elizabeth David then quotes one Yorkshire-born, Derbyshire-bred friend of hers as stating categorically, 'In Derbyshire and Yorkshire pikelets mean crumpets, the ones with holes', but another, also from Derbyshire, as saying, 'All muffins, crumpets and similar yeast cakes, of whatever size, are pikelets.'

Finally, I discovered on a later trip, the award-winning bakery Hambleton of Oakham sold something they called an English muffin. It was an asymmetrical cylinder, about 4cm high and 6cm in diameter: taller and narrower than a traditional holey crumpet, but much the same texture. Hambleton's brochure described them as hand-made (hence the appealing wonkiness of shape) and 'a breadier version of the crumpet', made from white French flour. 'After slow fermentation the bubbling dough is dropped into a ring and cooked on both sides on the griddle.'

Confused? I certainly was. But at least I now knew what a Welsh Cake was. And had permission to put chocolate in it.

Jo's northeastern connections meant she was also familiar with the Singing Hinny. This is another form of griddle cake, so rich that, as it cooks, it makes a singing or sizzling noise, which explains the first part of the name. The Visit South Tyneside website helped out with the second: 'A North Country housewife was baking this scone for tea and on repeatedly being asked by her children if it was ready to eat, her final reply was "No, it's just singing, hinnies".' So had they originated in Glasgow they might have been called singing hens, in Manchester singing chucks and in much of the rest of the country singing loves. It made me glad they were invented in Geordieland, home of the hinny and the pet.

Jane Grigson records that her South Shields grandmother called her 'hinny', as did everyone in shops and on the tram. She describes it as 'a kind word to grow up with', though she had a feeling that her southern relatives thought it 'common' and 'shuddered delicately when they heard it'. She's talking about a childhood before World War II, but reading this took me back to my early days as a student in Sheffield in the 1970s, when any of the lads who weren't local took a while to get used to being called 'love' on the bus – often by male conductors.

Singing Hinnies

Makes 6

225g plain flour
½ tsp each of cream of tartar and bicarbonate of soda
a pinch of fine salt
55g each of unsalted butter and lard, cut into cubes
85g currants
about 75ml milk

1. Sift the dry ingredients into a bowl, then rub in the butter and lard until the mixture resembles fine breadcrumbs. Add the currants, stir well, then carefully add just enough milk to make a firm dough.
2. Lightly grease a griddle or heavy-based frying pan and heat it until it sizzles.
3. On a lightly floured surface, roll the dough out to about 8mm thick. Cut into 6cm rounds, or divide into 6 equal pieces and shape into rounds.
4. Place the cakes on the heated griddle or frying pan and cook for 5–7 minutes on each side until golden brown. Serve hot, with butter.

Rather further north, the griddle cake emerges at times of celebration. The Bride Cake of Orkney and Shetland is basically a scone flavoured with caraway seeds; the bride's mother traditionally made them on the wedding day, then broke one over her daughter's head as she entered her new home for the first time as a married woman. (This was in the days before people disappeared to the Seychelles for a fortnight – these cakes would be pretty horrid if you left them that long.) The bride and groom had to eat it all, in order to ensure a happy marriage. Whether this meant scrabbling around on the floor in their finery in order to pick up the crumbs, I don't know.

Orkney Bride Cakes

Makes 8

50g unsalted butter
150g self-raising flour
25g caster sugar
15g caraway seeds
3–4 tbsp milk, to mix

1 Soften the butter slightly. Put the flour into a bowl, then rub in the butter until the mixture resembles fine breadcrumbs. Stir in the caster sugar and caraway seeds, then add just enough milk to make a firm dough.

2 On a lightly floured surface, roll out the dough to make an 18cm diameter circle, about 1cm thick. Cut into 8 wedges.

3 Lightly grease a griddle or heavy-based frying pan and heat it until it sizzles. Place the cakes on it, over a medium heat, and cook for 4–5 minutes each side, until golden brown.

4 Transfer the cakes to a wire rack to cool before crumbling over anyone; or, if there isn't a wedding in the offing, eat hot fresh from the griddle.

Back in Cardiff, the question of drop scones, crumpets and muffins had been thoroughly but inconclusively thrashed out and we felt we'd taken up enough of Jo's time. So we made our farewells and went for another stroll. As I said, the outside of the Pierhead building is in the best Victorian style of OTT Gothic; the inside doesn't let you down. It's recently been revamped and turned into a visitor centre for the Senedd, but it has 'listed building' written all over it. Tiles everywhere, even on the banister, and a covetable chunky staircase. You wouldn't want to sweep down it in a ball gown (too many corners, you'd be bound to trip over your hem), but it certainly gives the place gravitas.

As the administrative headquarters of the Port of Cardiff, the Pierhead would have needed all the gravitas it could get. In 1897 Cardiff was the largest coal-exporting port in the world. The worldwide price of exporting coal was set at Cardiff's Coal Exchange, where the world's first ever £1 million business deal – of any kind, not just coal – was struck in 1907. In 1896 the Port of Cardiff exported nearly 16 million tonnes of coal; in 1914 it was more than 26 million tonnes. By way of a random comparison, that's not much less than the whole of the US was exporting in 1945. We couldn't resist pointing this out to a couple of passing Americans, who had the grace to be impressed.

The Pierhead building doesn't have a café, so to pursue our research we went across the road to the Senedd. This entailed more security than my last visit to JFK Airport, as we put our bags and coats into plastic trays and stripped off our jewellery lest we set off the metal detector. There were eight security personnel to deal with the two of us, which, considering we'd only come for a cup of tea and a Welsh Cake, seemed a bit excessive. When we asked why, we were told that they were expecting the Chinese Ambassador and an entourage of about 150 in an hour or so's time. When the papers announce a new Sino-Welsh alliance, you heard it here first.

Once you're in, the Senedd is a gorgeous building, all swirling wood, but it has to be said that the Welsh Cakes left something to be desired. The café also sold Bara Brith, Welsh Butter Shortbread and other things that it boasted contained Welsh ingredients, but the catering firm was based in London and, considering this ought to be the showcase for all things Welsh, we were not impressed. Armed with our newly acquired understanding of the recipe, we decided that the Welsh Cakes contained plain flour and baking powder, lard rather than butter, too little spice and too much sugar. We expressed our opinion fairly frankly to the woman behind the counter and tried to persuade her to visit Fabulous Welshcakes. All things considered, she was remarkably civil to us.

As we left – a much easier process than coming in – we passed a table where goody bags and name badges were laid out in readiness for the Chinese visitors. One of the delegates, his badge told me, was from the Confucius Institute of Lampeter. It was a joyously bizarre juxtaposition that more than made up for the disappointing Welsh Cake.

Swapping one obliging friend-and-chauffeur for another, I headed north a couple of days later to check out the claim that Welsh Cakes were everywhere. I was aiming for Betws-y-Coed, unarguably in North Wales.

There's a touch of class about Betws-y-Coed. As the self-styled gateway to Snowdonia it has a constant flow of walkers and climbers, but there were also coachloads of refined couples from Scotland, doing tours of the local highlights, including the nearby waterfalls. A signpost outside the station announces that Swallow Falls are 5km away and Conwy Falls 3km; by contrast, Niagara is 7,227km and Victoria Falls 8,206km. 'Go local' is the clear message.

Going local, in a slightly less energetic fashion, was precisely what I was planning to do. What had brought me to Betws was the multi-award-winning Welshcakes Company – Cwmni Cacen Gri – run by Jen Barrie and Jo Wordsworth.

They were horrified when I suggested that Welsh Cakes were a southern invention. They're both local and use their own take on their grandmothers' recipes; it came as no surprise to learn that their secret lay in the blend of spices they'd chosen to use. Cacen Gri cakes are noticeably yellow, thanks to the Welsh butter and absolutely fresh organic eggs, both from a very local source. 'The hens are fed on grass,' Jen said, 'and I think that's the key, because it's so lush and green here. It makes a huge difference.'

They bake every day and use no preservatives, so although they do package the cakes for people to take home and say that they will keep for a week, there's no denying that they are at their best fresh from the griddle or at least later the same day. If you do keep them for a while, they advised, reheat them on a dry griddle or frying pan; adding butter to the pan is unnecessary, given how much there is in the cakes already.

They also make their own fudge and produce cakes to order, in a kitchen no bigger than the average garden shed. While we talked, Jen was busy mixing their own special Rocky Road fudge on a table about the size of the one in my kitchen (which is much the same size as anyone else's) and Jo was called away to take an order. 'It's hard to believe what we churn out from this table, because it's the only baking table we've got,' Jen said. 'But, having seen us on TV, people expect to see Jo and me behind the counter and we can only do so much.'

That's why they had – for the moment – turned down offers to expand and chosen to concentrate on consolidating the shop's reputation. In only the third year of their business, they just wanted 'to be very good at what we do'. Their visitors' book suggested that they were succeeding: fans ranged from the Samoan rugby team to 'Derek the Weather' from BBC Wales.

Like Jo in Cardiff, Jen and Jo produce Welsh Cake wedding favours and they bake three kinds of Welsh Cake every day. This always includes the traditional form, which I found a little on the cinnamony side, but then I've always thought that a quarter of a teaspoon of cinnamon goes a long way. Others will disagree. Of the other two, one is always a savoury – on that day it was Welsh Rarebit flavour, which was so delicious I wondered why more people hadn't thought of it. It was sugar-free – a pleasant change from the head-banging qualities of some of my recent researches – and as a concept it's surely no weirder than a cheese scone, and tastier than most of those.

All this is not to decry the Double Chocolate and Vanilla, which was the day's other flavour and which I managed to consume in its entirety when I was planning on having just a taste.

The Welsh Cake may be pan-Welsh, but there's no shortage of recipes that are unique to the north. Aberffraw Cakes (*Teisen 'Berffro* if you speak the language) are named after a village in Anglesey. I'd been intrigued because they appeared to be in the shape of a scallop and to have some connection with Santiago de Compostela. No one seemed to make them commercially any more, but Theodora Fitzgibbon's book *A Taste of Wales in Food and Pictures* (inherited by my current companion from her Welsh mother-in-law) shed light:

> *The Welsh name for a scallop shell is* cragen iago, *the shell of St James, and it was used as a badge by pilgrims who went to visit the shrine of St James at Compostela. These shells are used as a small cake tin in Anglesey, at Aberffraw, and the small cakes … resemble shortbread.*

She gave a recipe with equal parts sugar, flour and butter from which, despite several attempts, I couldn't produce anything other than a yellow sludgy mess. I was about to resign myself to not writing about them when, several months after my trip to Wales, I discovered the Aberffraw Biscuit Co. They hadn't existed when I was doing my initial research and in fact weren't due to launch their range for another two months. But James Shepherd, who had founded the company with his wife Natasha, was happy to talk on the phone. He told me that, as a keen amateur baker, he'd been watching last year's series of *The Great British Bake Off* when it featured a product from North Wales described as Britain's oldest biscuit. Despite both being from North Wales, James and Natasha had never heard of Aberffraw Biscuits, as the programme called them, and decided it would be a shame for this appealing piece of their heritage to be allowed to die. As James put it, 'All the tourist shops in North Wales were selling Scottish Shortbread. I've got nothing against that, but shouldn't they be selling Welsh Shortbread too?' He waxed eloquent about how much fun it had been going to Shell Island with his two small children, finding queen scallop shells and making the biscuits together. He then hastened to assure me that the ones the kids had made hadn't been for sale and that for commercial purposes they had evolved a more hygienic way of pressing and stamping the biscuits than using shells picked up on the beach.

The result is a round biscuit with a fluted shell pattern, which James believes resembles what the original must have been. They initially developed a stylised shell shape, rather like the oil company's logo, but decided this wasn't authentic: 'You can get too wrapped up in your product,' he said, 'so we've stripped it right down.'

The recipe, like the shape, is a simple one – just three ingredients, mixed by hand. As so often, this means the quality of the ingredients is paramount. Butter and flour are organic and sourced locally; caster sugar comes from the nearest possible – and indeed the only British – source, Silver Spoon in Bury St Edmunds. And because one product is never enough, they have a core range of four: traditional, chocolate, lemon and raisin, with the possibility of adding some other festive flavours in the run-up to Christmas. With an eye to another product I was going to be sampling in North Wales, they call the raisin flavour Bara Brith.

This is James and Natasha's recipe for their classic Aberffraw Biscuit.

Aberffraw Biscuits

Makes about 12

100g lightly salted butter, at room temperature
50g caster sugar, plus extra for dusting
150g plain flour
granulated sugar, for dusting

1 Preheat the oven to 160°C/325°F/ gas mark 3.

2 In a large bowl, cream the butter and sugar together until pale, light and fluffy. Sift in the flour and mix well to form a dough.

3 Dust a work surface lightly with caster sugar and carefully roll out the dough until about 1cm thick. (If your dough is too soft to work with, pop it in the fridge for 15 minutes first.)

4 If available, press the rounded back of a (thoroughly washed) scallop shell on to the dough. Then, using a round 6cm or 8cm biscuit cutter, cut a circular biscuit from the pressed dough. Repeat until all the dough is used up, then place each moulded biscuit on to a non-stick baking sheet. If you don't have a scallop shell then mark/score each round to imitate the scallop pattern.

5 Bake the biscuits in the preheated oven for about 15 minutes, then remove and leave to cool for 5 minutes. Dust generously with granulated sugar while still warm. Transfer immediately to a wire rack and allow to cool completely before storing in an airtight container. Enjoy on their own, with a cup of tea or with freshly whipped cream and jam.

Note: For a change, try adding the zest of a lemon or a handful of raisins or chocolate chips before rolling out the dough.

Other Welsh recipes that no one seems to make outside the home any more include *Teisen Lap*, also known as Moist Cake or Plate Cake, which contains sultanas and sour cream or buttermilk and, like the Welsh Cake, was popular with miners. Tinker Cakes (*Teisen Tincar*) are a bit like Welsh Cakes with grated apple in them and were made in the autumn, when the tinker came round. The friend who had married into a Welsh family told me that tinkers used to come every year to her husband's grandfather's place, sleep in the shed, sharpen and mend the tools and even, on one occasion, repair a clock that hadn't worked for ages. 'Oh, I can fix that,' said the tinker. He took it to bits before the appalled eyes of his clientele, put it back together again and it was fine. He'd earned his cake.

Tinker Cakes

Makes about 25

225g self-raising flour
110g unsalted butter
35g granulated sugar
1 medium apple, peeled, cored and grated
milk, to mix

1. Sift the flour into a bowl, then rub in the butter until the mixture resembles fine breadcrumbs. Stir in the sugar and grated apple. Carefully mix in just enough milk to make a soft dough.
2. Knead the dough quickly into a ball, then roll out to 5mm thick and cut into 5cm rounds.
3. Grease a griddle or heavy-based frying pan very lightly, and heat it until it sizzles. Cook the cakes for 2–3 minutes on each side, until golden brown. Serve hot or cold, either buttered or sugared.

The Welsh tradition that not only has survived, but is found everywhere in North Wales – and in the English border counties of Shropshire and Herefordshire too – is Bara Brith. To talk to people about that, we headed to the north coast to stay overnight in Llandudno. It was a beautiful evening for walking along the beach, but suddenly we seemed to have left Wales and entered Planet Seaside.

Llandudno bears much more resemblance to seaside resorts across England and Europe than it does to Betws-y-Coed, Llanrwst or any other of the very Welsh towns we'd been through earlier in the day. It's on a grand scale and has hotels called the Imperial and St George's, with palm trees outside them. The pier has a range of less up-market attractions such as a Tombstone Arizona 1896 shooting range, a bouncy castle and go-karting. There's also Happy Hands, an underwater manicure – you are invited to 'pop in and try it for yourself', as if there was any other way to have a manicure; a clairvoyant/medium called Spirit 2 Spirit; and a shop selling incredibly naff meerkat figures, including a beefeater and a bagpiper. In fact, apart from the bilingual signs everywhere, the only thing that reminded me I was in Wales was a shop selling scarves and gloves. As it happened I'd brought my own, and as the sun began to set I was glad of them.

Gorgeous though it was to look at on a sunny spring evening, Llandudno seemed to lack a useful commodity for those who had had only a few Welsh Cakes for lunch: restaurants. Most of the front is made up of B&Bs, many of them offering afternoon tea, but not dinner. A few of the grander hotels had restaurants that looked a bit – well, grand – and quite busy. The street behind the seafront had no shortage of fish and chip shops and a single pub that wasn't doing food, but nothing like a pizza place or a curry house that would have served the current needs. So, somewhat diffidently, I approached the maître d' of the Imperial and asked if he could fit us in.

Bless him, he didn't give a second glance to my trainers and scruffy fleece; he simply asked if we were residents in the hotel.

'No,' I replied.

'We do have a table,' he said, in a tone that suggested that if we had been residents he would have turned us away. Perhaps there were two madwomen staying in the hotel who looked a bit like us and had danced raucously on the tables the previous night before absconding with the coffee spoons. I'll never know. But they sat us in what might be called a loggia, at the front of the hotel, looking out over the sea. From the next room a harpist serenaded us with 'Moon River' and 'Somewhere Over The Rainbow' and we were fed a very good meal indeed. The menu offered vanilla fudge with the coffee, but they were very apologetic – there was no vanilla fudge today. Instead we got chocolate petits fours. We coped.

It was another beautiful morning when – fortified by the sort of breakfast you don't need when you have had chocolate petits fours the night before and are about to spend the morning sampling Bara Brith – we made our way along the coast to Rhos-on-Sea. The Tan Lan Bakery in Rhos is renowned for its Bara Brith and, while my friend took the air on the beach, I sat in the sun with a cup of tea and Master Baker Dean Geldart.

'Tan Lan' translates as 'fire on the hill' – a good name for a bakery, though perhaps less appropriate by the seaside. But Dean started his business, some 20 years ago, in Betws-y-Coed, where, as I had seen only the day before, there are plenty of hills. 'Bara Brith' means 'speckled bread', and, rather to my surprise, Dean told me that it originated in the mining communities of Scotland in the late 1800s; presumably it wasn't called Bara Brith there. It became popular in Wales, like so much of the rest of their baking, as a useful thing for wives to make for their husbands' lunches. Its advantage over some other baked goods is that it keeps soft and fresh for days and days – the generous amount of fruit sees to that.

Everyone has their own recipe for Bara Brith and Dean told me he'd tried loads before settling on the one he now uses: it's his take on something that is still acceptably traditional. A fruity mixture is soaked in tea for at least 24 hours and ideally 48, the idea being that it absorbs both the tea's flavours and, more importantly, its moisture. Dean uses currants and sultanas, as per the traditional recipes, but also adds cherries, brown sugar, black treacle, mixed spice, cinnamon and tea. A *lot* of strong Welsh tea. The fruit, of course, swells up, so that the currants and sultanas are almost back to the size of grapes. When you mix it, Dean warned, you have to be careful: 'You don't want to be knocking all that water out again.' After soaking, he adds self-raising flour and eggs – there's no fat at all.

Self-raising flour? Yes, because like Jo in Cardiff Bay, Dean doesn't want the tart taste of baking powder in Bara Brith. An alternative, which he uses for his scones, is to mix plain flour and a very expensive baking powder that doesn't leave an aftertaste. But when it comes to ingredients that don't affect the taste, he believes in using as few as possible. Self-raising flour is one less ingredient than plain flour plus baking powder, which means there is one less thing to go wrong. Some recipes also include marmalade, which Dean had tried and decided against. The treacle gives the bread a rich enough colour; marmalade, in his opinion, doesn't make much difference to the taste. 'So it's just another sugar. It doesn't need it.'

Soaking the fruit is absolutely crucial. Sometimes, during the summer, Dean will have two or three buckets of fruit soaking at once, just in case someone should say, 'We're going to need more Bara Brith tomorrow.'

'If I don't have the fruit ready,' he explained, 'they can't have it. I can make it, but it won't be right. So sometimes the fruit is soaking for two or three days, which is even better. The mixture is really thick and concentrated then. Like a good stock.'

This was a comparison I hadn't heard before, but Dean went on: 'When you're making a sauce, you reduce it and reduce it so that it gets stronger; that's what I do with the tea when I soak the fruit: it goes really black. You could do something similar with water, but it just wouldn't be nice on the palate.'

This is the reason you can't make Bara Brith in a hurry: if you skimp on soaking the fruit, you don't get the flavour. It's also the reason it tastes much nicer after two or three days: the fruit has been releasing its moisture back into the cake, which might otherwise be drying out by this time. 'It's a science,' Dean said. 'You've got to understand all the reactions that happen during baking. You've got to know what you're doing.'

On inspection, the Tan Lan Bara Brith proved to be a beautiful, well-risen loaf with a shiny toffee colour on top, but no glaze. Some recipes specify glazing with honey, but again Dean didn't see the need – for him, slow baking combined with the richness of the mixture produced the desired effect.

Although they are, of course, a bit busier in the summer – it's a seaside resort, after all – Dean and his wife Emma enjoy a loyal local trade all year round. 'People are changing their eating habits,' he said. 'They want to know where their food is coming from.' It wasn't only the local butcher who had benefited from the recent horsemeat scare – Dean and Emma had noticed an upturn too. An ill wind.

Bara Brith is ubiquitous in North Wales, so it didn't seem right to try it only once. The landlord of the Broadway, our B&B in Llandudno, had recommended a bakery in Conwy, so that was our next stop.

Like much of North Wales, Conwy is dominated by its castle and, in this case, a spectacular defensive wall. You sit on the waterfront with the castle to your right, glance up to the left and find a chunk of wall there. You amble to the other end of a shopping street and go through an arch in the wall. You do a circuit and head back down to the car park through another arch in the wall. But the wall is far from being complete: it's as if someone had decreed that there was too much wasted space inside it and decided to build a town there, then forgotten to maintain the wall itself.

On the Tan Lan website, Dean listed Bara Brith under cakes, but called it a tea *bread* and suggested eating it with Welsh butter. The Conwy Bakery version turned out to be more like a cake, softer and crumblier. My guess was that, like many recipes I'd found, it contained fat but not treacle. I'm not going to say it was better or worse, but it was completely different. As ever, two different bakers inherited two different recipes from an earlier generation and, by putting their own twists on them, came up with something to keep the traditionalists arguing.

Traditional Bara Brith

Makes 1 loaf cake

450g mixed currants and sultanas
300ml cold tea
175g Muscovado sugar
1 medium egg
1 tbsp finely grated orange zest
2 tbsp orange juice
1 tbsp runny honey, plus extra for glazing (optional)
450g self-raising flour
1 tsp mixed spice

1 Put the mixed fruit into a large bowl, pour over the tea, cover and leave to soak at least overnight.

2 The next day, preheat the oven to 160°C/325°F/gas mark 3. Grease a 900g loaf tin.

3 In a bowl, mix together the sugar, egg, orange zest, juice and honey. Add to the fruit, then sift in the flour and spice, and mix well. Pour the mixture into the prepared loaf tin.

4 Bake in the preheated oven for about 1¾ hours, until golden and firm to the touch in the middle. If you like, spread a little extra honey over the cake while it is still warm.

5 Allow to cool thoroughly, then store in an airtight container. This cake will become more flavoursome after a few days, as the moisture from the fruit seeps into the rest of the mixture. Serve in slices spread generously with butter.

Shropshire

Home of *the* Gingerbread?

HAVING DONE EVERYTHING WE INTENDED to do in Wales, we nipped over the border into Shropshire. That's because, for one of the most sparsely populated counties in the country, it has more than its fair share of baking specialities.

With its reputation for Michelin stars and its glitzy food festival, Ludlow is the culinary capital of – well, certainly Shropshire and some would say England. Yet we found a surprising lack of local baking. One deli sold a fruit cake made from local ingredients; the Castle Café had a Shropshire Apple and Sultana Cake; but the most popular baked good seemed to be Bara Brith, of which we'd seen plenty in the last couple of days. We were beginning to find Ludlow disappointing when we happened upon the Broad Bean Food Boutique. It offered a Shropshire Raspberry and Honey Cake, made by Cariad Cakes of Leintwardine, that looked (and later turned out to be) decidedly good.

I was getting cheeky by now, and the ladies in the shop looked friendly, so I asked if it was a genuine Shropshire tradition or if calling it 'Shropshire' was a marketing gesture. A bit of both, was the answer – both the raspberries and the honey were local, but Cariad's really traditional product was Shropshire Hills Fruit Cake, which contained winberries and Shropshire Lad Ale. I ordered one of these; it was not only fruity and beery but gently gingery as well. According to my road atlas, Leintwardine is actually in Herefordshire, but never mind; Cariad Cakes make good stuff.

From Ludlow to Market Drayton is but a step, and an essential one if you are interested in gingerbread. I knew that gingerbread and ginger biscuits of various kinds had been made all over the country, particularly in the North, for centuries and had been a feature of medieval fairs. Ginger, which originates in Asia, had been traded around the world for over 3,000 years; it was introduced to Ancient Rome by the Phoenicians (they did get that far, even if they never hit Cornwall). The Romans then spread it across Europe and it remained popular throughout the Middle Ages. Because it produced a large, solid rhizome that was easy to transport and came to no harm if it was at sea for a few months, it was comparatively cheap – at one time 50 times cheaper than pepper and goodness knows how many times cheaper than saffron.

When I say 'comparatively cheap' I don't mean 'really cheap'. I had read somewhere that in the Middle Ages, 'as little as just one pound was worth 1 shilling and 7 pence, approximately equivalent to the price of a sheep', though I must say that 1lb of ginger (454g in today's parlance) would last a good while in most kitchens. The point is that it was readily available and affordable to many, if not for every day then at least for special occasions. The earliest form of gingerbread was a thin, hard biscuit, often cut into imaginative shapes and figures. Across Europe, it was associated with festivals and weddings, with gingerbread figures given to the bride and groom to encourage fertility; in Bohemia the Guild of Gingerbread produced gingerbread images of the Madonna and Child. The modern gingerbread man probably developed from this Christian imagery.

But all that applies to a lot of places that made (and some that continue to make) gingerbread. Market Drayton had lifted itself above the crowd by calling itself 'the home of gingerbread'. This claim is somewhat undermined by the fact that gingerbread is no longer produced there – Billington's, the bakers who have been making it since 1817, are now based in Barnsley. But we found we could buy it at a splendid chocolate shop called Tuesday's.

Tuesday's would also have sold us a do-it-yourself gingerbread-decorating kit, but that was a sideline. They were pretty focused on chocolate. They had chocolate shoes filled with chocolates, chocolate rugby balls, chocolate birthday cards and an extraordinary range of truffles. I was tempted by the banoffee-flavoured one (among about 29 others), but felt that as I was there I should try the Market Drayton truffle: it looked a bit like a chocolate-coated walnut, but turned out to be very rich and smooth and decadent, with a fruity taste that might well have been the local damsons. I really didn't need more than one of it, but I bought a second for later, just in case, and found it had mysteriously disappeared within a very few minutes. Delicious chocolate has a way of doing that.

Market Drayton is a funny place. The Tudor House Hotel looked very old indeed, but much of the town was destroyed by fire in 1651 and it seems to have had a bit of an identity crisis since. A few new and appealing craft shops mingled oddly with the usual plethora of charity shops and supermarkets. It does have a tiny but enthusiastically run museum, though, where, for the princely sum of 50p, I bought a copy of *Shropshire's Spicy Secret* by Meg Pybus, acknowledged authority on gingerbread.

Expanding on the information I already had, Meg Pybus informed me that, while affordability and taste were two of ginger's attractions, it also had undoubted medicinal and more dubious aphrodisiac powers. The book even quoted an unnamed Frenchman who said that it conferred on those who used it 'absolute powers over any tigers they may happen to meet'. Meg rightly wondered how a trading standards officer would go about testing this claim.

So gingerbread became established and popular and, inevitably, subject to regional variations, as I would discover as I moved north and east. Every town used to have a gingerbread baker. A lot of them have fallen by the wayside, but Market Drayton held on to theirs for longer than most.

The town's connection with gingerbread is reinforced by the fact that Robert Clive – Clive of India – was a local boy, born a few kilometres away in 1725. His masterly generalship was responsible for the British defeat of the French-supported Nawab of Bengal's army in India, laying the foundations for the British Raj and giving us control of valuable ginger- and pepper-growing areas. For the first time, the Brits didn't have to negotiate with foreigners to secure a supply of spices. Clive spent the last few years of his life back in England, becoming among other things Lord Lieutenant of Shropshire, and there is no reason to doubt that he brought a taste for Indian spices, and a few samples, home with him. Trade routes with the West Indies were also up and running by this time, allowing the Market Drayton Gingerbread makers to add a further exotic ingredient to their mix – rum.

Many biscuits improve with dunking and Market Drayton Gingerbread is no exception. The difference here is that they don't do it with tea: in Market Drayton the traditional medium for dunking is port.

Yes, that's right. They dunk a gingerbread that already has rum in it into port. Legend has it that this was a favourite treat for farmers' wives, who would arrive at Billington's shop *discreetly veiled* (I'm quoting Meg Pybus here, but the italics are mine; what did they imagine people would think they were doing?) in order to indulge themselves. Given that farmers' wives would have lots of chores to keep them busy in the morning and evening, I'm guessing that this indulgence took place in the middle of the afternoon. There's more than a touch of Madame Bovary about it.

Well, don't knock it until you've tried it, they say, but I did try it and I am going to knock it. It's a most peculiar combination of tastes, with the port fighting against the ginger to the detriment of both. Stick to dunking in tea, is my advice.

The recipe I've given here is taken from *Traditional Food in Shropshire* by Peter Brears, who describes it as a 'home' version produced in the town in the 1930s, differing from the real thing in containing brandy rather than rum. I've restored the rum, because it is an intrinsic part of the tradition, but it's a matter of taste; I've also specified the amount of ginger, which was left vague in the original. A tablespoon may seem like a lot, but this is a very gingery gingerbread. It's also, as Peter Brears puts it, 'a real challenge to the teeth', so eat it when you're with people who won't thinking that dunking (in whichever medium you choose) is 'common'.

Market Drayton Gingerbread

Makes about 25

340g plain flour
110g unsalted butter
110g granulated sugar
1 tbsp ground ginger
a pinch of ground mace
12g chopped mixed peel
½ tbsp rum or brandy
1 medium egg, beaten
110g golden syrup or treacle

1. Put the flour in a large bowl, and rub the butter into the flour until the mixture resembles fine breadcrumbs. Mix in the rest of the dry ingredients.
2. In a separate bowl, mix together the rum or brandy, egg and syrup or treacle. Make a well in the centre of the flour mixture and pour the syrupy mixture into it. Stir well, then knead to form a firm dough. Cover and leave overnight.
3. Preheat the oven to 160°C/325°F/gas mark 3, and grease a baking sheet.
4. Form the dough into about 25 finger-sized rolls, around 10cm long, and arrange on the prepared baking sheet. Bake in the

preheated oven for about 20 minutes, until golden brown. Remove from the oven and allow to cool before removing to a wire rack.

All that said, Market Drayton doesn't claim to have invented gingerbread but (and now I felt I was getting to the root of the mystery) it claims to have the best. As the wrapping of Billington's Gingerbread says, and has said for many a long year, 'For QUALITY, PURITY and FLAVOUR we Challenge the World'. So Market Drayton is not the home of gingerbread but the home of *the* gingerbread. I wondered if this was bit of a marketing ploy. Or perhaps just a bit of a cheek.

Shrewsbury, another small step if you are pootling around Shropshire, is in a different league from Market Drayton. Costa, Starbucks and Caffè Nero have all infiltrated here, but it's the town's proud boast that it has more individual shops than it does multiples. Tanners the wine merchant, for example, was established in 1842 and is today an amalgamation of six companies that have been in business for a total of over 920 years. From the outside the premises look like an old coaching inn; inside you wander through room upon room of wine cellars stacked with bottles, as undisturbed as you would be in a good bookshop until you ask for help. Then you find that the staff are as knowledgeable and enthusiastic as they would be in – well, in a good bookshop.

Much of the rest of the town is in the same vein. We'd been recommended to have a light lunch (who needed more after two of Tuesday's chocolates?) at the 16th-century Draper's Hall, once the headquarters of Shrewsbury's most important guild. It didn't disappoint: it retains, as the guidebooks say, many original features, and its peppers roasted with mint and served with mint yogurt kept us going very nicely until the next round of tea and cake. And here's a touch of class: we had a bottle of mineral water and, still thirsty when it was time for the bill, we asked for some tap. The waiter brought it in a carafe and *gave us clean glasses*.

We'd come to Shrewsbury expecting not to find anyone making Shrewsbury Biscuits. Or Cake. As in Aberffraw, the two names seem to have been used interchangeably over the years, but in Shrewsbury they come down to the same thing – a particularly crumbly take on shortbread. Long before it turned into the sort of biscuit you might find in a sealed packet beside your bed in a not very imaginative hotel, it was famous throughout the country: in his play *The Way of the World* (1700), William Congreve described someone as being 'as short as a Shrewsbury biscuit', meaning short-tempered or brusque. It's had various flavours over the centuries – like many baked goods it was once flavoured with caraway and there remains a dispute among traditionalists as to whether it should contain dried fruit or lemon. I've chosen to include this 1823 recipe rather than one of the many others because the sherry and rosewater lend an interesting twist. I've reduced the quantity of caraway, though – a rather overpowering tablespoonful was specified in the original.

Shrewsbury Biscuits

Makes about 12

250g plain flour
1 tsp caraway seeds
½ tsp freshly grated nutmeg
175g granulated sugar
175g unsalted butter
1 medium egg, beaten
1 tbsp sherry
1 tbsp rosewater

1. Preheat the oven to 140°C/275°F/gas mark 1. Grease a baking sheet.
2. In a large bowl, mix the dry ingredients together, then rub in the butter until the mixture resembles fine breadcrumbs. Make a well in the centre, then work in the beaten egg, sherry and rosewater to form a dough.
3. On a lightly floured surface, knead lightly for a few minutes, then roll out to about 7mm thick. Cut into 10cm rounds and place these on the baking sheet. Prick the surface of each biscuit with a fork.
4. Bake in the preheated oven for about 25 minutes, until just starting to brown. Cool on the baking sheet for a few minutes before removing on to a wire rack.

When Laura Mason and Catherine Brown were researching their wonderful book *The Taste of Britain* in the 1990s, they found no one making Shrewsbury Biscuits and no one particularly interested in them. I knew that the WI had revived them, but the bakery they use isn't in Shropshire. However, the helpful guide produced by Shrewsbury Council told us that the Shrewsbury Bakehouse was famous for them.

No longer, we discovered. It's a lovely artisan bakery, but they stopped making the town's eponymous product a year or so ago. They found it didn't sell very well, the girl in the shop told us, and, because they don't use preservatives, it had a short shelf life. Apparently they had a lot of requests for them, but not enough to make it worth their while ...

A few doors up the hill, though, we found someone who *did* think it was worthwhile. Pomona Grocery sold psychedelically coloured cauliflowers, rounded courgettes and other fancy vegetables; it also had local cheeses, breads and, hey presto, Shrewsbury Biscuits. Hand-made in Shropshire Fruity Shrewsbury Biscuits, to be precise. When we enquired, the girl behind the counter said, 'I don't know why people don't make them here, but the only people who ask about them are tourists.'

At my friend's home that evening, we roped her husband into a blind tasting of two kinds of Shrewsbury Biscuit. The Hand-made Fruity ones were like a home-made shortbread: tasty but, despite their name, decidedly lacking in fruit. Taking our duties seriously, we counted a total of two currants in three biscuits; even allowing for the dispute over ingredients I mentioned a moment ago, this seemed to be sitting very much on the dried fruit fence. The competition was a more mass-produced shortcake biscuit, less fresh-tasting but undeniably fruitier. Both brands, it has to be said, dunked satisfactorily, maintaining firmness and texture (I did say we were taking it seriously). But we came to the sorrowful conclusion that perhaps the reason there isn't much demand for Shrewsbury Biscuits is that they aren't madly exciting.

6

Lancashire

'Everybody's Got To Be Somewhere'

THE IDEA THAT I'D BEEN WASTING MY TIME in Shrewsbury (particularly when it's such a lovely place and I had had tap water in a carafe) was too gloomy to contemplate, so on the train to Manchester next day I tried to think positively about Eccles Cakes.

Unfortunately my brain kept being sidetracked. If you are old enough to have been raised on *The Goon Show*, Eccles is neither a cake nor a place; it's the name of a particularly stupid character, always being lured into ridiculous and possibly life-threatening exploits by the nefarious Grytpype-Thynne. Once when Grytpype-Thynne needed someone to go off on a dangerous mission, he mused, 'Now who do I know who's a mug?' 'Well,' came Eccles's voice, 'I'd better go upstairs and pack.' Memories of this sort of nonsense may not have been the most useful way of passing the time, but they kept me amused until I got to Piccadilly Station and made my way to Ardwick, home of Lancashire Eccles Cakes Ltd.

Eccles Cakes are known to have been sold in the 1790s in a shop in Church Street, Eccles, by a man named James Birch. But they are much older than that – old enough to have been banned by Oliver Cromwell, almost 150 years earlier. In those days the town, like most others, held an annual fair to celebrate the founding of its church, and that is just the sort of thing that the Puritans hated; they thought it had pagan or, worse, Catholic associations, so out went the fair and with it went the cakes. Perhaps Mr Birch or his antecedents revived the tradition once the Puritans had been safely removed from power.

However, that was a couple of centuries ago and Mr Birch's business no longer exists; the mantle of chief Eccles Cake manufacturer has been taken on by Lancashire Eccles Cakes Ltd. It's a short bus ride from Piccadilly Station but, as the production director, Ian Edmonds, told me with the air of a man who has had to answer this question before, only 8km from Eccles as the crow flies.

In the 1920s Ian's grandfather, Sam Edmonds, started out with a horse-drawn cart, buying cakes from bakeries and supplying them to small shops around Manchester – wholesaling by any other name. Then it occurred to him that if he could make the cakes himself he'd improve his profit margin. With three of his sons, he started Edmonds Bakeries in Belle Vue, only about 3km further out of town from where his grandson and I were sitting some 90 years later. They made bread, cream cakes, 'morning goods' – all the sorts of things you'd expect from a general bakery, including a few Eccles Cakes.

This worked well until the emergence of the huge international bakeries in the 1960s; then the family decided they needed to specialise and Edmonds Eccles Cakes was born. Hearing this, I thought the story had a familiar ring to it: then, as now, big national and multi-national companies were muscling in on territory that had traditionally belonged to smaller, local ones; and the smaller ones had to produce something just that little bit better and more original in order to survive. Those big companies also took over a lot of smaller ones, so Ian's father found himself in the position of being MD of his family firm one day and a small cog in the wheels of a conglomerate the next.

So he did what anyone with any spirit would do: he left and started again, this time setting up Lancashire Eccles Cakes Ltd. Today it is the market leader – by a mile. It produces about 150,000 Real Lancashire Eccles Cakes a day and, although some of the process is automated, the pastry is still wrapped around the fruit by hand. Lots of other people, from artisan bakeries to supermarket suppliers, make Eccles Cakes, but if you see a packet of four in anything from a corner shop to Tesco, it's likely to be a Real Lancashire one.

One of the reasons why Eccles Cakes are so popular with bakers, Ian suggested, is that, unless you want to make a really good one, you can make them from scraps of puff pastry: 'You don't need it to rise like a vol-au-vent, you just need it flaky.' High-quality currants of the kind Ian uses are expensive these days, but again if you are not aiming for the best quality you can use leftovers from a fruit cake or anything else you might be baking.

Using up the scraps, I hasten to add, isn't the Lancashire Eccles Cakes way. For one thing, they make literally nothing but Eccles Cakes, so they don't have any scraps to use up. For another, they believe in using the best ingredients but, like Dean Geldart at Tan Lan, as few of them as possible. Their cakes don't contain spices – just fruit, butter and brown sugar, allowing the abundant fruit to complement the rich, buttery puff pastry. It's the philosophy espoused by many of today's celebrity chefs – good, unadulterated ingredients being allowed to speak for themselves.

Ian doesn't claim that their recipe is The Original or any more authentic than anyone else's, but it's the one Edmonds Bakeries were using in 1958, when they won First Prize for their Eccles Cakes in the Manchester Master Bakers' Bread and Confectionery Exhibition. The only thing that's changed is that they now use raisins as well as currants, simply because raisins are a seedless grape whereas currants are not. Replacing some of the currants with raisins reduced the amount of pip and improved what Ian called 'the eating quality'. They use only Vostizza currants, reckoned to be the best in the world in terms of both flavour and aroma; these have a European Protected Designation of Origin and come from a grape cultivated since the 12th century near Corinth in Greece. The name Corinth, I learned, is the origin of the word *currant*, so their local produce should be the real deal.

But even insisting on the world's greatest currant doesn't solve all the quality-control problems. If there is heavy rain before the harvest, the vine thinks it's 'in danger', to use Ian's words, so it produces extra pips to help it reproduce and ensure its future – which is fine for the grape but it makes the currant grittier. Lancashire Eccles Cakes Ltd buy the medium-sized currant, because although the smaller ones are likely to be less pippy, they have a higher proportion of skin, which makes them tougher. At the other end of the scale, large currants are juicy but there's more chance of pip. So, Goldilocks-like, something in the middle – with the addition of a few raisins – is just right.

Purists have been known to write and complain that something with raisins in it can't be called an Eccles Cake, but purists also write and complain that the company isn't based in Lancashire, so shouldn't be called Lancashire Eccles Cakes. Ian's attitude is, 'When my dad started the business, we were in Lancashire and we've only moved across the street, a stone's throw away. It's just that it's now called Greater Manchester. If you look at Lancashire Cricket Ground, that's not in Lancashire either.' He's right: since the reorganisation of local government that took place in the 1970s, Old Trafford has been an area of Stretford, in the Trafford borough of Greater Manchester – which to me sums up the immense complexity of the Greater Manchester metropolitan county. It has ten metropolitan boroughs, two of which (Salford and Manchester itself) are also cities. Eccles used to be in Lancashire, but is now officially a town in Salford. You can't blame people for ignoring the whole thing and still considering themselves Lancastrians.

Having learned more than I'd ever realised I needed to know about raisins and currants, I was hardly surprised when Ian said, 'Our one philosophy is we don't compromise on ingredients. It means we're probably putting the price up more than some of the supermarkets like, but we say, "We can keep the price down, but you'll get a cheaper cake. Let the customers decide."' It's a philosophy that's clearly working: they are, in the jargon of the trade, the number one selling cake in the convenience sector. As Ian said, 'For a small family business, making hand-made cakes, that's good.'

Florence White gives this 1904 recipe in her book *Good Things in England*. She specifies short pastry, but as the norm for Eccles Cakes today is puff, I've changed it.

Eccles Cakes

Makes about 12

200g puff pastry
caster sugar, for sprinkling

For the filling
120g currants
30g chopped mixed peel
½ tsp each of ground allspice and freshly grated nutmeg
55g granulated sugar
30g unsalted butter

1 Preheat the oven to 220°C/425°F/gas mark 7, and lightly grease a baking sheet.

2 Put all the ingredients for the filling into a pan, heat gently for a few minutes, then turn into a bowl to cool.

3 On a lightly floured surface, roll out the pastry to about 6mm thick, then cut into 6–7cm rounds.

4 Place a good tablespoon of the filling in the middle of each round of pastry. Gather up the edges, then turn over and press with a rolling pin into a flat cake. Make a hole in the centre of the top crust.

5 Place on the prepared baking sheet and bake in the preheated oven for 10–15 minutes. When cool, sprinkle with caster sugar.

Back near Piccadilly, I made a pleasing discovery. In Manchester you can get everywhere by tram. If you live in Manchester you probably know this, but to a Londoner, accustomed to going underground any time she wants to go anywhere in a hurry, it was very exciting. For less than £5 I bought a ticket that entitled me to go all over the place all day – a bargain that also stirred my usually dormant but sometimes surprisingly miserly Aberdonian blood.

My next destination was Radcliffe, one tram stop short of Bury, to the north of the city. This is the home of Newmans of Radcliffe, whose proprietor, Gary Newman, was going to explain the difference between an Eccles Cake and a Chorley Cake, both of which he makes. (In the course of our conversation we digressed into the subject of apostrophes; Newmans, with no apostrophe either before or after the s, was his chosen style.)

At a glance, the two cakes look similar. Roundish, flattish, 10cm across, about the size of a crumpet but fractionally thinner. But this is just the Newmans way. The Chorley Cakes that I had bought (in an investigative spirit) in a supermarket in Exeter and the Real Lancashire Eccles Cakes are about two-thirds that diameter and double the depth.

The difference between the two is that Chorley Cakes, Newmans style, are made from shortcrust pastry with no sugar on top; Eccles Cakes are puff pastry and lavishly sprinkled with sugar. Both have the same filling: nothing more than currants, which have been washed, drained and sweetened with sugar. Some Eccles Cakes makers blend the fruit with melted butter and brown sugar to produce something more like a paste, but in Newmans' version, as in Ian Edmonds', the individual currants are very much in evidence. There is even, for the unsweet-toothed or the health-conscious, a 'no added sugar' Chorley Cake, which means the currants really are left to speak for themselves.

Not all recipes for Chorley Cakes are so straightforward: this one includes a number of other ingredients that you can put in or leave out according to taste, and according to the quality of your currants.

Chorley Cakes

Makes about 16

For the pastry
225g plain flour
60g each of unsalted butter and lard
a few tbsp cold water, to bind

For the filling
30g unsalted butter
170g currants
1 tbsp soft brown sugar
¼ tsp each of freshly grated nutmeg and mixed spice
60g chopped mixed peel

1. For the pastry, put the flour in a large bowl. Rub the fat into the flour until the mixture resembles fine breadcrumbs. Add just enough water to form a dough. Wrap in clingfilm and keep in the fridge until you're ready to use it.
2. Preheat the oven to 200°C/400°F/gas mark 6. Grease a baking sheet.
3. For the filling, melt the butter over a low heat. Remove from the heat, then mix in the currants, sugar and spices. Allow to cool thoroughly, then stir in the mixed peel.
4. On a lightly floured surface, roll out the pastry to about 4mm thick and cut into 10cm rounds.
5. Place a tablespoon of the filling in the centre of each round. Dampen the edges of the pastry with milk and gather together to form parcels. Turn over and, using a floured rolling pin, roll each one out gently until you can just see the fruit through the pastry. Prick the top with a fork, then place on the prepared baking sheet.

6 Bake the cakes in the preheated oven for about 20 minutes, until lightly browned. Cool on the baking sheet before removing to a wire rack.

Newmans have a substantial and eye-catching sideline in celebration cakes, but they are basically a small family baker. The unconventional shape of the Chorley and Eccles Cakes is part of the 'hand-made' look. Gary showed me the bakery, where six women were working round a table to put the Chorley Cakes together. There was a machine that chopped a batch of pastry into 36 equal pieces; everything else – the rolling out, the filling and the sealing of the edges – was done by hand. 'There isn't a way of automating it fully,' Gary said. 'We've looked into it, and other bigger companies have automated part of the process, but some of it still has to be done by hand.'

In the days when Eccles and Chorley Cakes were being made in the home to use up leftovers, Gary reckons they would have been made in a less labour-intensive way. Instead of making a parcel of fruit surrounded by pastry, the housewife would have mixed the fruit into the pastry before cutting out, producing something like a fruit scone, but with pastry instead of dough. 'That would have been a really easy way of sweetening something up – just mixing fruit or peel into the pastry, without messing about doing all the pursing.'

The cakes I was sampling were at room temperature, but Gary waxed eloquent about eating them warm from the oven. 'We also do a mince pie at Christmas,' he said, 'and of course they have to be tested. That's another of my jobs.' He grinned as if to indicate this wasn't the most arduous of his responsibilities.

With the rise of interest in local products generally, Newmans had a claim to fame that I hadn't heard anywhere else: they featured on a Lancashire version of the Monopoly board. About ten years ago, when this was being developed, the producers wanted to feature a maker of Chorley Cakes and apparently couldn't find one in Chorley.* So they approached Newmans. 'Strictly speaking we're not in Lancashire any more, we're Greater Manchester, but we were allowed on because of the connection with Chorley.' (Chorley is northwest of Manchester, well on the way to Preston; no messing about with boundaries and metropolitan counties has moved it out of Lancashire.) The Monopoly publicity did a lot to put Chorley Cakes back on the local culinary map.

We talked about the possibility of either Chorley or Eccles Cakes being given Protected Geographical Indication, like Cornish Pasties, but Gary didn't think this was likely. 'Maybe it's not as important to the towns as the Cornish Pasty is to Cornwall. Maybe it's the tourist industry that dominates that.' There certainly wasn't, to his knowledge, an Olde Original Cake Shoppe in either Chorley or Eccles, and no one claiming to have Ye Original Recipe.

Newmans also make something that they call English Parkin or, for some customers, Lancashire Parkin. Most people think of Yorkshire as the home of Parkin, and there is a decided difference between the two: both are a sort of spicy gingerbread, but, according to Gary, 'Yorkshire Parkin can be very moist – sometimes too moist if you don't like that sort of thing – very sticky and treacly and rich. Our Parkin has a lot of syrup, but no treacle. It's much drier, more of a cake, whereas although Yorkshire Parkin is a cake too, you could almost class it as a pudding.'

When I came to taste it I found that the striking feature of Lancashire Parkin was that it was quite amazingly crumbly. How something that has syrup in it can fall apart so readily, I have no idea. I'd advise eating it with a teaspoon and/or in a room you were planning to vacuum in about three minutes' time. Otherwise you'd leave so much behind you'd feel obliged to lick the

* That may or may not have been true then, but it isn't now – Morris's Quality Bakers make Chorley Cakes and their postal address is Coppull, Chorley.

plate, which means you'd have to be choosy about where you were and who you were with. But it's good: not too gingery, not too syrupy; you could at least contemplate having a second helping.

Lancashire Parkin

Makes 12–16

225g medium oatmeal
75g plain flour
1 tsp ground ginger
50g soft brown sugar
a pinch of fine salt
½ tsp bicarbonate of soda
110g unsalted butter
225g golden syrup
30ml milk

1. Preheat the oven to 150°C/300°F/gas mark 2. Grease and line an 18cm square shallow baking tin, or a rectangular one of similar dimensions.
2. Mix the oatmeal, flour, ginger, brown sugar, salt and bicarbonate of soda together in a large bowl.
3. In a small pan, slowly melt the butter and syrup together, then add to the dry ingredients. Stir in with just enough milk to produce a slightly runny dough.
4. Pour into the prepared tin and bake in the preheated oven for 1¼ hours. Allow to cool in the tin, then cut into 12–16 squares or slices.

One stop on the tram back towards Manchester is Whitefield, home of Slattery Patissier and Chocolatier. I wanted to talk to John Slattery about his two local specialities, Manchester Tart and Simnel Cake, but I wasn't going to refuse a tour of the chocolate-making facilities. As we went around, I was struck by how friendly everyone in Manchester, or certainly in Slattery, was. 'Are you all right?' or, in the local patois, 'Yaw right?' obviously meant little more than 'Hello', but people said it as if they were expecting – and interested in – an answer. I discovered that evening that it was an even more versatile expression than I'd realised. As used by the hotel barman, it clearly meant, 'Good evening, madam. What can I get you to drink?'

Slattery, John told me, had become a 'destination shop' – a place to which you brought your friends from out of town to show them something special – and I wasn't surprised. It's in a 100-year-old building that used to be a pub and occupies three floors, including a bistro; baking, chocolate-making and teaching areas; and a fabulous ground-floor shop. My first thought when I walked in had been, 'Wow!', which was clearly the desired reaction. The bakery was behind glass, so that the public could stand and watch bread being made; at the time of my visit work had just started on an extended chocolate area, so that we'd soon be able to do the same with the chocolates.

Even without that amenity there was chocolate of every description as far as the eye could see. The shop window was full of chocolate cakes decorated in chocolate, with chocolate brides and grooms, chocolate spirals, white chocolate rose petals, chocolate ruffles, chocolate pearls, chocolate lace work. 'We can do almost anything with chocolate,' John said. 'We can shape it, we can colour it. It's a lovely medium to work with.' Everything was hand-made: there were machines to temper the chocolate and keep it at the right temperature, but all the crafting and sculpting was done by hand by a talented team of 12 cake decorators.,

Tempering chocolate is the key to its quality. It's the same process that results in tempered steel, only not at anything like such a high temperature, and the point is to give the chocolate a pleasing gloss when it's set and to make it crisp and snappy when you bite into it. Also, when you pour well-tempered chocolate into a mould, it shrinks slightly as it sets and comes out of the mould cleanly.

Like a lot of baking, it's all about chemistry – in this case the chemistry of the five different fat crystals in cocoa butter. One sets and is stable at 28°C; the other four set at varying temperatures between 28°C and 44°C, but are not stable. So heating, cooling and then heating again are carefully controlled parts of the process. At 44°C, I could see in the tempering vat in front of me, chocolate is very pourable, but as it cools it becomes thicker and more viscous, which is what you want. That tiny bit of shrinkage that happens in the mould is the key to the chocolate perfection that is Slattery's USP.

There was a lot more to it than this – 'It's quite technical,' John said, with gentle understatement – but if I didn't take in all the details it's not because he didn't explain it properly, it's because I was too busy drooling.

The result of this expert activity was evident on the shop floor: there were chocolates, chocolate truffles, chocolate 'slates' on which you could pipe greetings from 'Gone Fishing' to 'Good Luck in Your New Home', and chocolate novelty items – chocolate teddy bears, chocolate dogs, chocolate iPhones, chocolate lipsticks, chocolate shoes, chocolate CDs. There was a chocolate 'Big Breakfast' bar with fried eggs, sausages and bacon, all made of chocolate; and the healthy option, the chocolate 'five a day' bar, with carrots, cauliflower, peas, corn and cabbage in green, orange and yellow chocolate.

It seems almost incidental to the Slattery business that they make cakes. But they do – everything from lunchtime takeaways such as muffins to gateaux that were every bit as glamorous as I would have expected, having been in the place half an hour. Specifically for the purposes of my research, they make Manchester Tart, sometimes called Manchester Pudding, which in the 1960s and '70s in the North of England was a commonplace school-dinner pudding to which no one gave much thought. A friend of mine had it at school in Liverpool; Dean from the Tan Lan Bakery remembered it in North Wales. This is an updated version of Mrs Beeton's recipe.

Manchester Tart

Makes 1 x 20cm tart

180g puff pastry
a few tbsp your favourite flavour of jam
icing sugar, to sprinkle

For the filling
300ml milk
a strip of lemon peel, about 5cm long
85g fresh white breadcrumbs
2 medium eggs, plus 2 extra yolks
55g unsalted butter
2–3 tbsp caster sugar, to taste
3 tbsp brandy

1. For the filling, put the milk and lemon peel in a small pan and warm gently until the milk is just steaming. Remove from the heat, cover and leave to infuse for half an hour.
2. Put the breadcrumbs in a bowl, and strain the milk on to them. Return to the pan and boil for 2–3 minutes. Remove from the heat and add the eggs, butter, sugar and brandy. Stir well together and leave to cool thoroughly.
3. Meanwhile, preheat the oven to 180°C/350°F/gas mark 4.
4. On a lightly floured surface, roll out the puff pastry and use it to line a pie dish about 20cm in diameter and 5cm deep. Spread the base of the pastry with a thick layer of jam. Pour the cold custard mixture on to the jam.

5 Place in the preheated oven and bake for about 45 minutes until the custard has risen a little and has just set. Serve cold, with a little sifted icing sugar sprinkled over.

I'm guessing that most school-dinner versions did without the brandy. They also made Manchester Tart in a single dish, as Mrs Beeton did, whereas Slattery makes individual tarts. They spread a layer of jam in the pastry case, top it with coconut and then pour on a vanilla custard. Once it's baked but while it's still hot they sprinkle it with caster sugar (to stop a skin forming) and toasted coconut.

Why coconut? Mrs Beeton doesn't mention it and John admitted to having no idea. 'From the coconut mines in Didsbury?' he suggested, with a nod towards Ken Dodd and his jam butties.

Some recipes contain sliced banana instead of or in addition to jam; if you want to throw caution to the winds, feel free to use both. It's a simple recipe that can be made delicious by the use of high-quality ingredients and has become popular again in much the same way as traditional puddings such as Spotted Dick have – they fall out of favour, people become nostalgic for them, they are revived and, as John put it, 'it all comes around again in a big circle'.

Slattery's other local speciality is the Simnel Cake, which probably has a more complicated history than anything else in this book. Its origins are linked to Mothering Sunday, also known as Laetare or Rejoicing Sunday. The reason for the rejoicing was that it was just over halfway through Lent (hence yet another name, Mid-Lent Sunday); the end of fasting was in sight and the Lenten restrictions – on diet and on other things, such as playing the organ in church – were put aside for the day. Mothering Sunday had nothing to do with mothers; it was the day on which people made a point of worshipping at their 'mother church', the principal church or cathedral in an area. Later it became a day when everyone went to visit their mothers with gifts of flowers and cake.

Mothering Sunday was and is three weeks before Easter Sunday, which meant that, as often as not, it fell close to Lady Day, 25 March, which is sacred to Christ's mother, the Virgin Mary, known to many Catholics as Our Lady. Over the years the whole business of mother churches and mothers became inextricably linked and, in most people's minds, cheerfully confused. That confusion has also extended to the fact that most of us now ignore the connection with the mother church or with a female parent and instead associate Simnel Cake with Easter.

The predominant flavour of a modern Simnel is almond, from the almond paste that sandwiches it together, covers the top and produces the 11 almond balls that decorate it. They represent Christ's 12 disciples minus Judas Iscariot, who had blotted his copybook by the time the cake was created.

The name Simnel probably derives from *simila*, the fine flour from which it used to be made. If that's too prosaic for you, though, there's a 19th-century Wiltshire poem attributing it to a married couple called Simon and Nell, who argued about whether to boil or bake a spare piece of dough. They ended up agreeing to do both, and indeed early recipes do instruct you to boil the mixture first and then bake the result. Even so, I think we can safely pooh-pooh the idea that Simon and Nell put their names together to produce Simnel. If anybody takes you up on this, you can cite as your authority Miles Coverdale's 1535 translation of the Old Testament, where a verse in Ezekiel refers to eating 'symnels, honny & oyle'. (Some 75 years later the King James Version, perhaps aiming for a wider audience, settled for 'fine flour'.)

For no reason that I can discover, the three places that became famous for their Simnel Cake were Shrewsbury in Shropshire, Bury in Lancashire and Devizes in Wiltshire. In Devizes the cake was made in a star shape, of which sadly the poem about Simon and Nell makes no mention, and an early recipe contains currants, saffron and lots of lemon peel but no almonds.

According to Shropshire food enthusiast and publisher David Burnett, the local Simnel Cake has more or less died out. In Henry VIII's time, he had told me in Ludlow, the crust had to be as hard as wood and cut with a saw because it couldn't be cut with a knife. You could drop it from a great height and it wouldn't break. 'But of course you could take the lid off with a knife, going round the rim, which is probably what they did, and put the lid back on when they had taken out what was inside. It was like a sort of uncooked fruit cake – very delicious.'

All very well, but it caused confusion in its time. In 1864 Chambers' *Book of Days* reported that one person, who had never seen a Shropshire Simnel Cake before, ordered it to be boiled to soften it; another, having been given one as a present, assumed it was a footstool. The same book records that the cakes were rather expensive: 'some of the large ones selling for as much as half-a-guinea, or even, we believe, a guinea, while smaller ones may be had for half-a-crown'. Those sums equate to 52½p, £1.05 and 12½p respectively – expensive indeed when the average farm hand was earning the equivalent of 70p a week and a professional man who could afford to employ two maids might be on £14. Shrewsbury Simnels were about 40cm in diameter, 7.5cm high and decorated round the edge with spiky triangles to give a crown-like effect. The pastry case had saffron in it; the filling contained candied peel, currants, raisins, nutmeg, cinnamon, allspice and ginger. But not almonds. Where all the marzipan came from remained a mystery.

This recipe, published in the 1970s, merely says 'traditional at Easter' and is what most people would nowadays think of as a Simnel Cake, without attributing it to any particular part of the country.

Simnel Cake

Makes 1 x 20cm cake

150g unsalted butter
120g granulated sugar
2 tsp golden syrup
3 medium eggs, beaten
240g self-raising flour
1 tsp baking powder
360g mixed dried fruit
30g chopped mixed peel
½ tsp each of mixed spice and ground cinnamon
¼ tsp ground cloves
a little milk, for mixing

For the filling and topping
450g almond paste, plus about 150g extra for decorating
2 tbsp apricot jam, warmed

1. Preheat the oven to 150°C/300°F/gas mark 2. Grease and line a 20cm diameter round cake tin.
2. In a large bowl, cream the butter and sugar together until white and fluffy. Gently warm the syrup in a small pan until it runs. Beat the eggs in a small bowl, mix in the warmed syrup, then stir this into the butter mixture. Mix the flour, baking powder, fruit, peel and spices together and fold into the mixture to form a fairly stiff dough. Add a little milk if it seems too dry.
3. Put half the mixture into the prepared tin. Divide the 450g almond paste in two, then roll out one half to the fit the cake tin (it should be about 6mm thick). Leave just a little space all round so that it doesn't touch the edges of the tin. Lay this circle of almond paste over the top of the cake mixture in the tin. Press down lightly to get rid of any air bubbles, then add

the rest of the cake mixture. Wrap the remaining almond paste in clingfilm until you are ready to use it.

4 Bake the cake in the preheated oven for about 2¼ hours, until well risen and firm to the touch. Allow to cool in the tin.

5 When the cake is completely cold, spread the top with the warmed apricot jam. Roll out the remaining almond paste into a circle as before and cover the cake with it. Use the extra almond paste to form 11 balls, and position them in a circle around the edge. Brown slightly under a hot grill. Watch carefully, as this will take only a moment or two. The almond topping should be no more than lightly toasted.

The Foods of England website suggests that the Bury Simnel Cake came to prominence 'because of a series of promotions for the town carried out in the early 19th century, which included the presentation of a 70lb Bury Simnel to Queen Victoria in 1863 and the monster 170lb Bury Simnel displayed at the "National Free-Trade Bazaar" held at the Covent Garden Theatre in London in 1845'. (For those who think in metric, those cakes weighed over 30kg and 75kg respectively.) The website also includes a cutting from the *Manchester Courier and Lancashire General Advertiser* dated Wednesday 5 April 1848, which tells us that on Mid-Lent Sunday three days previously:

> *The town was never so throng [busy] before; upwards of 10,000 persons travelled on the East Lancashire line of Railway. There was not a single case of disorderly conduct brought before the magistrates on Monday. We understand that upwards of £1,000 has this year been expended in Bury in Simnel cakes.*

Not a single case of disorderly conduct indeed. That has to be the town's PR department working overtime. Nevertheless, £1,000 is an extraordinary figure. An average of 2 shillings (10p) a head – you could have bought 12 twopenny buns for that.

I'd taken it into my head that Bury Simnel Cakes were the ones with the almond balls on top, but John Slattery's answer was simply, 'No.' The Bury Simnel Cake is more like a scone. It contains a variety of dried fruit – currants, sultanas, raisins – like a fruit cake; it also has cinnamon and mixed spice in it, and sliced almonds sprinkled on the top, but no layer of marzipan in the middle. It's round, perhaps 15cm across, 3–5cm high and dome-shaped. The dough is moulded into a ball and pressed out a little before it's baked; then in the oven it flows very slightly to give a not-quite-perfect shape.

The label on Slattery's Simnel Cake suggested that it was very nice buttered, but as John said, 'Anything's better eaten buttered.'

Bury Simnel Cake

Makes 1 cake

40g unsalted butter, softened
40g lard
225g self-raising flour
½ tsp ground cinnamon
½–1 tsp freshly grated nutmeg
135g granulated sugar
110g each of currants and sultanas
60g chopped mixed peel
60g ground almonds
1 large egg
a little milk

1. Preheat the oven to 180°C/350°F/gas mark 4. Grease and flour a baking sheet.
2. In a large bowl, rub the fat into the flour until the mixture resembles fine breadcrumbs. Stir in the spices, sugar, fruit, peel and ground almonds and mix well (it's probably easier to do this with your hands).
3. In a separate bowl, mix the egg lightly – do not beat – and add to the mixture. Mix to produce a very stiff dough, adding a little milk if necessary.
4. On a lightly floured surface form the dough into a ball and press down to form a shallow dome shape about 3–5cm high and 15cm across. Place on the baking sheet and brush the top with milk.
5. Bake in the preheated oven for about 35–40 minutes (it will spread a little as it cooks), until a skewer inserted into the middle comes out clean. Transfer carefully to a wire rack and serve in wedges, warm or cold, with butter.

Back on the tram, I realised that if I headed into Manchester proper on the blue line and then changed to the pink line, I could get to Eccles. It was a fair way to go, but I'd already established that the trams were quick and efficient; my ticket would take me there for nothing, so, although I knew that the Original Eccles Cake Shop no longer existed, it had to be worth having a look. Half an hour later I had a moment of alarm when an announcement told me that the next stop was Anchorage – I know I'd been thinking that you could get anywhere in Manchester by tram, but that was further than I'd intended going. It turned out we were passing through the Salford Quays area and Anchorage was the name of one of the quays and of an office development on it. Silly me.

Apart from the cake, Eccles' main claim to fame is that William Huskisson MP died here, the first person ever to do so after being run over by a train. You might have thought this was something a town would keep quiet about, but the Friends of Eccles Station had been busy making their station look attractive and there were notices all along the platforms about its history. 'Exciting but dangerous – a fatality on the opening day' was the heading for the poster about Mr Huskisson.

The day in question was 15 September 1830, and the occasion was the opening ceremony for the world's first scheduled passenger railway, the Liverpool to Manchester line. As MP for Liverpool, Huskisson was one of those present; so was the then Prime Minister, the Duke of Wellington, with whom Huskisson had recently fallen out. During a scheduled stop for the eight trains involved to take on water, Huskisson went over to the Duke's carriage to try to make his peace and was promptly knocked down by one of the other trains (it was, as railway buffs will know, George Stephenson's famous *Rocket*). The poster detailed the various mishaps which the accident-prone MP had already suffered – the poor man was obviously a catastrophe waiting to happen and should never have been allowed anywhere near anything more powerful than a pushbike. With his leg mangled and bleeding profusely he was hastened away to the nearest place where he could be looked after, the vicarage in Eccles. Four surgeons from Manchester soon arrived and noted his symptoms (detailed on the poster without a trace of a comma):

> *in great pain and suffering spasms countenance pale and ghastly forehead covered with cold perspiration cold and stiff at extremities difficult respiration great constitutional alarm.*

With all that to contend with and four doctors trying to build up his strength so that they could amputate his leg, it's hardly surprising that Mr Huskisson died later the same day.

I'm telling you all this because otherwise Eccles seemed a dreary place, even on a sunny day. One café did offer Eccles Cakes, but otherwise it looked as if you could buy them only in the two chain bakeries, neither of which was enticing. Surely the town was missing a trick here? I'd read all that stuff about Huskisson, dutifully admired the Grade I listed church, checked out the bakeries, seen all I felt like seeing of Eccles and was ready to catch the tram back into Manchester in the space of about 20 minutes. I contemplated getting off at Anchorage to see if anyone there made Baked Alaska, but decided that was likely to lead to further disappointment.

As I left, wondering why anyone would choose to live in this place, I remembered that another *Goon Show* character, Neddie Seagoon, once found Eccles in the coal cellar. He asked, 'What are you doing down here?' Came the reply: 'Everybody's got to be somewhere.' That may be the answer to my question.

7

The Lake District

Mint, Ginger and a Dash of Rum

From Manchester it was northward, ever northward, to visit another obliging friend who lives just outside Penrith and had offered to chauffeur me round the Lake District and the Scottish Borders.

Driving back south along the A6 next morning, heading for the Southern Lakes, it was hard to imagine that this had once been the main road between the Midlands and Scotland. Even outside the tourist season, with the caravans fewer and further between than they would be later in the year, the nearby M6 rattled with lorries that would have been hard pushed to negotiate some of these bends. As if it knew we were on a cake-reconnoitring trip, a sign warned 'Road liable to icing', which probably wasn't meant to be funny at all.

In fact, I was taking time off from cake for the first part of the day because, despite its name, Kendal Mint Cake isn't a cake at all. But its name, its fame and the fact that it is so closely connected with a place all encouraged me to stretch a point. It's made by three local firms, one of which is George Romney of Kendal.

Founded in 1918 by a confectionery wholesaler called Sam Clarke, Romney's is now run by his great-grandson John Barron. (It's named after the road where Sam lived, which was in turn named after the portrait painter George Romney, who died in Kendal in 1802.) Unable to find a reliable supply of Kendal Mint Cake for his various customers, Sam had bought a recipe and set about making it himself.

Like an improbable number of other foodstuffs, Mint Cake is said to have been created by accident. (I'd find this again in Grantham and in Bakewell, to name but two.) A confectioner named Joseph Wiper, intending to produce glacier mints one day in 1869, let his attention wander just long enough for the mixture to become cloudy. The result was to make the name of Kendal world famous.

For the first 40 years of its life, though, Kendal Mint Cake was little known outside the North of England. It wasn't until Joseph retired in 1910 and left the business to his great-nephew, Robert Wiper, that anyone really exploited its potential as a quick-fix source of energy. Robert supplied it to Sir Ernest Shackleton's Imperial Trans-Antarctic Expedition in 1914 and seven years later to George Mallory's first attempt to reach the summit of Mount Everest. Neither of these expeditions achieved its goals, but both are regarded as great feats of endurance from which all concerned returned with their lives intact. And their breath remarkably fresh.

Fast-forward to 1953, when another attempt on Everest was being planned. Romney's by this time routinely advertised Kendal Mint Cake in climbing magazines, and at the last minute the organisers of the Everest expedition approached them to see if they could supply a quantity, specially packed to withstand the altitude, within seven days. They did, of course, or I wouldn't be telling you this story. Sugar was still rationed, so Romney's staff gave up their sweet coupons to ensure that the company could rise to the challenge but also to prevent any suggestion that the deal was being done on the black market. (The coupons were, touchingly, later reissued to them by the Ministry of Food.)

So, after the first successful ascent of the world's highest mountain, Edmund Hillary and Tenzing Norgay ate Kendal Mint Cake on the 8,848-metre summit; Tenzing even left some behind to appease his gods. You can't buy publicity like that – a fact that is reflected on the packaging to this day: the label shows four Lake District scenes, a portrait of George Romney and the words 'Romney's Everest Kendal Mint Cake'.

Wiper's and Romney's continued as separate entities until 1987, when the last Mr Wiper sold his firm and his recipes to Romney's, who continue to use both the name and some of the methods of production. Most of this I had gleaned from the website, but the current managing director was sure to be able to tell me more.

John Barron came as a surprise. I'd made my appointment through the Office Administrator, which sounded a bit grand, so I was expecting a middle-aged suit; John was a good 15 years younger than I had envisaged and wearing the whites that showed he'd just come off the factory floor. He had a tiny and cluttered office, in which wearing a suit would have been decidedly out of place, but said they were hoping to expand soon. What he would really like would be a shop, a tea room and an area where the public could watch the products being made, perhaps even participate in making them. (What a winner that would be. Some friends of mine once went to a vineyard in France and came back with wine labelled *mis en bouteille par l'acheteur*; 20 years on I can still remember how chuffed they were.)

John didn't know why Joseph Wiper decided to call his mistake a Mint Cake, but a combination of his best guess and mine was that it was a continuation of the accident: Joseph starting pouring the spoiled mixture away and found it formed something like a cake. Or at least something more like a cake than the individual sweets he'd been intending to make. He tasted it and decided there was nothing wrong with it – it was just a bit softer than it should have been. It was cloudy, but as long as he wasn't calling it a glacier mint, did that matter? Great brands have surely been created from less promising beginnings.

As for the two brand names, Wiper's and Romney's contain the same basic ingredients – water, sugar, glucose and mint – but Wiper's has slightly less glucose and is boiled to a higher temperature, making it slightly harder and slightly more crystalline. You'll notice the repeated use of 'slightly' there – John reckoned there weren't many people who could tell the two apart in a blind tasting. Romney's 'original' is white, but from an early stage they've also been making a brown version, using brown sugar. Nowadays, of course, diversity rules, so they produce an aniseed-flavoured winter candy, a chocolate-covered version, a rum-and-butter flavour and, by request from certain customers, a chilli flavour. They also make fudge (including a chilli fudge) and toffee on the premises.

Business has changed a lot in the last 20 years or so: many of the corner shops, newsagents and sweet shops that used to be Romney's core business have gone, subsumed by the ubiquitous supermarkets, but they've been replaced by the almost equally ubiquitous outdoor shops, so that walkers and climbers looking for maps and waterproofs – in the Lakes and around the country – also have the opportunity to stock up on Kendal Mint Cake.

Shelf life isn't a problem. Officially it's a year, but John had recently heard about somebody finding a Mint Cake that was 60 years old. Would it be edible, they had asked him. 'I said yes. There's nothing in it that will harm you. The only thing is that the mintiness will definitely decrease.' It's an interesting insight into 'best before' dates. 'Best before' means 'best before'; it doesn't, at least as far as Kendal Mint Cake is concerned, mean 'completely awful or poisonous afterwards'.

Whatever it's like after 60 years, it's certainly minty when it's being made. Romney's use a mint concentrate that's powerful enough to make your eyes water when you're pouring it into the vat. They often have TV crews filming a bit of local history in the factory and presenters always want to be 'interactive' – to have a go at whatever is going on. 'Their eyes are just streaming,' John said. 'Even the cameraman is struggling.'

I remarked that when we were coming into the office, we had accidentally gone in the wrong door, closer to the heat of the action, and the smell of mint was overwhelming.

'Yeah, and they're making fudge today. There isn't any mint around.'

Alongside their other flavours, Romney's now make an 'extra strong' Mint Cake – presumably behind heavy-duty goggles.

Because fudge was on the menu that day, fudge-making was what we saw, but the production methods are much the same. The area was surprisingly small: about two average-sized garages end to end. At one end was an enormous vat: it took two men to crank the handle to tip it over and pour the fudge mix into four copper pans. The big vat was a modern contrivance acquired to meet health and safety standards, but the smaller pans had been in use for 80 years. There were about 75kg of fudge: it was bubbling away merrily and looked very hot indeed. We kept our distance, but the operatives didn't seem in the least concerned. They took a spatula and scraped out the remaining mixture, just as you would with a cake mix at home. It was all very hands-on and it was easy to see that the more adventurous members of the public would love joining in.

From the coppers the mix was poured into silicone moulds about 30cm long, marked out into domino shapes, six across and six down. This gives great flexibility in terms of the 'cakes' it can produce. The 85g bar that many climbers go for is two dominoes wide and three long, but for another customer Romney's produce a longer, thinner version (one domino by seven), and their individual after-dinner chocolate mints are a single domino each. We were offered some of these straight off the chocolate machine; they were very crunchy, very chocolaty and, as you might expect, very minty. It was a good taste to take away with us.

Romney's premises are on the outskirts of Kendal, but to continue our journey we drove through the town. It's pretty. Everywhere in the Southern Lakes is pretty. Grasmere, our next stop, is almost offensively pretty. The souvenir shops are in the best possible taste; the

River Rothay and the bridge over it are straight off a chocolate box. William Wordsworth and various members of his family are buried in the churchyard, and just up the road from it the Wordsworth Daffodil Garden invites you to plant a daffodil for yourself or a loved one. We were there at the right time of year and although I won't claim to rival Wordsworth's 'ten thousand saw I at a glance' – not least because it didn't occur to me to count them – there were certainly daffodils aplenty, in the garden, in the churchyard and by the side of the road. Did I mention it was pretty?

Grasmere church is dedicated to St Oswald, which intrigued me: I knew he'd got about a bit but hadn't realised he'd made it to Cumbria, or whatever it was called in the seventh century. Oswestry in Shropshire is said to be named after him, because he died in battle near there; he was also instrumental in founding the monasteries at Jarrow and Whitby, not exactly a stone's throw away. Another story associates him with Bamburgh, where, in the middle of dinner with St Aidan, he insisted on giving his food to the beggars outside. Aidan, deeply moved by the gesture, clutched Oswald's right hand and said, 'May this hand never perish.' Some believe it never did and that it lies unperished in a casket in the church at Bamburgh, though Oswald's head is said to be in Durham, an arm may be in Peterborough and, if you believe this sort of thing, he performed a number of posthumous miracles at Bardney, near Lincoln.

When I say he got about a bit, you understand, it wasn't always in one piece.

There's a charming ceremony associated with his church in Grasmere. It's called the Rushbearing and was traditionally performed on St Oswald's Day, 5 August. Latterly it's been brought forward to July so that local children can take part in it before they disperse for their hols. Back in Wordsworth's time and beyond, it was traditional to strew rushes on the floor of the church, for the practical reasons that until 1841 the 'floor' was actually made of earth and until 1823 deceased parishioners were buried underneath it. Sweet-smelling rushes had their uses.

The 'bearings' are garlands, decorated crosses or other traditional decorations, each with its own symbolism. A procession of local children led by six 'rush maidens' carries them through the village and adorns the church with them. The children are then (and finally we come to the reason I am telling you all this) given a gift of local gingerbread. A visitor in 1789 reported that, once this was done, the villagers were met at the church door 'by a fiddler who plays before them to the public house, where the evening is spent in all kinds of rustic merriment'. I think we can safely draw a veil over any more details.

Grasmere isn't the only part of the Lake District where Rushbearing takes place; this is a recipe for the gingerbread that used to be distributed after a similar ceremony in Ambleside in the middle of the 20th century.

Lakeland Gingerbread

Makes as many pieces as you like

170g granulated sugar
115g margarine
350ml milk
4 rounded tbsp golden syrup
2 tsp each of bicarbonate of soda and baking powder
450g plain flour
6 level tsp ground ginger

1 Preheat the oven to 160°C/325°F/gas mark 3. Grease and line a large baking tin, about 24 x 30cm.

2 Melt the sugar, margarine, milk and syrup together in a saucepan over a gentle heat: do not allow to boil. Remove

from the heat, add the baking powder and bicarbonate of soda, and stir well.

3 Sift the flour into a large bowl with the ground ginger, then add the syrupy mixture and beat until well amalgamated.

4 Pour the mixture into the prepared tin and bake in the preheated oven for about 45 minutes, until golden brown. Allow to cool in the tin for 10 minutes, then turn out on to a wire rack and cut into squares or rectangles, as large or as small as you like.

That recipe makes something a bit like the gingerbread given out during today's Grasmere ceremony, which is thick, spongy and has 'Saint Oswald' etched into each piece. Although it's very different from Sarah Nelson's Celebrated Grasmere Gingerbread®, it's supplied by The Grasmere Gingerbread Company, which is run by Joanne and Andrew Hunter and was the reason we'd come to Grasmere. Sarah Nelson's Grasmere Gingerbread is sold here and only here (other than by mail order), in a tiny shop sandwiched between the church and the Daffodil Garden. The shop is so unassuming that it would be easy to walk past it without giving it a second glance, but it brings people back to Grasmere again and again.

Joanne Hunter, my companion and I met across the street from the shop, in an office with a meeting room, a kitchen, a staff room and other facilities of a kind I hadn't seen everywhere I'd been recently. A plate of Grasmere Gingerbread was waiting on the table and she served us tea in a Sarah Nelson Grasmere Gingerbread mug.

Grasmere Gingerbread was quite unlike any other kind I'd had; Joanne described it as a cross between a cake and a biscuit, crispy and chewy, quite crumbly and very gingery, and we munched happily as she told us its story.

Sarah Nelson, née Kemp, was born into a poor family in 1815, went into domestic service at an early age, worked diligently and rose through the ranks to become a cook. After her marriage she made cakes and pastries for a certain Lady Farquhar at Dale Lodge in Grasmere and became a protégée of Her Ladyship's Swiss chef. (Recent research by an American enthusiast has unearthed the fact that the chef was not French, as had previously been believed. This may, I speculate, help explain why Grasmere Gingerbread evolved the way it did – it's more like the hard spiced biscuit the Swiss call *Basler läckerli* or *leckerli* than it is like the French *pain d'épices,* which is on the borderline between a cake and a bread.)

Around 1850, Sarah and her family rented Gate Cottage, built two centuries earlier as the village school but by then too small for that purpose. Saddled with a ne'er-do-well husband and needing to increase her income, Sarah started to make and sell gingerbread.

It was a shrewd 'right place, right time' decision. It's not a coincidence that 1850 was the year Wordsworth died. Tourism as a concept was perhaps in toddlerhood rather than infancy: the Kendal and Windermere Railway had opened three years earlier and visitors now flocked to the Lakes to absorb the atmosphere and admire the scenery that had so inspired Wordsworth and his circle. In that respect, Sarah Nelson's cottage was in a particularly fortunate location. What is now the Wordsworth Hotel used to be the coaching inn where travellers coming up from Windermere Station would be set down. Whether they were staying in Grasmere or just changing horses on their way north, they would want to visit Wordsworth's grave. To do that they had to walk past Sarah's shop and plenty of them took the opportunity to pick up a snack.

To attract this passing trade, Sarah set up a table top on a tree trunk in front of her gate, dressed herself in a white starched apron and sold the hungry and thirsty travellers 'aerated water', Helvellyn Cake and gingerbread.

No one is sure what Helvellyn Cake was, but Joanne reckoned Sarah was shrewd enough to create something to take advantage of the interest in the nearby peak – it had cropped up in a lot of Wordsworth's poems and his friend Samuel Taylor Coleridge had even worked Helvellyn into a medieval romance called *The Knight's Tomb*. It begins:

Where is the grave of Sir Arthur O'Kellyn?
Where may the grave of that good man be? –
By the side of a spring, on the breast of Helvellyn,
Under the twigs of a young birch tree!

It may be the most forced rhyme ever written, but Coleridge was passionate about the Lake District and finding rhymes for Helvellyn can't have been easy.

Taking advantage of the new tourist trade wasn't Sarah's only savvy decision: she not only kept her recipe a secret but made a point of emphasising its uniqueness. She put the words 'None Genuine Without Trade Mark' on her wrappers from an early stage, and even went to the trouble and expense of consulting a solicitor and registering Grasmere Gingerbread as a trade mark to prevent other people from making and selling anything under that name. The trade mark number – 169,213 – is still on the packaging. This seems an extra-ordinary thing for an uneducated working-class woman of the period to have done, especially since the concept of registering a trade mark didn't come into being in the UK until 1875, when Sarah was 60. But Joanne has the paperwork to prove that it's true. She obtained the correspondence from the Patent Office a decade ago, when the company was approaching its 150th birthday, and she told me that seeing Sarah's signature on the documents had made her feel quite humble. 'It's an honour to be part of a tradition,' she added. 'I want to protect this little piece of history.'

Sarah died in 1904, at the then remarkable age of 88. Having no surviving children, she left her recipe to two nieces, but they were in their sixties and not interested in running a business. They sold it to a lady called Daisy Hotson, in whose hands the business expanded sufficiently for her to want to take on a partner. Two partners, in fact – Jack and Mary Wilson, who eventually sold it to their nephew, Gerald Wilson, and his wife Margaret. Joanne is Gerald and Margaret's daughter, and when they retired ten years or so ago she took over.

She was about a year old when her parents bought the business, so she has well and truly grown up with Grasmere Gingerbread. Yet, she told us, she doesn't know the recipe. Despite being a member of the family by marriage rather than by blood, her husband Andrew does, because he does the mixing, a heavy, physical job that involves lifting huge bowls. Apart from one electric mixer, the entire method of making the gingerbread is as it was in Sarah's day and Andrew literally puts his hands through every bit of mixture himself. As for the other members of the bakery staff, the qualities that make the recipe special can be divided into three categories – ingredients, quantities and methodology – and everyone knows the bits they need to know.

When Joanne took us across the road to show us the shop and bakery, it became obvious why she needed an office. Although the amount of gingerbread they produce is large enough to require brawny men to lift the mixing bowls, the shop remains absolutely tiny – there was room for perhaps four customers.

Along the narrow corridor we came to Andrew's retreat, into which many executives would have been hard pushed to fit a mini-bar. He said he'd mixed one batch of gingerbread this morning and would make another later in the day, when he could get back into the bakery. Three people were working in the room containing the ovens and the cooling racks and that left no space for anyone else. It was in this very room that Sarah had done her baking 150 years ago. The mixing room behind was even smaller, having once been the cottage's bedroom.

Like many producers of unique products, Joanne had been approached with the suggestion that she branch out, sell to supermarkets, enter a bigger league. But, as so often, shelf life was a stumbling block.

'Compared to Sarah's time, the business is huge,' she explained. 'But what makes the product special is that it's not supermarket material. Because it's a Victorian recipe, it doesn't have any additives or preservatives, so, as with biscuits you make at home, you bake them, you eat them and after a week you put any left over in the bin. It's the same principle here. It hasn't got the shelf life that lots of people expect. They think they are going to take it home and put it away and it's going to last for ever. Then they're disappointed when they get it out and it doesn't taste right. But it's meant to be eaten freshly baked, like bread.'

She admitted that they would love the opportunity, at some point, to tweak the recipe so that the gingerbread could be vacuum-packed and keep longer.

'But even if we did that we'd never mass produce it so that it could go on supermarket shelves. As far as we're concerned, this is not just about producing a product. As Andrew says, we're like a small blip in the history of the gingerbread. It's about your passion and your belief and your roots and how you want to hold on to all that. People aren't just buying a packet of gingerbread; they're buying the smell, the history, the whole experience.'

Sarah's legacy is obviously very important to Joanne and Andrew. Like the Wordsworths, she is buried in St Oswald's churchyard – you can see her grave from the bakery window. Sometimes, when Andrew has been on his own in the shop, he has felt her there, keeping an eye ...

'I hope she agrees with what we're doing,' Joanne said, with what seemed like heartfelt concern.

Despite the emphasis on Grasmere Gingerbread, Joanne and Andrew are far from being one-trick ponies. I'd spotted Rum Butter on the shop's shelves and expressed surprise at seeing it in the spring. Lots of people had apparently said the same thing, but Joanne was adamant it wasn't just for Christmas.

There's a strong rum tradition in Cumbria, dating back to the days when Whitehaven was second only to London as the largest port in England. In the 17th and 18th centuries rum, sugar and spices from the West Indies poured in, crossing the fells on pack horses and, for those who could afford them or had the wit to avoid the customs duties, literally spicing up what was otherwise a bland diet. So engrained in local culture did rum become that a *Lakeland Cookery Book* published in the 1970s could contain this recipe with no explanation of why it included something called Jamaica Cake.

Jamaica Cake

Makes 1 loaf cake

115g self-raising flour
½ tsp ground ginger
30g cocoa powder
115g semolina
150ml milk
150g margarine
115g dark Muscovado sugar
1 good tbsp golden syrup
2 tsp coffee essence
1 tsp vanilla essence
1 medium egg, beaten

For the filling
85g soft brown sugar
40g unsalted butter
2 tsp rum

1 Preheat the oven to 180°C/350°F/gas mark 4. Grease and line a 900g loaf tin.

2 Sift the flour, ginger and cocoa together into a large bowl, then stir in the semolina.

3 Warm the milk until it is just tepid (don't let it boil), then add the margarine, sugar, syrup and coffee and vanilla essences. Continue to heat very gently, stirring, until everything has melted and is well combined. Pour on to the flour mixture, along with the beaten egg. Mix well and turn into the prepared loaf tin.

4 Bake in the preheated oven for 1 hour. Remove from the oven and leave to cool in the tin overnight.

5 The next day, make the filling by beating all the ingredients together. Split the cake into three horizontally and sandwich together with the filling. Serve in slices.

One legend has it that Rum Butter was invented after a merchant ship was wrecked off the Cumbrian coast. Members of the crew were salvaging the cargo when they caught sight of a party of customs officers, so they secreted themselves in a cave until the officers had disappeared. That bit seems quite plausible – there is a history of smuggling in this part of the country, as in most others that have a sea coast. It happened that the men had a barrel of sugar, a barrel of rum and a barrel of butter with them, but these had been damaged in the wreck and the rum seeped out into the butter and the sugar. The tide came in (which, given that the men were seamen, you might think they would have predicted), cutting off their exit from the cave, so while they were waiting for it to recede they sustained themselves with the newly created Rum Butter.

A lot of stories claim that products were invented by accident; not many of them suggest that they came about through the intervention of Mother Nature or perhaps the god Neptune.

Back in those days, Rum Butter had nothing to do with Christmas pudding; in fact, Christmas pudding as we know it didn't exist until Victorian times. Instead, the butter was served at christenings in a special bowl, which would pass down through the generations of a family as an heirloom. Any rum left over was used to 'wet the baby's head'; Cumbrians claim that this is where the custom and the expression came from. According to tradition, the first woman to put her knife into the Rum Butter would be the next to conceive. (A bit less easy to engineer than choosing which friend is going to catch your bridal bouquet, surely?) Once the butter was all eaten, the bowl would obviously be sticky; coins would be thrown into it, and the more that stuck to the bowl the richer the baby would be.

Joanne maintained that the important thing about Cumbrian Rum Butter – as opposed to some pale imitations found in supermarkets at Christmas – was that it contained rum, rather than rum essence. Plus cinnamon and nutmeg if you like. Slop a decent-sized glass of rum into 250g butter and 450g caster sugar. After all, it's a christening – you aren't (I hope) planning to drive home. As for the Rum Butter bowls, if you don't happen to have an heirloom in your family, spread the butter on crackers. It does away with some of the ritual, but will still fur up your arteries and get you mildly sloshed.

Cumbrian Rum Butter is a truly local thing: Joanne called it the West Coast marmalade. When they go to shows in Whitehaven, she told us, they sell masses of it, whereas in other parts of the county, never mind other parts of the country, people haven't heard of it. Joanne remembered her grandmother making it when she was a child and being allowed to scrape out the bowl and spread it on gingerbread – really sickly and fattening, she admitted, but a fond childhood memory. Her grandmother came from Workington, on the coast, and Rum Butter was something she made as a matter of course. Joanne's team still make it in her grandmother's big enamel bowl, using Lamb's Navy Rum, 'a good, strong, dark Demerara rum'. They've tried local rum, but they prefer to stick to the tradition. 'It's good, so why change it?'

Joanne was also adamant – and the label on the jar reinforced this – that Rum Butter shouldn't be kept in the fridge. 'Sugar crystallises in the fridge. The alcohol and the sugar act as natural preservatives for the butter, and that's how the product evolved, long before we had fridges.'

The thought that Rum Butter was particular to the Whitehaven area rather than to the whole county reminded me that the place we now call Cumbria is a 1970s agglomeration of several historic counties – Cumberland, Westmorland, the northern part of Lancashire and a section of the West Riding of Yorkshire – all of which had their own specialities. Nevertheless, I was intrigued (reading up about this some time later) to come across a recipe for Cumberland Courting Cake. It was in a book published in 1960, when Cumberland was still Cumberland and courting was a word people could use without giggling (sexual intercourse, as Philip Larkin memorably remarked, didn't begin for another three years). It isn't a cake so much as an iced tart.

Cumberland Courting Cake

Makes 1 x 20cm cake

200g shortcrust pastry
300ml thick sweet apple sauce

For the filling
55g unsalted butter
30g granulated sugar
1 medium egg
115g plain flour

For the topping
55g icing sugar
55g unsalted butter
about 1 tbsp milk

1. Preheat the oven to 200°C/400°F/gas mark 6. Grease and line a 20cm diameter round baking tin.
2. Roll out the pastry to about 4mm thick, and use to line the tin completely, sides and base. Cover the bottom with apple sauce.
3. For the filling, in a large bowl cream together the butter and sugar until white, then add the egg and mix in the flour. Spread this mixture on top of the apple, covering it completely.
4. Bake in the preheated oven for 30 minutes, then leave until cold.
5. For the topping, in a small bowl cream together the icing sugar and butter. Carefully add only enough milk to produce a spreading consistency, and spread on top of the cake.

Further research told me that the future Duke and Duchess of Cambridge were presented with a Courting Cake when, as a betrothed couple, they visited Witton Park in Lancashire in 2011. The article I read claimed it as a Lancashire custom, but then it was in *Lancashire Life*, so they had their own angle on it. William and Kate were given two layers of heart-shaped shortbread sandwiched together with strawberry jam, but the article explained that the traditional version was something between a firm sponge and a shortbread, filled with strawberries or raspberries. Making a present of it to the royal couple slightly missed the point that it was supposed to be a gift *from* the bride-to-be to her intended. It was a token of her love and devotion, not to mention a before-it's-too-late-to-back-out demonstration of her baking ability.

What was odd about this was that my Cumberland recipe wasn't anything like the one described by *Lancashire Life*. We're not talking 'variations on a theme' here; it was absolutely and utterly different. Even odder, it was in a book of 'family recipes' obviously aimed at women who were not only too busy to make their own pastry but presumably already married. Yet it was still called a Courting Cake. How many 1960s housewives lined a pastry case with apple and poured batter on top of it with the specific intention of proving to their husbands that they still loved them and could still produce a decent pudding? I have no idea, but I suspect not many.

Intrigued by what Joanne had told us about rum, we decided to drop in on the Rum Story in Whitehaven. It's not exactly a museum, more what tends nowadays to be called 'an experience', and it has the evocative strapline 'The Dark Spirit of Whitehaven'. I learned a lot.

The 17th and 18th centuries saw many people in Europe enjoying luxury imported goods for the first time. Tea, coffee and chocolate became popular but they tasted bitter. The answer, of course, if you could afford it, was to add sugar.

Sugar had been imported into the New World by the Spaniards, but it was the British who revolutionised its production, beginning in Barbados in the 1620s and aided by a massive amount of slave labour. Britain's Caribbean economy, the museum told me, came to be dominated by sugar and the rum produced from it. By the 1770s the Caribbean islands were supplying a quarter of all goods imported into Britain and a lot of that was sugar. No wonder we became notorious for our bad teeth.

An interesting aside on smuggling habits: the Isle of Man was called 'the Warehouse of Frauds'. Duties there were much lower than elsewhere, which encouraged Cumbrian smugglers to buy goods legitimately on the island and smuggle them back to the mainland. Though from the sound of it the average 18th-century Cumbrian didn't need much encouragement to smuggle anything from anywhere to anywhere.

Even though we declined the tot of rum offered at the end of the tour, it was too late to get from Whitehaven to Keswick before the shops shut. That was the next morning's task.

There's a lot to be said for Keswick. It's so much more *real* than Grasmere. Where Grasmere is full of places for tourists to spend money, Keswick abounds in places where walkers and climbers can invest in gear that will help them not to perish chillily on the Fells. There *is* scenery in Grasmere, of course there is, but it's much gentler: the sort of scenery you look at and admire from the comfort of a tea room rather than putting on your boots and getting involved in it. Keswick is at the other end of the Lake District, the more rugged, outdoorsy end, with the higher peaks, and it's a different world. Or so my friend who lives there reckons.

One of the reasons I wanted to go to Keswick was that it has a Booth's supermarket. Booth's specialise in local food produced on a small scale and as a result were able to sell me a Cumberland

Rum Nicky, made by the Appleby Bakery, just the other side of the M6.

The history of Rum Nicky begins in the glory days of Whitehaven, when, in addition to rum and molasses, dates, ginger and other spices passed through the port. According to the label on the packet, seamen's bonuses were paid in the form of goods that their ship was carrying and it was from these that they invented a date, rum and ginger flan. It is assumed that the name 'nicky' derives from the fact that other ingredients needed to complete the recipe were often nicked from the ship.

Appleby's Cumberland Rum Nicky comes in a rectangle, about 20cm long, 9cm wide and only 1cm deep. The filling sits on a thin pastry base and is topped with lattice-worked pastry. It's undeniably attractive: unlike, say, an Eccles Cake or a Banbury Cake, its dark inner richness is on display; and the proportion of filling to pastry (or goo to stodge, if you prefer) is generous. Somewhat to my surprise, as I don't much like rum, it's delicious: there's a pleasing non-specific alcoholiness to it rather than a strong taste of the spirit.

Cumberland Rum Nicky

Makes 1 tart

For the pastry

150g salted butter
75g icing sugar
2 medium egg yolks
finely grated zest of 1 orange
1 tsp rum
250g plain flour

For the filling

200g pitted dates, finely chopped
85g sultanas
50g stem ginger, finely chopped

1 apple, peeled, cored and grated
140g unsalted butter
70g soft light brown sugar
5 tbsp rum

1 To make the pastry, in a large bowl beat the butter, icing sugar, egg yolks, orange zest and rum together. Stir in the flour until you have a firm dough. Wrap the dough in clingfilm and place in the fridge for 30 minutes.

2 On a lightly floured surface, roll out three-quarters of the pastry to a rectangle to fit your shallow baking tin, preferably about 20 x 9cm. Place the pastry in the bottom of the tin. Wrap the remaining pastry up again and put it back in the fridge

3 Meanwhile, preheat the oven to 180°C/350°F/gas mark 4.

4 In a bowl, combine the dates, sultanas, ginger and grated apple and spread on top of the pastry.

5 Beat the butter and sugar together, then add the rum a tablespoon at a time. Don't let the mixture get too runny – it should be an easy spreading consistency. Spread it over the fruit mixture.

6 Roll out the remaining pastry thinly and cut into thin strips. Criss-cross these on top of the fruit mixture to give a lattice effect.

7 Place the tin in the preheated oven and bake for 10–15 minutes, then reduce the heat to 160°C/325°F/gas mark 3 and bake for another 30 minutes or until the lattice topping is golden brown. Serve hot or cold with Cumberland Rum Butter.

I'd also, on the recommendation of my local friend, scheduled a visit to Bryson's of Keswick – tea room and craft bakery – because they produce a lot of Lakeland specialities. According to the company's head baker, Paul Carter, John Bryson was a baker from Berwick-on-Tweed who came over to Keswick in the 1940s. He had in theory retired and handed the business over to his sons when Paul arrived 30 years ago, though 'like a lot of people who work in this trade, and particularly in a family business, he never really retired. He pretty much had to be shown the door when it was sold.' It was sold to Debra Travis, the current owner and managing director, and is, Paul said, still very much a family business – just not the original family.

Back in the '40s, John found that local tastes in baked goods were very different from what they had been back home. He had to develop new lines and Lakeland Plum Bread was one of them. Unless you have a very refined palate you may be hard pushed to tell it apart from Lincolnshire Plum Bread or the Yorkshire version made by Botham's of Whitby, but Bryson's have developed a unique way of serving it. Go to their sandwich-bar area and ask for their Signature. You'll get a sandwich made from Plum Bread with crumbly Lancashire cheese and apple chutney, and I'll be very surprised if you don't come back for another next time you're in town.

Another Bryson's special is the Borrowdale Tea Bread, which contains almost no fat and only a little sugar. Instead it has a lot of very, very strong tea, in which currants and sultanas are soaked. 'This is a way of getting lots of liquid into a cake. Flour can carry only so much liquid, but with a tea bread the water is trapped in the fruit.' In the past, Paul told me, he had made tea bread to a client's specification and included honey, cinnamon and ginger, but he wasn't happy about it: 'They've all got fairly strong tastes. You add that to something with a subtle taste like tea and you just can't taste what you're supposed to taste.' The predominant tastes in a tea bread, in his opinion, should be tea and fruit – you don't want other ingredients fighting each other.

If this sounds familiar, it's because it's very close to what Dean Geldart of Tan Lan said about his Bara Brith. Nice to hear two experts agreeing with each other. This isn't Bryson's recipe, but it's a traditional Lakeland one.

Borrowdale Tea Bread

Makes 1 loaf cake

450g mixed dried fruit
175ml strong tea
170g soft brown sugar
1 medium egg
30g unsalted butter, melted
255g plain flour
½ tsp bicarbonate of soda
1–2 tbsp milk

1. Soak the fruit overnight in the tea.
2. The next day, preheat the oven to 180°C/350°F/gas mark 4. Grease and line a 900g loaf tin.
3. Stir the sugar into the soaked fruit. Beat the egg and melted butter together in a small bowl, and add to the fruit. Sift the flour and bicarbonate of soda into the mixture and fold in. Carefully add just enough milk to make a soft dough.
4. Turn the mixture into the prepared tin and bake in the preheated oven for 1½ hours.
5. Remove from the oven, and leave to stand for 5 minutes, then turn out on to a wire rack to cool. Serve sliced and spread with butter.

Bryson's Simnel Cake isn't particularly traditional, but they sell about 10 tonnes a year, which is a lot for a business that has only three shops. It's based on their own extremely popular fruit cake. Paul was as discreet as everyone else I'd met about the details of recipes, but he did admit that one of the secrets of the fruit cake was that they baked it at a low temperature for about 30 per cent longer than most other bakers would, to produce an unusual toffee-fudge flavour. They don't cream the batter to fill it full of air – it has to be fairly dense. Nor do they add spices: as with the Tea Bread, they let the fruit do the work. For the Simnel Cake they simply sandwich a layer of marzipan in the middle before baking, then cover the cake with marzipan and decorate it with daffodils. As I'd already discovered, everybody does Simnel Cake differently. This was the design Paul had been using for Bryson's for 30 years, but it wasn't what he'd used when he was working for his father as a young man.

The issue of John Bryson's having to adapt recipes when he moved from Berwick to Keswick set Paul off on an intriguing train of thought. Tastes across the country are quite different, he said. Think about the way we're all being encouraged to reduce our salt intake. In London, bread bakers would traditionally put about three and a half ounces of salt to a stone of dough, and it crept up the further north you went: in Sunderland, where Paul did his training, it was four ounces; in Scotland it was five. It doesn't matter if you don't know what a stone or an ounce is – you can see that the difference is significant. It doesn't quite explain why the people of Lakeland found John Bryson's fruit cake too wet or too dry (all these years later Paul couldn't remember which way round it was) and it's less valid now that you can buy muffins in Aberdeen and Eccles Cakes in Dover, but it's something to add to the 'nowt so queer as folk' melting pot.

8

The Borders

Where the **** is Ecclefechan?

I'D BEEN VERY LUCKY ON MY TRAVELS SO FAR. While the UK was suffering the worst spring in living memory, I had been to the seaside three times – in Cornwall, North Wales and Cumbria – and had glorious sunshine on each occasion. But on the day I planned to visit the Scottish Borders the weather reverted to type. A damp mist enveloped us from the moment we left Carlisle to the moment we descended from the moors along the windy A7 through Hawick and Selkirk into Galashiels. I mean windy in the sense that it winds, but it was pretty blowy as well.

To me, Galashiels and the other Border towns will always be associated with the mellifluous tones of Bill McLaren, 'the voice of rugby'. 'They'll be dancing in the streets of Gala tonight,' he would say on many a Saturday afternoon in my youth, in those long-ago days when Scotland scoring tries and winning matches were common occurrences.

So I had been very excited to find a bakery in Galashiels, Alex. Dalgetty & Sons, that made a wide range of the Scottish products I wanted to talk about: Border Tart, Scotch Black Bun, Selkirk Bannocks and the wonderfully named Ecclefechan Tart. (I also liked the meticulous use of the full stop after Alex. It was like putting an apostrophe at the start of 'cello or 'bus.) You can buy Dalgetty's products on Amazon, so I was expecting a large unit on a characterless industrial estate on the fringes of town. The man I was meeting had signed himself 'Craig Murray, Director', so I was expecting a 50-something in a suit.

As with John Barron in Kendal a few days earlier, I could hardly have been more wrong. Dalgetty's offices and bakery occupy four houses in a terrace near the centre of Galashiels; they looked a bit boarded up, but a discreet sign on one door admitted that they took deliveries there and a little further along the row was a similarly understated invitation to call there for office enquiries.

We knocked and were invited in by a young man in jeans who turned out to be Craig; his mother was a Dalgetty, so although he doesn't bear the name he is very much part of the heritage. The door opened straight into the office, where there was one other person, sitting at the only desk, counting cash. The entire room would have fitted comfortably into my living room and it had clearly been a bit of a squeeze to bring in two extra chairs.

The premises may not be ideal, but one of the reason Dalgetty's stay there is that the original brick ovens are built into the walls of the bakery, behind the office. If the firm were to move, these would have to be left behind and they would be impossible to replicate. The ovens have stone bases and that's where most of the heat comes from – cooking from the bottom up, quite different from a conventional modern oven. Moving would mean changing not just their baking methods but also their recipes, and it wouldn't be the same. That's also one of the reasons Craig doesn't share recipes – although his Selkirk Bannock recipe, for example, is fairly straightforward, the process is not and you simply couldn't do it at home.

As for their products, one thing that had been bothering me was why there seemed to be so many different versions of the Border Tart. I'd even read that Border Tart and Ecclefechan Tart were the same thing, but Dalgetty's versions were completely different. So was there an authentic, traditional version?

'Border Tarts vary from baker to baker,' Craig said, 'and each baker probably has his own version. We're one of the oldest bakeries still going; there are fewer and fewer bakeries about, not just in the Borders but in the whole country. Any bakeries that do survive are probably quite old and their recipes probably go back as long as the companies do. So I'm not going to say that our Border Tart is any more authentic than anyone else's – but it's authentic to us, to Galashiels and Melrose. Others will be authentic to their part of the world.'

The Dalgetty's Border Tart is a short-pastry case filled with sponge which is 'lightly fruited' with sultanas and cherries and has coconut and almonds in it. To be honest, I haven't found a recipe anywhere else that's anything like it, which is why I haven't included it here. Their Ecclefechan Tart is not a sponge: it's much heavier and richer, made with brown sugar, lots of butter and lots of fruit. The butter and sugar aren't creamed, as they would be for a sponge recipe, they're just blended together. It is exceptionally gorgeous, but very sweet: you really don't need more than a mouthful at any one sitting. So what were its origins?

'Dunno,' said Craig. I liked this man. 'I know we're nowhere near Ecclefechan.' Quite true. Ecclefechan is in the old county of Dumfriesshire, over 100km away if you stick to sensible roads. 'But we sell hundreds of them, and we supply a lot of them into Dumfries. I don't know if anyone makes them down there.'

Craig makes the tart to a recipe found in a cookery book dating back about 100 years, so, as he said, 'It's authentic as far as that goes.' They used to make a lot in his grandfather's day, then for some reason stopped until only a few years ago, when a wholesaler in Dumfries asked if Dalgetty's could supply them. They did – at first just for that wholesaler, but now to customers all over the country. But it did sound as if the man in Dumfries hadn't been able to find them closer to home. I'd planned to go to Ecclefechan later in the day, so I hoped to find out.

Noticeable in both of these tarts was the quality of the pastry, which was something Craig felt strongly about. 'It can easily be ignored, but it's what makes the flavour. If your pastry isn't tasty, it doesn't matter what you put inside it, it's going to affect the flavour. Ours is egg-based and that makes all the difference.'

Ecclefechan Tart

Makes 1 x 20cm tart

For the pastry
100g plain flour
50g cold unsalted butter
25g caster sugar
1 medium egg yolk
1–2 tbsp cold water

For the filling
125g unsalted butter
200g soft brown sugar
2 medium eggs, beaten
1 tbsp white wine vinegar
50g shelled walnuts, chopped
250g dried mixed fruit
50g glacé cherries, chopped

1. First make the pastry. Put the flour into a large bowl. Cut the butter into cubes and rub into the flour until the mixture resembles fine breadcrumbs. Add the sugar and mix well. Add the egg yolk and just enough cold water to make the mixture hold together. Cover with clingfilm and keep in the fridge for 30 minutes.
2. Line the base and sides of a 20cm diameter loose-bottomed flan tin with the pastry and prick the base with a fork. Put the pastry case back in the fridge while you make the filling.
3. Preheat the oven to 190°C/375°F/gas mark 5.

4 For the filling, melt the butter in a small pan over a low heat and allow it to cool. In a bowl, combine the sugar, melted butter and beaten eggs. Stir in the vinegar, walnuts, dried fruit and cherries, then pour into the pastry case.

5 Bake in the preheated oven for 25–30 minutes, turning the flan tin halfway through the cooking time, until the pastry is golden and the filling has puffed up slightly and is lightly browned. Serve immediately, or allow to cool for 10 minutes in the tin, then turn out on to a wire rack to cool completely.

As for Scotch Black Bun, it's historically a Hogmanay tradition, but Craig now makes it all year round – once a week from January to September, then every day in order to build up stocks for Christmas and New Year. Although it's called a bun, it's not a conventional bun shape; it's more of a slab. It's a very rich mixture of fruit, dough, caramel and sugar, covered top and bottom with a thin layer of pastry. In Dalgetty's version the same starter mix that goes to make the pastry goes into the fruit; because it contains yeast and has a lengthy fermentation period, the fruit comes out tasting and smelling lusciously alcoholic. The recipe I've given here is perhaps easier for the home cook, and if it doesn't come out boozy enough, you can add a slurp or two of whisky to the filling at the same time as you add the milk. It's for Hogmanay, after all.

Scotch Black Bun

Makes 1 large bun

For the pastry

225g plain flour
1 tsp baking powder
a pinch of fine salt
110g unsalted butter
1 medium egg yolk, beaten
a few tbsp cold water
1 medium egg, beaten, to glaze

For the filling

225g plain flour
110g granulated sugar
2 tsp each of ground ginger, cinnamon and allspice
1 tsp each of bicarbonate of soda and cream of tartar
400g each of currants and large raisins
50g chopped mixed peel
50g blanched almonds, chopped
about 150ml milk

1 First make the pastry. Sift the flour, baking powder and salt into a large bowl. Rub in the butter until the mixture resembles fine breadcrumbs, then add the egg yolk and just enough cold water to make a stiff dough. Wrap in clingfilm and leave to rest in the fridge for 30 minutes.

2 Grease a 20cm diameter round cake tin, or a square or rectangular one of similar size. Preheat the oven to 200°C/400°F/gas mark 6.

3 Roll out two-thirds of the pastry thinly and use it to line the base and sides of the tin. Roll out the remainder to the right size and shape to make a lid. Return all the pastry to the fridge while you make the filling.

4 For the filling, sieve the dry ingredients together, then add the fruit, peel and nuts, then mix thoroughly with the milk. Pack into the pastry case. Turn over the top edges of the pastry, dampen and cover with the lid, pressing the edges well together so that the lid doesn't shrink away while it's baking. Brush with beaten egg, prick the lid well with a fork, then plunge a skewer right down through the filling about 6 times.

5 Bake the bun in the preheated oven for 1 hour, then reduce the heat to 160°C/325°F/gas mark 3 and continue baking for a further 2 hours. Keep an eye on the bun to make sure the top is not burning and if necessary cover with greaseproof paper or foil.

6 Allow the bun to cool in the tin for 2 hours, then transfer to a wire rack. Once the bun is completely cold, wrap in foil and store in an airtight tin. It can be eaten after a few days but is best after a few weeks. Cut into wedges or small squares or rectangles. It's rich!

Dalgetty's was established in the 1890s by Craig's great-great-great-grandfather, Alexander, who had previously worked just a few kilometres down the road in Selkirk for a man named Robert Douglas. It was Robert Douglas who invented perhaps the Borders' most famous product, the Selkirk Bannock, but when Alexander set up on his own in Galashiels, he brought the recipe with him and his descendants still produce bannocks to that recipe.

'Bannock's the Scottish word for any free-flowing bakery product,' Craig explained. So much for my Scottish ancestry: I didn't know that. 'By that, I mean it's not cooked in a tin, and a bakery product that's not cooked in a tin generally ends up round. That's why a Fife Bannock can be an oatcake and a Selkirk Bannock can be a fruit bread and they can both still be bannocks.'

You're aye learnin', as my grandmother would have said.

With all his products, Craig is aiming for the top end of the market: for the Selkirk Bannock he insists on the best quality butter and sultanas. 'I could buy cheaper sultanas, but it would affect the product, so I don't.'

Even in these difficult times, he feels this is the key to the business's success. 'Particularly in the last few years, when people haven't been spending so much money, there's always the temptation to cut back, to cheapen your product so that you still sell as many. But we've always resisted. We stick to making good-quality products and so far it's working: if people know something's nice, and it's worth the money, they'll still buy it. It cheapens the company name, too, if you start cutting corners.'

As with almost every regional speciality I'd come across, people have their own variations on the Selkirk Bannock. Many use a combination of butter and lard, and many recipes use more sugar than this one from the Scottish cookery writer Sue Lawrence. She prefers to let the richness come from the dried fruit.

Sue Lawrence's Selkirk Bannock

Makes 1 bannock

900g strong white flour
a pinch of fine salt
2 x 7g sachets fast-action dried yeast
55g caster sugar
170g unsalted butter
about 500ml milk
340g sultanas
110g chopped mixed peel
1 medium egg, beaten, to glaze

1. Place the flour and salt in a bowl, then make a well in the centre. Add the fast-action dried yeast directly to the flour mixture along with the sugar.

2. Place the butter and milk in a small saucepan and heat together until the butter has melted, then allow to cool until lukewarm. Pour this liquid into the well in the flour, and combine to a soft – but not sticky – dough, adding more warm milk if you feel the dough is too dry.

3. Turn the dough on to a lightly floured surface and knead for at least 10 minutes, or until smooth and elastic. If you do not knead thoroughly at this stage, the bannock will be heavy and dense. Place the kneaded dough in a lightly oiled bowl, cover with clingfilm and leave in a warm place for about 2 hours, until well risen.

4. On a lightly floured surface, work the sultanas and peel into the risen dough, a third at a time, using well-floured hands. Knead until the fruit is evenly distributed. Then shape into a bannock – that is, a round dome 25cm in diameter.

5. Brush the top and sides with beaten egg, then place on a baking sheet and leave somewhere warm for about an hour, until well risen.

6. Preheat the oven to 220°C/425°F/gas mark 7.

7. Bake the bannock in the preheated oven for 15 minutes, then lower the heat to 190°C/375°F/gas mark 5 and continue to bake for a further 20–25 minutes. If necessary, cover with foil after about 10 minutes to prevent the fruit from burning.

8. Remove the bannock from the oven, tap the base to make sure it is cooked – it should sound hollow – then transfer to a

wire rack to cool completely. Serve in slices, either freshly baked or toasted, spread with butter.

Note: This recipe makes 1 large bannock, but the dough can be halved and baked as 2 smaller cakes (reduce the cooking time by 5–10 minutes). Once cooked the bannock freezes well.

Although Dalgetty's has a shop in Gala, only a few minutes away from the office and bakery, Craig recommended a visit to his shop and tea room in Melrose, not only because we could have lunch there but because Melrose was a nicer place to wander around. How right he was: it is surely one of the prettiest towns in the Borders. The ruins of its Cistercian abbey retain sufficient structure to give a feel of what it must have been like in its 13th-century heyday. Standing in the street, you look straight down the nave to where the altar would have been; the framework of the windows is still in place and you can paint your own stained glass in your head. If you are of a historical (or macabre) bent, the list of abbey highlights is headed by the stone marker indicating where Robert the Bruce's heart is buried. The rest of him is in Dunfermline Abbey, but on his deathbed he particularly asked that his heart be removed and taken on a crusade; on its return it was buried in Melrose at the request of his son, by then King David II. Archaeological excavations in the 1990s brought to light a casket that experts believe is more than likely to contain the heart, and that is what lies beneath the stone. Not quite on a par with finding Richard III in a car park, but not bad.

A ghoulish pattern seemed to be emerging here. In Ludlow I had found myself in the church of St Laurence, where there is another royal heart, that of Henry VIII's elder brother Arthur. On the information board, 'heart' was in inverted commas. When I asked, I was told that it was a euphemism for his insides (itself a euphemism,

I venture to suggest). The rest of Arthur's body is in Worcester, but he had been taken ill in Ludlow and died there unexpectedly (leaving Catherine of Aragon a young widow and setting off a chain of events that has sparked many a TV costume drama). It took a while for his funeral procession to be organised. So basically they took his guts out to stop the body going off before it could be buried.

If history and regal bodily organs are not your thing, look around the edges of Melrose Abbey's roof for the carving of a pig playing the bagpipes. Later in my trip I would see human buskers playing the pipes in the street in both Aberdeen and Dundee, but this little piggy was decidedly jollier. Not to mention quieter, which is always a consideration with bagpipes.

However, it was too cold and wet to hang about admiring pigs. Dalgetty's tea room supplied just what we needed on such a day – a bowl of warming leek and potato soup, accompanied by soft, warm and delicious herby bread. It was a lovely, light but still cosy room, with well-informed, friendly staff – further evidence of Craig's desire not to cut corners. There was only one loo, but it was enormous – bigger than the bedroom I would pay £80 a night for in Edinburgh later in the week – with ads for Dalgetty's shortbread and the Original Selkirk Bannock on the wall. Back in the tea room the walls were decorated with photos of the brick ovens, showing how and where Dalgetty's baking was done. One of the pictures showed bannocks being put into the oven on an enormous tray with a handle – very much 'don't try this at home'.

While we were there we did something we couldn't do anywhere else in the world – buy a Melrose Tart. It's a pastry case whose sugary, gingery sponge filling is flavoured with honey, then topped with bright yellow icing and the words 'Melrose Tart' piped on in black. Craig's father had invented this for the town's Millennium celebrations. All the key ingredients had a local resonance: in the Middle Ages the monks at the abbey kept bees and produced honey; a few centuries later a local joiner called Robert Waugh made his fortune in sugar in Jamaica and brought both that and the ginger back home with him; and, perhaps most importantly, yellow and black are the Melrose rugby colours. Melrose Tart is available only in Dalgetty's in Melrose – they don't even sell it in the Galashiels shop – and it seemed to me to embody the essence of what I set out to find in this book. It's a cake that is intimately linked to a specific place, using local ingredients and invoking local traditions – yet as I write this it's only 13 years old.

The other unique offering from Dalgetty's in Melrose is a bread-and-butter pudding based on the Selkirk Bannock. Bannocks are often served toasted with butter at teatime – self-indulgent, perhaps, but nothing too over the top. The Original Selkirk Bannock Bread-and-Butter Pudding, on the other hand, is decadence on a plate. It's dead easy – make a simple (but undeniably rich) vanilla custard, pour it over the sliced bannocks and bake – but the result is stupendous. Craig, who was surprisingly slim for a man who had this recipe at his fingertips, may not share his other secrets, but he heartily recommended this one.

Dalgetty's Famous Original Bread and Butter Pudding

Serves 4

1 Dalgetty's Famous Original Selkirk Bannock
about 50g unsalted butter
300ml single cream
a few drops of vanilla essence
1 tbsp granulated sugar
4 medium egg yolks
a dash of brandy (optional)

1. Preheat the oven to 200°C/400°F/gas mark 6.
2. Slice the bannock into approximately 1cm slices and spread thinly with butter. Divide between 4 x 9cm ramekins, allowing space for the custard to run between the slices. Put the ramekins on to a baking sheet.
3. In a small pan bring the cream almost to the boil with a spot of vanilla essence. Allow to cool for 15 minutes.
4. In another, larger, pan beat the sugar into the egg yolks and brandy, if using. Slowly add the cooled cream, stirring constantly on a low heat. Continue stirring on a low heat for approximately 10 minutes, until the custard starts to thicken. Don't let it thicken too much – it's important that it be fairly runny.
5. Pour the custard into the bannock-filled ramekins, leaving some of the bannock exposed. Put the baking sheet into the preheated oven and bake for about 8 minutes or until the exposed bannock starts to caramelise. Serve immediately.

What with one thing and another, we were feeling much warmer as we left Melrose. Next stop was Selkirk itself, where there is a shop on the market place called Grieves Snack Attack. Large letters above its front windows proclaim it as the home of the Original Selkirk Bannock and there is a plaque confirming what Craig Murray had told us: Robert Douglas opened a bakery here in 1859 and spread the fame of the Selkirk Bannock throughout the world. He obviously didn't invent it, though, because Walter Scott mentioned it in *The Bride of Lammermoor*, published in 1819 but set 100 years earlier. Luxuriating in the preparations for a celebration, Scott wrote:

> *Never had there been such slaughtering of capons, and fat geese, and barndoor fowls; never such boiling of 'reested' hams; never such making of car-cakes and sweet scones, Selkirk bannocks, cookies, and petticoat-tails—delicacies little known to the present generation.*

I briefly wondered what car-cakes could have been in 1819, a quarter of a century before Karl Benz was born, but felt that might be a wild goose chase too far.

Scott was closely connected with Selkirk: he was Sheriff-Depute of the county from 1804 to 1832, and the courtroom where he sat has been turned into a mini-museum. Entry was not only free but was via a lane with the irresistible name of Fleshmarket Close. Plus it was raining again and this was a good excuse to spend a few minutes indoors.

As a Sheriff, Scott seems to have been benevolent, letting the most common offenders – poachers – off lightly. He also had a surprisingly modern take on the petty financial disputes that came before him. In his journal dated 12 December 1825, he wrote:

> *There is something sickening in seeing poor devils drawn into great expenses about trifles by interested attorneys ... Very few cases come before the Sheriff Court of Selkirkshire that ought to come anywhere. Wretched wranglings about a few pounds, begun in spleen and carried on from obstinacy, and at length.*

So true, Walter, so true. As for his literary legacy, the museum had this frank assessment:

> *Through his literature Scott created a romantic heritage for the Borders. Although not always historically correct, this romantic view has endured and even in Scott's lifetime drew visitors to the area.*

Well, I've only read *Ivanhoe*, which is set in England during the Crusades (and which when I was small was also a TV series starring a young Roger Moore and having few pretensions to historical accuracy), but I was still drawn to Scott's romantic view of the Borders. It's a place it would be easy to be romantic about, if only it would stop raining.

In Snack Attack, where we of course bought and savoured a Selkirk Bannock, they also sold Hawick Balls. These sound even funnier if you know that the place is pronounced Hoick. The friendly woman behind the counter told us they were a boiled mint sweet made famous by none other than Bill McLaren, who had drawn me to the Borders even more strongly than Walter Scott and almost as strongly as Ecclefechan Tart. There ensued a conversation – not entirely initiated by me, I promise – about how rugby had never been the same since he retired. Sensing a kindred spirit, the woman gave me detailed instructions on how to find the bust which had been erected only two months earlier in the park behind the rugby ground in Hawick, the great man's home town. Despite the weather and the difficulty we had finding it, it turned out to be a delightful little park and the woman in Snack Attack was quite right when she said that the statue had captured the spirit of the man. I had my photo taken beside it – me in bright pink raincoat, Bill in glistening bronze – and was filled with childish joy.

It was just as well, because we needed all the enthusiasm we could muster when we got to Ecclefechan. It was, to all intents and purposes, shut, and there was so little life to it that we couldn't see what difference it would make if it were open. The expression 'You'll have had your tea?' sprang to mind.

Ecclefechan is famous – if at all – as the birthplace of the historian Thomas Carlyle. He understandably left as soon as he could and eventually married and moved to London, where you can visit his house in Chelsea. It's owned by the National Trust and their website informed me that the Carlyles 'became an unusual but much-loved celebrity couple of the 19th-century literary world'. That's a supremely tactful way of putting it: it was said of Thomas and Jane Carlyle that it was just as well they had married each other, because it meant two people were miserable instead of four.

As you come into Ecclefechan from the north there's a statue of Thomas sitting in a dressing gown, bearded and wistful, a slight air of Abraham Lincoln about him. But that's the high spot: his birthplace (owned by the National Trust for Scotland) is open only over the Easter weekend and from June to September. Do people flock? I wonder. Do they buy Ecclefechan Tart? I doubt it. There wasn't anywhere that looked as if it would sell it. And do you know what? It was raining.

I told a friend later about this dreary town and she recalled passing through it a few years ago, on the way to a holiday further north, and desperate for something to eat. 'It was shut then, too. So was Lockerbie. I've never been so grateful for a motorway service station with plastic-wrapped sandwiches.'

After Dalgetty's soup and Selkirk's Bannock we didn't sink as low as service-station sandwiches, but we did think, 'Oh sod it', and went home.

9

Scotland

From Granite to Paving Stones

SETTING OUT ONCE MORE FROM PENRITH, I made the slightly perverse decision to whizz through much of Scotland on the train and head for Aberdeen. I was then going to work my way down the east coast to Edinburgh and catch a train back to London from there. This was largely because, sadly, I couldn't find a cake-related excuse to stop in Glasgow and have tea in the gorgeous Willow Tea Rooms, designed by Charles Rennie Mackintosh. Their website offered me a lavish-sounding afternoon tea served on a traditional three-tiered cake stand, including sandwiches, scone with cream and strawberry jam and much more. I'd been there before, years ago, and knew it was fabulous – there just wasn't anything particularly Glaswegian about three-tiered cake stands and scones with cream and jam. Though it did occur to me belatedly to wonder whether they would put the cream or the jam on first.

Aberdeen is the home of the Buttery or Rowie, a roll normally eaten at breakfast. It might not have made it into this book if Aberdeen hadn't also been the home of my ancestors. I hadn't been there for 40 years and was anxious to revisit, so I let it sneak in.

Not sure what to expect, I bought a Stuart MacBride novel – a thriller set in the Granite City – to give me a bit of ambience. The weather plays an important part in the book: it's December, there's a serial killer at large and the police keep having to go out in freezing conditions to look at yet another corpse. At one point, a new Geordie recruit to the force remarks, 'I'm used to rain, like, but this place takes the biscuit.'* He's warned that it won't stop raining until March. 'Don't you listen to DS McRae,' intervenes the commanding officer, 'he's pulling your leg ... Don't lie to the poor constable. This is Aberdeen. It never stops raining.'

Not true. I was there in April and it was snowing.

I was staying at a slightly away-from-the-centre hotel called Simpson's because it was convenient for my ancestor-hunting. It turned out to have one of the nicest restaurants in Aberdeen. Certainly my fellow diners on Saturday night thought so. The couple at the next table were celebrating their wedding anniversary and the jolly foursome beyond were clearly regulars. Smoked trout with haggis, leeks and fried duck egg wasn't a combination I'd necessarily have thought of conjuring at home, but it was very good.

In due course, a sweet young waiter persuaded me to try the chocolate brownie with hot chocolate sauce and dark cherry ice cream, though I'm not going to pretend I took much persuading. He also suggested that a Grand Marnier would go well with it. After I'd agreed, he came back with profuse apologies: they'd run out of Grand Marnier, but he had copious quantities of Cointreau. I told him that copious quantities would be a mistake, but a sensible quantity would be nice and that is what he brought me. I felt a certain smugness: if I woke up next morning feeling slightly heavy headed and thinking, 'Why did I have that Cointreau?', for once I would have an unanswerable response: 'Because they'd run out of Grand Marnier.'

At a sleepless, thirsty three o'clock in the morning, this conversation didn't sound as droll as it had four hours earlier.

Lovely though Simpson's was, it didn't do Butteries. I had a toned-down version of the full Scottish – *sans* black pudding – no

---

* Actually, Stuart MacBride's characters have a rather robust vocabulary. I've related these bits of dialogue in pre-watershed form.

complaints there. But the pastries on the buffet table were of the delicate, two-bites-and-you're-done *pain au chocolat* variety. Not what I was looking for. So at ten o'clock on a snowy Sunday morning, having had enough dinner and breakfast not to need lunch any time soon, tired, mildly hung-over but undaunted, I set off in search of a mid-morning snack.

Aberdeen is at its best in what the locals would call *dreich* weather. There's something about granite and gloom that makes them go well together. And anyway, within half an hour it had stopped snowing and turned into what, if this had been November rather than April, would have been a perfectly pleasant day.

But the hunt for Butteries was surprisingly difficult. Choosing a Sunday to do my tourist thing in Aberdeen turned out to be a mistake, as lots of it was shut. I walked all the way up to the King's College campus – one of the two ancient seats of learning that allow Aberdeen to boast it had two universities at a time when there were only two in the whole of England. (The other is Marischal College, whose gloriously ornate town-centre headquarters, one of the largest granite buildings in the world, now house the City Council.) King's is also the place that enabled my parents to study, meet, graduate and, after a decent interval, produce my siblings and me, so it was a reasonable destination for a pilgrimage. There were several appealing-looking cafés and bakeries, as you'd expect in a student area, but they were closed. It took me a while to realise that the reason why the place was so quiet was not that no self-respecting student would be out and about before noon on a Sunday, but that it was the Easter holidays and there were no students, self-respecting or otherwise, around at all. I wasn't going to find anything useful in this part of town.

Back in the centre I found a bakery that would have sold me Butteries earlier in the day, but it was lunchtime by now and they had all gone. In Union Terrace, overlooking the pretty little town-centre park, there was a remarkably cosmopolitan food market. I could have bought exotic meats such as springbok, ostrich, kangaroo and crocodile; I could have bought baklava, viennoiserie, Belgian waffles, hot chocolate in 20 different flavours; and I could have bought Fiery Dragon cheese, whatever that was. But this wasn't a place you'd expect to offer an unassuming local product, and it didn't.

I had high hopes of the art gallery café, but for some reason the gallery didn't open as billed at one o'clock, nor indeed at half-past. The noticeboard outside gave me one last hope – its sister museum. Aberdeen has, of course, been a seaport for hundreds of years (the harbour is in the *Guinness Book of Business Records* as being the oldest surviving business in Britain, dating back to 1136) and in the harbour area I found all the sorts of things you'd expect: sturdy ships built with an eye more for practicality than for beauty; lots of Irish pubs; and a maritime museum. With a café. That sold Butteries.

They looked rather like shapeless croissants, so I asked the man behind the counter, 'These are Butteries, aren't they?'

He looked surprised.

'Yes,' he said. Then, perhaps feeling that more was required of him, 'They're a special Aberdeen thing.'

I assured him that I knew this, I just wanted to be certain I was eating the right thing. He poured my tea, took my money and seemed glad to be rid of me.

They tasted a bit like shapeless croissants too. Only duller. I was glad I'd done some ancestor worshipping and not come all this way just to eat this.

That said, it's a nice museum. They recommend you start at the top and work down, so I obediently got into the lift and was told to press '5' to get to Level 3. The Irish influence hadn't confined itself to the pubs.

The view across the harbour showed row upon row of terraced granite houses. Every bit as disciplined as Bath, but greyer, in keeping with the city's dour reputation. In addition to a 3D experience of life on an offshore oil rig (not for me, thank you), there was a fascinating list of the goods that had been imported and exported through Aberdeen harbour down the years. In the 17th century, goods totalling about 4,000 tonnes a year included apples, bark, beef, coal, linen, onions, soap, stockings and vinegar; in the 19th century a much longer list (518,698 tonnes of goods in 1874) ran alphabetically from ale to wood and included eggs, esparto grass, guano, manufactured manure and sugar. By 2005 the tonnage was up to almost 5 million and was almost entirely to do with the oil industry, although we did have the first mention of granite; there were also fresh and frozen fish, and potatoes, presumably to allow the importers of the fish to make chips to go with it.

The museum closed at three on a Sunday, so I headed for my hotel. An hour later, back with Stuart MacBride, I read a Glaswegian character's view of the local delicacy: 'Only an Aberdonian could come up with a roll that looks like a cowpat.' It wasn't until a couple of days later, when I was a long way south of Aberdeen, that I discovered exactly how unjust that remark and my reaction in the Maritime Museum café were.

Somebody in heaven was smiling on me, because the sun came out the next morning, which meant that on the train from Aberdeen to Dundee I had the most glorious view. For the first part of the journey the railway runs very close to the sea. Hardy souls were playing golf on the links courses, giving a whole new meaning to the concept of a water hazard. Below them were rocky inlets like minuscule fjords. Do they have selkies in the east of Scotland? I don't know, but if they do this is where they live.

I arrived in Dundee with the preconception that nobody there made Dundee Cake any more. Indeed, the cookery writer Sue Lawrence, raised in Dundee, mentions in one of her books that she has never seen a Dundonian eating it. My online researches had found a local baker, Goodfellow & Steven, but no mention of the local speciality. Instead, I had bought (via Amazon!) Dundee Cake from three different suppliers: one based in Wales, one in Staffordshire and one in Leicestershire. Two of the three despatched their cakes only in boxes of six, so I reached Dundee secure in the knowledge that, if I couldn't find it there, I had a lifetime's supply – 13 cakes weighing in at about 400g each – sitting on my kitchen table.

Like my speculations about temperance hotels, my views on Dundee Cake turned out to be nonsense. It was too early for me to check into my B&B, so I wandered about and one of the first shops that caught my eye was a bakery. It was called Clark's and it did indeed sell Dundee Cake. The helpful assistant suggested that if I wanted to know more about the cake's history I should ring her boss, Alan Clark, which I duly did. He told me about the campaign to have the cake granted Protected Geographical Indication by the European Union. As with the Cornish Pasty, this would mean agreeing on a definitive recipe and that, in order for the product to be sold as Dundee Cake, at least one of the stages of production, processing or preparation would have to take place within a specified distance of Dundee. Various other local bakers, notably Goodfellow & Steven, were involved in the campaign, which Alan said would take three or four years to achieve its aim. It's become a cliché to say that PGI is a bit like the French *appellation contrôlée*; in fact it would give Dundee Cake the same status as not only the Cornish Pasty, but also the Melton Mowbray Pork Pie, the Arbroath Smokie and a Scottish cheese with the rather rubbery-sounding name of Traditional Ayrshire Dunlop.

Returning to my B&B, the Aabalree in Union Street, I found that it was two doors along from Goodfellow & Steven's shop, which sold a gifty version of Dundee Cake, in a decidedly cute and reusable jute bag. The only one of my samples that was round, it was also, at 750g, the most substantial and is said to be made to an Original Recipe: 'an orange, lightly fruited cake, with its distinctive whole almond decoration on top'. I can excuse my wrong-headedness about the local bakers only by the facts that Clark's didn't have a website and the Goodfellow & Steven's site laid a lot of emphasis on bespoke cake-decorating for special occasions. Once I got there, there was no lack of opportunity to buy Dundee Cake in Dundee.

According to tradition – and this one is generally considered to be nearer the truth than many – Dundee Cake was invented in the 19th century by the local marmalade maker, Keiller's. Keiller's no longer exists as an independent company, though it did give its name to a singularly unattractive shopping centre in the city, now renamed the Forum. (The Overgate Centre is much pleasanter, even if it isn't named after a marmalade.) Dundee was at the time a major trading port and specifically an important whaling centre, but what Keiller's imported were Seville oranges in order to make their marmalade. They are said to have created Dundee Cake as a way of using the orangey leftovers. Take a conventional sultana cake recipe, darken it with Demerara sugar, add orange peel and other by-products of the marmalade process and there you are. Oh, and because you are doing business with Spain to get your oranges, you have no trouble importing almonds for decoration.

When I told the landlord of the Aabalree, John Bell, why I was in Dundee he expressed great enthusiasm for cake in general and his wife's baking abilities in particular. But he was disparaging about the local product. Fine in very small doses, was his view, but too rich, too much stuff in it. He liked his cake plainer. The best way to eat Dundee Cake, he reckoned, was fried for breakfast, but even then it wasn't a patch on a clootie dumpling, the traditional steamed pudding which is first steamed in a cloth (or 'clootie') lined with flour to give it a bit of a crust, then 'finished off' in a low oven or in front of the fire. The clootie traditionally had sixpences in it and could be decorated with candles to make a birthday cake, or served with cream and sugar as a pudding. Not something I'd thought of frying and having with bacon and eggs, but then this was Scotland. An English friend of mine had told me he'd recently had a deep-fried Mars Bar in Glasgow – 'Not as bad as you'd think,' was his verdict. But I didn't get the impression he'd had it for breakfast.

Over the following weeks, I sampled five types of Dundee Cake – the three I'd already bought and the two I acquired in its home city. They varied enormously in colour, texture, orangeyness and quantity of almonds. I'm happy to report that I thought the Dundee-made ones were by far the best, though I gave a Welsh one to a friend who was having work done on her house and garden and it received a unanimous seal of approval from the plasterer, the decorator, the electrician and the landscape architect. I should also note that I tried one fried, with bacon, mushrooms and baked beans, and either it is an acquired taste or I should have taken the almonds off the top first.

Here's a classic version that you can eat at whatever time of day seems right to you.

Dundee Cake

Makes 1 x 20cm cake

150g unsalted butter or margarine
150g caster sugar
3 medium eggs, beaten
225g self-raising flour
110g raisins
55g each of sultanas and currants
55g fresh orange peel, or mixed orange and lemon peel, finely sliced
12 drops almond essence
1 tbsp milk
30g blanched almonds

1 Preheat the oven to 150°C/300°F/gas mark 2. Grease a 20cm diameter round cake tin and line it with a double layer of greaseproof paper.

2 In a large bowl, beat the butter and sugar together to a soft cream, then add the beaten eggs and beat until smooth. Gently stir in all the rest of the ingredients, except for the almonds.

3 Turn the mixture into the prepared tin and arrange the almonds over the top. Bake in the preheated oven for 1½–2 hours, until a skewer inserted into the middle comes out clean. As soon as the cake is a golden brown colour, cover it with greaseproof paper or foil to prevent the almonds hardening and losing their flavour.

4 Allow the cake to cool in the tin. Once it is completely cold, wrap in foil or greaseproof paper and store in an airtight tin. The cake will improve by keeping for a few weeks.

It may sound as if I had had a busy day learning about Dundee Cake, but by the time I'd finished talking to John it was just coming up to noon. As I was staying the night in Dundee, I had the afternoon free for further exploring. I knew that Kirriemuir Gingerbread was no longer made in Kirriemuir – it's made in Shotts, and I had an appointment to go there next day. But Kirriemuir is the birthplace of JM Barrie, author of *Peter Pan*; as someone in her fifties who was making a career out of travelling round the country eating cake, I liked the idea of visiting the place that had spawned the boy who wouldn't grow up. Plus it was easily accessible by bus. You went through Forfar, home of the Forfar Bridie – the local equivalent of a Cornish Pasty, though I daresay the people of Forfar wouldn't thank me for saying so.

Kirriemuir, according to the Visit Angus website, is 'a charming and historic town [whose] narrow streets are lined with traditional red sandstone houses, friendly shops and galleries, interesting museums, cosy cafés and welcoming pubs, not to mention some of the best ice cream in Tayside'. On the day of my visit it was cold, inclined to be snowy and largely shut. It bills itself as the Gateway to the Glens, but even the Gateway to the Glens Museum was closed. The man in the one gift shop that was open asked me if that day was a holiday – a question I felt I should have been asking him.

However, JM Barrie's house was open and justified my trip. On his desk in one of the downstairs rooms lay the original play version of *Peter Pan*, typed on an unimaginably old and smudgy typewriter. I flipped through to the end and read about Wendy coming back to visit Peter when she was visibly older and he had not aged at all. He didn't really remember their adventures or care much about them. It seemed terribly sad: the one who refused to grow up was left behind as others matured. Perhaps I shouldn't devote the rest of my life to eating cake after all.

I'd got off the bus in a one-way system and it wasn't at all clear where the 'return' stop was, so I asked the girl in Barrie's house if she knew. She very kindly googled it and produced precise information. I thanked her profusely and as I was leaving she said, 'See you later.'

'Oh, I hope not,' I said.

She looked surprised.

'If you see me later, it means your instructions are wrong and I am completely lost,' I explained.

She looked a bit blank but smiled politely. I then went to buy a few bits in the Co-op, where the woman also said, 'See you later.' I didn't try the same gag again. It hadn't been particularly funny the first time and didn't bear repeating.

The bus arrived, precisely when and where I'd been told it would, by the statue of Peter Pan, opposite the gift shop called The Wendy House and the sadly boarded up Hook's Hotel.

So why had that charming but cold and closed little town, devoted to Peter Pan and the Glens, given birth to its own gingerbread?

That question was answered the next day, when I visited Bells Foods in Shotts, makers of the famous Bells Scotch Pie and owners of the Kirriemuir Gingerbread brand. James Stuart, Bells' director of sales and marketing, had kindly offered to pick me up at the station. I was early, so I spent five minutes walking up and down the road before I phoned him to say I'd arrived. My impression was, 'This is a funny place. What's it doing here?' It's about halfway between Edinburgh and Glasgow and today obviously a commuter town for both, but how did it start?

James turned out to be a jovial soul from northern Glasgow. 'It's a funny place, Shotts,' he said, without my asking, as he drove me up to the bakery. 'Old mining town, but that's all gone now. One of the coldest places in Scotland, too.' It's situated on high ground, so the snow lingers longer than it does elsewhere, and it also catches the haar, the cold sea mist rolling in from the east coast some 40km away. He didn't say the population was funny, too, in an inbred sort of way, but somehow I picked up that impression. Where he comes from they presumably have a broader gene pool.

Shotts is also the home of one of Her Majesty's larger establishments and many of the nastiest people in Scotland are banged up there. Bells supplies the prison with pies and the joke goes that one is served up to an inmate on the day of his release.

'Not another **** Bells pie!' he groans. 'I'm going out today and I bet my missus'll've got me a Bells pie for a treat. So I'll be back in here tomorrow, because I'll have **** killed her.'

Bells is a family business dating from the early 1930s, with a third generation now involved. Donald Bell started making scones and selling them door to door and the business expanded from there. In the 1950s Donald went 'down south', as the Scots say when they mean England, and discovered a product that was new to Scotland – puff pastry being sold in a packet. As anyone who has tried it at home knows, puff pastry is fiddly, so it was a great convenience for butchers who were making their own pies to be able to buy it ready prepared. Branching out from packets of pastry, Bells began making pie cases and the pies themselves and now dominate the (substantial) pie market in Scotland.

So where does Kirriemuir Gingerbread come in? Independently of Bells it was, as the name suggests, originally made in Kirriemuir, by a man called Walter Burnett, whose name still appears on the packaging. Bells bought the brand in 1975 and make it to the original recipe. It's what James calls a 'scratch' recipe – it is made from scratch in the Bells factory, just as you would make it at home (if it weren't a closely guarded secret). There is also an iced version, whose recipe has been modified slightly to stop the treacle and other ingredients filtering through the icing and discolouring it.

Marketing Kirriemuir Gingerbread obviously keeps James on his toes. The cake market is changing, he told me: not many people now produce a 'slicing' cake for visitors who come for afternoon tea. They're more likely to invite you round after work and open a bottle of wine. Also, he thought that ginger appealed to a more mature palate – it's an adult taste, unless you go for the über-bland gingerbread men aimed at children. Not only that, but there are lots of people who like just a hint of ginger and then there are connoisseurs who will eat pure stem ginger and cry for it to be stronger. But this latter group is a niche market. It's a subtle juggling act for the seller of gingerbread.

It occurred to me that I'd found the Melrose Tart a bit gingery, but hadn't liked to say so. I wondered what Peter Pan would have had to say about this.

Grown up or not, what exactly *is* Kirriemuir Gingerbread? It's a cake rather than a biscuit, a circle about 12cm across and 3cm deep. According to James, some people eat it dry, some with butter, some toasted. (But not, so far as I know, fried for breakfast.) Personally, I thought it was good just as a cake – syrupy and slightly gooey in texture, with a few currants that took me by surprise because I wasn't expecting them in a ginger cake. As for the gingeriness, the first bite had quite a kick in it and then it seemed to relax, as if it had made its point.

But I'm getting ahead of myself. I need to go back to the morning after my visit to Kirriemuir, when I was having breakfast in Dundee. Linda the landlady shared her husband's dismissiveness of Dundee Cake, but was very enthusiastic about her own home-baked gingerbread. So much so that she shared the recipe with me. It was her variation on one that had been published in a newspaper a few years earlier, said to have been the Queen Mother's favourite. She gave me a sample, wrapped in tin foil, to take away. Neither of us mentioned the word Kirriemuir, but this wasn't far off – there were no currants, and there were both treacle and syrup, but it was chewy, cakey and pleasingly sticky.

Linda's Gingerbread

Makes 1 loaf cake

225g self-raising flour
1 tsp bicarbonate of soda
1 tbsp ground ginger
1 tsp each of ground cinnamon and mixed spice
110g unsalted butter, melted
110g black treacle
110g golden syrup
110g dark Muscovado sugar
280ml milk
1 large free-range egg, beaten

1. Preheat the oven to 180°C/350°F/gas mark 4. Grease and line a 900g loaf tin.

2. In a large bowl, mix the flour with the bicarbonate of soda and the spices, then add the melted butter. Put the treacle, syrup, sugar and milk in a pan and warm over a low heat, stirring frequently, until the treacle and syrup have melted and the sugar dissolved. Whisk this mixture into the flour and butter, then add the egg and whisk until smooth.

3 Pour this mixture into the prepared tin and bake in the preheated oven for 45–60 minutes. Cool on a wire rack, then wrap in greaseproof paper or foil and store for 2 days before eating. Serve sliced and spread with butter.

Another brief train journey brought me to Cupar, former county town of Fife and now home of bakers Fisher & Donaldson, founded in 1919. They produce a wide range of baked goods on a Scottish theme, lots of them based on local ingredients, especially Fifeshire oats. But I was there because Fisher & Donaldson are the only people in the world who make Paving Stones. Sandy Milne, great-great-great-great-nephew of William Fisher, one of the founders, now runs the business with his brother Eric and had sent me a cheery email in response to my request for a meeting: 'Please let me know you can be here before 10.00 a.m. and we can see the Paving Stones being made. Takes about 15 minutes, bring a camera.'

I assumed that – like most bakers – they started ludicrously early and that ten o'clock was the end of the shift. Not so. The Paving Stones were being baked in my honour. Not only that but, despite the fact that I arrived just a few minutes before ten, there was time for a cup of tea and a chat before we went into the bakery. So, never one to hide my ignorance under a bushel, I began by asking, 'Can you tell me what they are?'

Paving Stones are a finger-shaped, spicy, dryish biscuit containing a few currants, covered in boiled icing sugar. In their day the spiciness and the sugar coating would have made them a huge treat; by today's more exotic standards they might be considered a little dull, but the coating is unusual and gives them a certain nostalgic charm. The currants, as Sandy put it, 'create some slight diversion, but you aren't going to mistake them for a fruit slice'. They're called Paving Stones because they're hard – he bashed one on the table to demonstrate.

Then he realised he wasn't doing a very strong sell and added apologetically, 'But you know, they're nice. They really are nice. And pretty useful for dunking in your tea.'

Fisher & Donaldson's bakehouse had been converted from what must have been the biggest garage this side of Detroit – certainly bigger than I was expecting from something hidden away 'behind the shop'. A batch of biscuits, newly baked, was piled on an oiled table, waiting for the bakers to pour a jam pan of hot syrup over them. We debated whether the syrup was heated to 240°C or 240°F. Sandy's view was that it must be Fahrenheit ('We're a bit old-fashioned here'), but no one seemed sure, not even Marie, who was wielding the thermometer. We agreed – and I subsequently discovered that we were right – that 240°C would be pretty damned hot. In fact, it's hotter than Fahrenheit 451, the temperature at which paper burns, but it seemed typical of F&D's easy-going approach that we were having the conversation at all. Anyway, they recommended you didn't put your fingers too close to it.

Marie and a companion, using two paddles each, deftly tossed the Paving Stones in the sugar. It's a process that simply couldn't be done by machine. As I watched, the biscuits turned from plain gingery brown to glossy, glistening gingery brown to the distinctive patchy white as the sugar cooled and hardened. The result was a big, sticky mass that needed to be separated into individual fingers – something else that couldn't be done by machine and which was made much easier by the fact that you can't break the things by dropping them on the table. Sandy had obviously thought better of underselling his favourite product and remarked that it was a sort of Scottish biscotti. OK, you wouldn't always have it in preference to a Kit Kat, but back in the day, before chocolate reached our shores and when ginger was one of the few spices that were widely available, this would have been a high treat. Have our palates become more sophisticated? Less sophisticated? Or are we just spoiled? We ate another Paving Stone each and contemplated.

Fisher & Donaldson have another unique product: the endearingly named Puggy or Puggie Bun: an equally old-fashioned biscuit/cookie/gingerbread wrapped in a pastry case and flattened into a disc. The top of the case is then scored to produce a feature that isn't often seen in baking: a tiger stripe.

I asked what puggy meant, rather hoping that it would be Gaelic for tiger. But no. Sandy wasn't sure, but said there was an expression 'as fou as a puggy' – fou being Scottish for 'full' or 'drunk'. A puggy is also a colloquial local name for a one-armed bandit. So why it has come to be used as the name for a tiger-striped ginger cake remains a mystery. Again, at one time these were very popular as a ship's biscuit, but now F&D are the only people who make them. They aren't a big seller, any more than the Paving Stones are – the locals don't buy them every day as a matter of course, in the way that Aberdonians buy Butteries – but Sandy couldn't bear to see them die out, which is what would happen if he stopped making them.

Mention of Butteries, though, led to my road to Damascus moment about them. Sandy went away and returned with a couple on a plate. It was at least an hour and a half since I had eaten a substantial breakfast in Dundee, and I'd had nothing but two Paving Stones in the meantime, so I showed willing. They were utterly delicious. They looked like shapeless croissants, but they were buttery and flaky and fresh and gorgeous. The reason for this is that they contained butter.

D'oh?

Well, yes, believe it or not, the traditional Aberdeen Buttery is made with lard. It was Sue Lawrence, on a visit to F&D, who suggested that they make them with butter. (In her book *On Baking* she says that some recipes stipulate three parts butter to four parts flour, which really does sound like Cholesterol City: she reduces it to one to four and still makes something dangerously moreish.)

Judging by the way Sandy talked about Butteries, Sue had touched a chord: 'I've always thought butter was the most sublime fat,' he told me, rising to eloquence. 'Who doesn't love butter on potatoes? Who doesn't love butter on peas with mint? Who doesn't love toast with butter? Toast with marmalade is fine, but you've got to have butter as well. So, thanks to Sue Lawrence, we started making Butteries with butter and we've never looked back – we sell *loads* of Butteries – and they are a different product altogether because they're made with butter.' I was recording our conversation and when I played it back later it was obvious that we were both talking with our mouths full for quite some time.

The reason Butteries exist is that they are full of fat, so a fisherman going to sea for a week could take them and, as Sandy put it, choosing his words carefully, 'By the time seven days were up they were still slightly palatable.' His were obviously fresh that morning, which gave them an advantage, but I couldn't imagine they would ever sink to being 'slightly palatable'. They were also quite salty, so I asked if they used salted butter. No, was the answer: they took a big lump of dough and a big lump of butter, then someone scattered a handful of salt over them. Sandy admitted to liking the salty taste but he had occasionally had issues with staff being too heavy-handed with it. 'I've often thought we should have some kind of measure,' he said disarmingly, 'but we aren't that sort of business.'

F&D are also one of the few companies that make oatmeal shortbread; under licence for another local company they make oatcakes, flapjacks and rolled oat bannocks, too. The bannocks are a bit like oatcakes, but made in a very old-fashioned way, with the same sort of rolled oats that are used to make porridge. As a result they are much chunkier and oatier than most oatcakes, which are made with oatmeal flour. All these products use oats sourced in the county of Fife – no mean task, apparently, but it's a selling point that goes down well with the tourists who come for the golf and the scenery, and with the wealthy locals, of whom there is no shortage. There are plenty of high-priced properties in the area, attracting the sort of people who are happy to pay good money for better quality shortbread made from local oats.

I left Fisher & Donaldson with a carrier bag full of goodies and the promise that a couple of Puggy Buns, which were in the oven at that moment, would be in the post to me in a couple of days. They were, and I followed the instructions: split them, toasted them lightly, buttered them and had them with tea. They were pleasant without being earth-shattering, but they were so pretty on my kitchen table that I took a photo of them for posterity. It isn't every day the post brings you a tiger-striped bun.

My visit to Fisher & Donaldson had certainly reawakened my enthusiasm for Butteries. This recipe was given to a friend many years ago by the landlady of a long-since vanished B&B in Banchory, Aberdeenshire. The original contained equal parts lard and margarine, but I think we all know better now.

Aberdeen Butteries

Makes 12–15

125ml warm water
1 level tsp fine salt
1 heaped tsp granulated sugar
225g plain flour
1 tsp dried yeast
115g unsalted butter, softened

1 Pour the warm water into a large bowl with the salt and sugar. Add the flour, sprinkle the yeast over the top and mix to a dough. Cover with a tea-towel and leave in a warm place until doubled or trebled in volume (about 30–45 minutes).

2 Add the softened butter to the flour mixture and beat until it is incorporated. The mixture will look like very wet bread dough or 'stringy' cake batter. Cover and leave to double in volume again.

3 Preheat the oven to 220°C/425°F/gas mark 7, and lightly grease two baking sheets.

4 Place 12–15 dessertspoons of the mixture on the prepared baking sheets and bake in the preheated oven for 20–30 minutes, until golden brown. Serve the butteries as soon as they are cool enough to eat. (They can be reheated up to a few hours after baking, but are definitely best on the same day.)

By train, Cupar is roughly midway between Dundee and Edinburgh, so I continued on my way. I was hoping to learn a bit more about the history of shortbread in Edinburgh, but first I had to negotiate Waverley Station. It's vast and intimidating, a bit like Grand Central Station in New York, except that Grand Central probably doesn't have a pasty shop. There are many stations throughout Britain where you turn right down a platform and find you are on 2a; if you go left you are on 2b. At Waverley, you follow the signs to platform 2, turn left and find you are on platform 19. If I ever moved to Edinburgh I'd have to find a way of getting used to this. Or go by bus.

I'd booked a hotel close to the station and found that, like a great deal of Edinburgh, it was at the top of a steep hill. To reach my room I was told to take the lift to the top floor and go through the door to my left. Only when I was through this door did I realise I now had to descend a spiral staircase in order to get to journey's end. It was a bit of a struggle with a suitcase, a laptop and a bag full of Paving Stones and oatcakes. I was obviously in some sort of annex, but for the life of me I couldn't work out the geography of the place. It seemed a rather perverse way of carrying Edinburgh's hilliness over into the residential experience.

I'd arranged to talk to Anthony Laing, proprietor of Shortbread House of Edinburgh, next morning. His office was a bit out of town and I set off to walk. It was drizzling. Even so, the young woman in front of me was in bare feet. She was wearing a strapless, backless top and a very short skirt and was carrying a pair of boots with strikingly high and skinny heels. If she had also been carrying a banner with the words 'I accidentally didn't go home last night' it could not have been more obvious.

Everyone coming towards me, passing the girl, clearly had the same thought. There were quite a few of them: it was a quarter to nine and Edinburgh was going to work. Anyone on their own smirked to themselves; anyone with a companion turned to them, grinned and whispered.

There was one exception. A homeless man, huddled in hoody and blanket on the pavement, gave her a deeply sorrowful look, as if he had a daughter, or even a granddaughter, her age.

Central Edinburgh is a bit like central Paris or the part of London around the Royal Albert Hall – full of confidence, imposing buildings and statues, although the magnificent Scott Monument could have done with a clean and the easily overlooked statue of David Livingstone next to it looked as if it was a pigeon favourite. But the road out towards Leith, where I was heading, was cosmopolitan in the extreme. I passed a big Polish deli-cum-supermarket with a poster in the window advertising Thai boxing; almost directly across the street was a Russian Baltic food shop next door to a log-fired pizza restaurant. Within 100 metres there was a large Chinese supermarket and a large Irish pub; but then, lest I should think there was nothing of Scotland left, there was a café called The Tattie Creel, which offered, among other things, baked potatoes and that embodiment of warming Scottish cookery, stovies.

After all this multi-culturalism, I came to the little industrial estate where Shortbread House had its headquarters. The company doesn't have a shop or showroom; it's a high-end business supplying Harvey Nichols, Fortnum & Mason and similar emporia. Most of the year it produces about 5 tonnes of shortbread (in various guises) a week;

at Christmas that goes up to about 9 tonnes. A lot of biscuits in a small space, where the vast majority of the work is done by hand and produces a minor but noticeable irregularity from biscuit to biscuit. Looking through the office window down into the bakery itself, I saw people pouring flour from one bowl to another, patting out dough by hand and using the sort of biscuit cutter I would use if I was doing the same thing in my own kitchen. Practically the only thing that was mechanised was the electric beater, and you'd probably use a scaled-down version of that to cream butter and sugar if you were making shortbread at home.

I'd read websites that said shortbread was a favourite of Mary, Queen of Scots, and might have been brought from France to Scotland with her. Some even say that she invented it, but if you consider that she died at the age of 44, having been imprisoned for most of the last 20 years of her life, and that she also spoke six languages, played several musical instruments, went in for equestrianism and falconry, played golf at the Old Course at Musselburgh and put in a lot of work on her tapestry, you can't help wondering where she could have found the time.

There's also the suggestion that the famous petticoat tails might take their name from *petites galettes*, a similar buttery biscuit made in France, but this is pooh-poohed by the people who think that petticoat-tail shortbread looks like – well, petticoat tails, the individually wired sections of the full petticoat worn in the 16th century. By, possibly, Mary, Queen of Scots.

When I asked Anthony Laing about this, he looked apologetic: 'We've all been reading the same websites.' The real origins are not terribly clear.

The traditional recipe is generally agreed upon: three parts flour to two butter and one sugar. To this Shortbread House adds rice flour, which gives a slightly crisper texture than the cornflour many other manufacturers use. They also add vegetable shortening, not by any means in order to save on butter, but to make it 'shorter' and crumblier.

I found this recipe in a 1920s cookbook – it came immediately after another one headed 'Economical Shortbread', which didn't have rice flour and used margarine rather than butter. I didn't feel like trying that. You'll notice that this one, contrary to tradition, has equal parts flour and butter. It isn't called 'rich' for nothing.

Rich Shortbread

Makes as many as you like

225g plain flour
40g rice flour
⅛ tsp fine salt
110g caster sugar
225g unsalted butter

1 Sift the flours, sugar and salt together into a large warmed bowl. Slightly warm the butter and rub it in until the mixture resembles fine breadcrumbs. Continue rubbing until the mixture begins to bind, then turn out on to a lightly floured surface.

2 Knead as you would bread until it is a soft, pliable dough. Roll out lightly and form into the desired shape – square, rectangular or circular (for petticoat tails). Allow to dry for an hour before baking.

3 Preheat the oven to 160°C/325°F/gas mark 3 and grease a suitably sized round tin or a baking sheet.

4 Carefully lift the shortbread on to the baking sheet or into the tin, and bake in the preheated oven until a light biscuit colour, about 45 minutes – it should still be a little soft. Without removing the shortbread from the tin or baking sheet, cut it into fingers, squares or petticoat-tail wedges while it is still hot.

Allow to cool for at least 30 minutes before moving on to a wire rack to cool completely and become crisp.

An interesting addition to the North/South divide debate: it's said that when William Crawford & Sons, who had been making shortbread in Edinburgh since 1813, expanded south of the border in the 1890s, the English thought the biscuits were too thick. So in the early years of the 20th century Crawford's Liverpool factory started making a slimmer product. Another for the 'nowt so queer as folk' department, I feel.

Anthony Laing's shortbread was labelled with a shorter shelf life than other, more mass-produced versions, but the truth is that all shortbread deteriorates from the day it is made, so he wanted people to eat it when it was as fresh as possible. 'It doesn't go off. We had an incident the other day with someone eating it when it was over two years old and they said it was delicious.' I didn't tell him about the 60-year-old Kendal Mint Cake. It would have smacked of one-upmanship.

Anthony had been running Shortbread House since 1989, having taken it over from a lady called Anna Wilson. She had sold her shortbread only in Edinburgh and had only one recipe. Nowadays shops want more than one product for a display, so as Anthony's business grew it diversified: they still use Anna's recipe and Anna's suppliers, but they now produce Stem Ginger Shortbread, Lemon Shortbread, Chocolate and Orange Shortbread, Macadamia Shortbread and Oaties with Chocolate Chips, to name but a few. Unusually for a Scottish shortbread manufacturer, there isn't a tartan in sight: the packaging has a repeating pattern of thistles on a background that changes colour according to the flavour: blue/dark orange for stem ginger, yellow for chocolate and orange, pale green for macadamia. There are also shortbread 'minis' in little containers with clip tops like metallic Kilner jars. It's all very elegant and understated; when I later walked into a touristy shop in Princes Street the array of tartan tins from various other manufacturers struck me as more than a little brash.

By the time I left Scotland, I'd eaten a lot of sweet sugary stuff in an alarmingly short space of time (it wasn't much more than 48 hours since I'd left Aberdeen), and if I had to award a Palme d'Or it would go to Shortbread House's Lemon Shortbread; though those oaty, chocolate chippy ones, both from Shortbread House and from Fisher & Donaldson, were pretty special too. And I couldn't help sharing some of Sandy Milne's affection for the Paving Stones he'd made especially for me.

10

Somerset and Dorset

Of Knob Throwing and Lard

THE REASON I CAME STRAIGHT HOME from Scotland, rather than stopping off in Yorkshire and the Midlands, was that I had a number of events to attend on fixed dates. The first of these was on the first Sunday in May.

I hadn't intended to write about the Dorset Knob: despite the fact that it is, according to the tin, 'made to the original Moores family recipe in the heart of Dorset', which made it an ideal contender, it is also 'a double baked *savoury* biscuit' and therefore outside my self-imposed remit.

I changed my mind when I found out about the Dorset Knob Throwing Contest and Frome Valley Food Fest. At a food fest in Dorset I could reasonably hope to find local cake, but the real attraction was the totally English lunacy of organising a festival around biscuit tossing.

The fest takes place in the village of Cattistock, which, in the absence of a bus service on Sundays in May, is a pricey taxi ride from Yeovil. But I discovered that if I came down the day before and got off the train at the station before Yeovil Junction, the trip became less whimsical and potentially very productive. I would be in Sherborne, home of Oxfords Bakery, who would, with any luck, sell me a Lardy Cake.

Sherborne was – on a sunny Saturday lunchtime – bustling and beautiful. There was a pleasing absence of chain stores and an equally pleasing presence of historic buildings. The pharmacy, for example, was housed in an old coaching inn, and although it had been a pharmacy since 1790 they told me that the original wine cellars were still down below.

The main shopping street boasted two 'artisan bakers' – Oxfords and Mortimers, the latter a branch of a business based in Yeovil. Even though it was early May, Mortimers sold me Easter Biscuits, a Somerset speciality which they told me they now made all year round. Historically these have also been called Sedgemoor Easter Cakes, but Biscuit is more accurate – they're a rich, spicy shortbread studded with currants. Florence White's *Good Things in England* gives a recipe dated 1904 and remarks that 'these somewhat resemble Shrewsbury Cakes', but I found a recipe I thought was more interesting in Nicola Cox's *Country Cooking from Farthinghoe*. She describes Easter Cakes as 'not as crisp as a biscuit or as crumbly as a cake' and adds that 'the brandy makes all the difference'. Whether she means in terms of authenticity or of taste she doesn't say, but I think I can guess.

Nicola Cox's Somerset Easter Cakes

Makes about 25

225g plain flour
100g unsalted butter
100g currants
100g caster sugar
½ tsp each of ground cinnamon and mixed spice
1 medium egg
2 tbsp brandy

1. Preheat the oven to 180°C/350°F/gas mark 4. Grease a baking sheet.

2. Put the flour into a large bowl, and rub the butter into the flour until it resembles fine breadcrumbs. Add the currants, sugar, cinnamon and mixed spice. Whisk the egg and brandy together and add to bind the mixture.

3. Draw the dough together, knead very lightly on a lightly floured surface, and roll out to 1cm thickness. Cut into 5cm rounds with a fluted cutter and place on the prepared baking sheet.

4. Bake in the preheated oven for 20–25 minutes until light golden and cooked through. Keep an eye on them for the last few minutes as they burn easily. Cool on a rack and store in a tin.

Like many biscuits/cakes with a Christian connection, Easter Cakes were traditionally tied up in bundles of three, to represent the Holy Trinity. They were given as a present on Easter Sunday, when the restrictions of Lent were over. Mortimers sold them in sixes, but there'd be nothing to stop you dividing each packet in two and gift-wrapping them next time you were visiting a Christian biscuit-eating friend. Or even a Christian-biscuit eating friend.

The connection with Sedgemoor is a fanciful one, methinks. Sedgemoor is a low-lying, marshy part of the Somerset Levels and the site of the battle that put an end to the Monmouth Rebellion. The Duke of Monmouth was the illegitimate son of Charles II, who died early in 1685 and was succeeded by his brother, James II. James had the advantage of being the legitimate heir and the disadvantage of being a Catholic, and a deeply unpopular one at that. As a Protestant, Monmouth was able to lead an uprising against James, but was eventually defeated at Sedgemoor.

That much is history. The rest isn't. As he fled from the battlefield, Monmouth is said to have fallen into a ditch, where he was found by a kindly woman who fed him up with her home-baked biscuits. I'm sorry to be sceptical, but apart from the improbability of anyone inventing a new cake in these circumstances rather than giving her patient whatever she had to hand, we have the problem that the Battle of Sedgemoor took place on 6 July – even allowing for the moveability of feasts, a long way from Easter. But never mind. It's an excuse for more biscuits.

Oxfords did, as I had hoped, supply me with a Lardy Cake. There's argument about its origins, inevitably: Jane Grigson, among others, says it's a Wiltshire speciality. She describes Wiltshire as 'cheese and pig country', where lard abounded and Lardies were invented as a way of using up the fat once the pig was slaughtered. They were the big treat on baking day.

Wiltshire may have invented the Lardy but, as I'd discovered by venturing further south and west, it doesn't have a monopoly. In addition to the one I'd just bought in Dorset, Elizabeth David gives both a Northumberland and a Suffolk version, I'd come across one recipe billed as being from Surrey, and a friend of mine who grew up in Gloucestershire said she'd never seen it anywhere but there. The best story, though, came from another friend, raised in Berkshire in the 1950s. His godfather, Jack Palmer, used to come round with gifts of biscuits. It was never quite clear to my friend and his sister, both very young at the time, whether or not Uncle Jack was related to the Palmers of Huntley & Palmers, but he certainly had ready access to their products. Biscuits were exciting enough in this period of post-war austerity, but occasionally Jack would turn up with a Lardy Cake and that was the highlight of the children's week. 'I was fascinated,' my friend said. 'It looked like the cake equivalent of a collapsed volcano, or a Yorkshire pudding covered with some sort of sweet sauce. The centre was gloriously mushy, with a hard, treacly coating, and it certainly made it easier to listen to Uncle Jack boring on to my mother.'

'Collapsed volcano' almost exactly described what I had bought from Oxfords. They bake it in the oven they've been using since 1911. It's made from a moist dough with currants in it, kneaded, then spread with equal parts lard and brown sugar and folded over. The baking tin is lined with syrup so that the cake has a golden glaze when turned out. The result, they say, is like a gooey, chewy tea cake. After one bite you can absolutely see why Jane Grigson was able to write, 'In bakeries, you see plump middle-aged persons struggling with base desire – and losing. "A bloomer, a Hovis, thank you, that's all ... oh, and put in a couple of lardies."' Base desire is what Lardies are all about, as I was to discover a number of times over the next few weeks.

The next day, for example, I tried one from a stall run by Sgt Bun Bakery of Weymouth. Flatter and lighter in colour than Oxfords', it was certainly gooey, the consistency more of a doughnut than of a cake, with sultanas, spices and – well, goo. It wasn't something you could eat three helpings of. Not in quick succession, anyway. Then a couple of weeks later I found myself in the gorgeous Oxford covered market and tried one from the Nash's of Bicester stall – or rather I tried a square from a cake that had been baked in a slab and looked satisfyingly like a sunken Yorkshire pudding. The coating was not only deliciously caramelly, but it had a crunchiness that I assumed was due to the use of granulated sugar. It added a pleasing new twist.

One of the bakeries most famous for Lardies is the Cotswolds firm of Huffkins. They have shops in Burford, Stow-on-the-Wold, Cheltenham and Witney; Witney is also where the bakery is. It's a pretty town, with a brook babbling through it, a butter cross and no shortage of thatch or Virginia creeper. It's the only place I've ever seen a cello shop – though I admit that up to that point I hadn't been looking – and it also boasted a goldsmiths called We Three Kings; whether they did a sideline in frankincense and myrrh wasn't clear.

I was in Witney at half-term, with my eight-year-old godson Kit (probably the most assiduous cake researcher involved in this book) and his mother; I left them in Huffkins tea room and went to visit the bakery manager, Lorna Bennett-Murdoch. She told me that Lardies were originally made with just currants, but that recipes vary as you move around the counties; Huffkins use both currants and sultanas, but no spice. Rather to my surprise, the other thing they don't use is lard. They've replaced this with margarine, making the cakes acceptable to vegetarians, non-pork eaters and anyone else who doesn't choose to include rendered pig fat in their teatime treat. This runs directly contrary to Elizabeth David's view that genuine pork lard is essential to a good Lardy, but her book on bread and yeast cookery was published in 1977, before cholesterol was a word on everyone's lips.

Having by now tasted several different Lardy Cakes, I mentioned that one seemed to have a layer of something soft in it, almost like a fruit purée, but presumably this was the fat? Yes, said Lorna, that would have been the fat seeping through the sugar: a lot of people make Lardies in layers, rather like a lasagne, with a layer of dough, a layer of sugar and fat, and a layer of fruit. At Huffkins, they combine the fruit with the dough, roll it out, spread it with a mixture of margarine and sugar and roll it up like a Swiss Roll. It's baked in a tin that is also lined with margarine and sugar; this forms a toffee-like base that runs down the side of the cake when it's turned out. It's then sliced so that a single portion looks like something between a caramelised Swiss Roll and a flattened Chelsea Bun.

I asked Lorna if there was a dispute about the Lardy Cake recipe: was Huffkins' version any more 'original' than anyone else's? 'With a lot of our cakes,' she said, 'if we think we want to change a recipe, we put out samples and get customer feedback. So we give customers the taste they want, rather than what's expected. With the Lardies, the only thing we've changed is the type of sugar we use, to get the best toffee effect. But we sell so many now that we daren't change it.' People do make special trips to sample Huffkins' Lardies, or they taste them in the tea room and then go round to the shop to buy some to take home. Lorna even told me about a customer in London who rang up once a year to order 12 large cakes, which he put in his freezer – 'It probably costs as much for postage as it does for the Lardies.' He presumably took them out of the freezer one by one and warmed them up. 'They freeze really well,' Lorna said, 'but they do taste much better warmed up. You get the soft toffeeness of them.'

I can vouch for this, because by the time I got back to Kit and his mother they had consumed both a Lardy Cake and a Millionaire's Shortbread. Millionaire's Shortbread – apparently invented in Australia – falls outside the scope of this book, but I mention it because it came with not only a cake fork but also a cake knife, which pleased the youngest member of the party enormously.

As for the Lardy, they confirmed that warm was the best way to eat it. 'It was a little bit too hot when it arrived,' they said. 'We were too eager to eat it. But we did like it warm.' It was swirly, like a meringue, Kit told me, and the raisins were like the raisins you have in a madeleine. Not an observation many eight-year-olds would have made, but I did say his research was assiduous. When I asked if it was sticky, though, he reverted to being eight years old and giggled. 'Yes, it was sticky. Any cake is sticky.'

I was surprised that it wasn't stickier than 'any cake'. His mother elaborated, 'It wasn't sticky like a Danish Pastry. It tasted as if it *ought* to be sticky, but it wasn't the sort of cloying sticky that sticks the tongue to the top of your mouth.'

So it was sticky in the most positive, least oleaginous sense of the word.

A postscript on the whole subject of Lardy Cake. Back home, I tasted yet another sample I'd brought back with me and decided that neither my arteries nor the interests of research required me to eat the whole thing. I put the remains on my balcony for the birds. When I say 'birds' I mean mostly 'London pigeons', the ones that prowl round Trafalgar Square and consume discarded KFC, containers and all. It took them *two days* to dispose of it. That's how powerful it was. Whoever coined the expression 'One bite is never enough' hadn't eaten Lardy Cake.

Want to try it for yourself? Here is one version of many.

Lardy Cake

Makes 1 cake

For the dough
1 tsp dried yeast
150ml warm water
1 tsp granulated sugar
225g strong plain flour
1 tsp fine salt

For the filling
75g lard or margarine
75g currants or sultanas
75g granulated sugar

For the glaze
milk and extra sugar

1. In a large bowl, crumble the fresh yeast or sprinkle the dried yeast on to a few teaspoons of the warm water, then mix in the sugar. Leave in a warm place until frothy.

2. Add the flour, salt and the rest of the water and mix to make a dough. Knead well on a lightly floured surface, then return to the cleaned bowl, cover with a tea-towel, and leave to rise until doubled in size, about an hour.

3 Preheat the oven to 200°C/400°F/gas mark 6, and have ready a 20cm square cake tin.

4 To make the filling, mix the lard or margarine, fruit and sugar together and divide into 3 portions.

5 Roll out the dough into an oblong shape about 5mm thick. Spread one portion of the fruit mixture on to two-thirds of the dough. Fold the dough into three by folding over the empty third, then folding again. Turn it through 90° and roll it out again. Spread another third of the fruit over two-thirds of the dough and repeat the process; roll again and repeat again with the rest of the fruit.

6 Form the dough into a square and place in the cake tin. Score the top diagonally both ways. Brush with a little milk and sprinkle with sugar.

7 Bake in the preheated oven for 35–40 minutes. Remove from the oven, then leave to stand in the tin for a few minutes to absorb any free lard. Remove from the tin and, when cold, cut into slices or squares.

On that Saturday in Sherborne, all those Lardy Cake excesses were in the future. Let's go back to Dorset, Somerset and Knob throwing. Yeovil, six minutes further along the railway line from Sherborne, is, at first glance, a different proposition altogether. In Sherborne you stroll across a pretty little park from the station and are in the centre of things in five minutes; Yeovil Junction is a 45-minute walk from town, along pedestrian-unfriendly country roads. The few taxis that had come to meet the train had been snapped up by the time I got there and a sign at the bus stop said firmly that buses were not necessarily timed to meet trains and would not be held up if a train was delayed. But there were three other people waiting and the timetable suggested a bus was due in five minutes, so I didn't despair. In five minutes a bus did indeed turn up and I couldn't help imagining how disappointed the grumpy person who'd painted the sign would have been if he'd known how smoothly that part of my journey had gone. Serves you right, you miserable so-and-so.

Once there, I dropped my bag at my hotel and set off to do the sights. It didn't take me long. The Tourist Information Centre didn't open on a Saturday and, if the size of the type on the map outside its door was anything to go by, the most important place around was Tesco. Mortimers bakery was closed, as was the church, so I meandered into the award-winning Sienna Deli. There was a Saffron Cake sitting on a wire rack, but they told me it was just out of the oven and needed to cool and dry out a little before it could be served.

'Is it a local speciality?' I asked, knowing full well it wasn't.

'Well, it's a Cornish speciality,' came the reply, 'but I had some saffron and it sounded good.'

Fair enough, I thought, and had an excellent cheese scone with my tea.

Afterwards I went into the local WH Smith and found the section headed 'Local interest'. It took a broad-brush approach to the concept of 'local' and included Professor Brian Cox's *Wonders of the Solar System*, a large illustrated book called *Universe: the definitive visual guide* and Richard Dawkins' *The God Delusion*. Waterstones did better: in addition to plenty of maps and guides, it offered *Somerset Cricket: the glory years* (a slimmish volume) and *Yeovil Cinemas Through Time*, which had apparently sold over 250,000 copies. The words 'sublime' and 'ridiculous' battled for supremacy in my brain.

So to the highlight of my weekend. The Dorset Knob Throwing and Frome Valley Food Fest took place on the Cattistock football pitch, with another large field designated as the car park. As I walked towards the entrance, I heard 'A Nightingale Sang In Berkeley Square' over the Tannoy. It was a beautiful morning and this set the mood. Sunny but surreal.

I paid £2.50 and they stamped my hand, something that hadn't happened to me since I last went to a disco, as we used to call them, some decades ago. (The stamp washed off within two days, suggesting that ink is one of the many things they don't make the way they used to.) Round the edge of the field was a circle of marquees, most of them offering local wares: jams, chutneys, honeys, bison and venison, cheese, pasties and – thank goodness, said the part of my conscience that was calling this jaunt a business trip – cakes.

There was a makeshift pub that looked like a cross between a bouncy castle and the witch's house in *Hansel and Gretel*; it was selling Badger, a local beer, and had no shortage of customers at a quarter past ten in the morning. I spotted a young man wearing a T-shirt that proclaimed 'I love a good Piddle', suggesting that he supported the rival Dorset brewery. But considering that the centrepiece of the Fest was tossing Knobs, it wasn't only the Piddle Brewery that offered opportunities for sub-*Men Behaving Badly* humour.

The festival was in its sixth year and even at that early hour people were queuing up to test their skill. The Knob-throwing pitch had been marked out in 2-metre intervals and little flags showed the length of the best throw so far for males, females and under-12s. The previous year the winning man had thrown a bit over 29 metres, the winning woman 26.45 metres. The Dorset Knob looks a bit like a small bun, but it's hard and crunchy. There was a bucketful from which punters helped themselves – you got three Knobs for a pound, but could have as many goes as you liked, as long as you kept paying. There were clear regulations about throwing – underarm only, one foot must remain on the ground at all times and should the Knob break upon landing the umpire would decide which bit of it counted as the final resting place. I do like rules that think of everything. A party of lads measured the distances, moved the flags if necessary and gathered up the debris as if they were collecting golf balls on a driving range. The field was spattered with dandelions and, continuing the golfing theme, I wondered if these constituted a natural hazard.

If this seems a bit energetic – shame on you. There were three-year-olds competing and taking it as seriously as only three-year-olds can, although they had no sense of direction at all. But if you think your strength lies in something more subtle, there were Knob Darts and the Knob Pyramid. For the darts, imagine the wire segments of a dart board, plus the numbers, laid out on the grass: you lobbed the Knobs into the segments and scored according to darts rules. Three Knobs for a pound and the highest score at the end of the day won a tenner. The pyramid was an upright triangle of hardboard with six small flowerpots fixed on to it. Each pot was marked with a score: get the Knob into the flowerpot and win that number of points. Again, £10 at the end of the day for the winner. Or there was Hunt the Knob, the Knob and Spoon Race and the rather terrifying prospect of the Knob-Eating Contest. There was also ferret racing – the only event of the day, apart from eating and drinking, that didn't involve Knobs. It was all utterly insane and wonderful and you could buy a T-shirt that said 'I've thrown a Dorset Knob'. I didn't, because I hadn't, because my throwing has always been rubbish and I didn't want to be shown up by three-year-olds, even if they were three-year-olds I was never likely to meet again.

Moores – the makers of the Dorset Knob – had a stand in the big tent and offered me half a Knob spread with Dorset Blue Vinny cheese. The cheese was creamy and tasty and at first the biscuit was rather nothingy under it. Then I realised that it was the perfect texture. Never mind the taste – the crunchiness and the creaminess were made for each other. The recipe is simple, I was told – flour, yeast, water, vegetable oil and sugar – but the biscuits are quite difficult to make. According to the tin, the traditional Dorset way to eat Knobs is with tea, but I imagine this would be a bit dull. With the local cheese, however – absolutely worth the trip. And frankly, it could taste of anything or nothing and, as long as it inspired an event like this, you'd forgive it.

In the course of my travels round the field I'd also found three versions of Dorset Apple Cake, but nobody I asked seemed clear on what made a Dorset Apple Cake different from any other. 'The spices?' suggested the lady from the WI, but very much with a question mark. 'Cinnamon and allspice,' said someone else, but the consensus seemed to be that everyone had their own recipe. There are lots of recipes for Somerset Apple Cake too and, considering that the county boundary is no more than 10km away, it's safe to assume that there is overlap.

There was certainly variety. The WI version was a soft, beautifully home-baked cake, with only a hint of apple and only a hint of spice. It was a cake with apple in it, rather than an Apple Cake, if that doesn't sound too daft. But again, if you can judge food by texture alone, it was lovely.

Sgt Bun's of Weymouth produced something very different: it had a layer of apples at the bottom, a more solid texture, a generous sprinkling of sugar on the top and sultanas within. Not very spicy, but certainly appley, with a firmer crust.

The third came from a friendly man wearing a Court, Coffee and Catering apron, who told me he used to have a Royal Warrant to supply Christmas puddings to the Prince of Wales. For his Apple Cake he insisted on Bramleys and lots of cinnamon, and he used an oven that threw the air in from three sides, which gave a very even bake. His was a noticeably tall cake – perhaps 12cm high – and much darker than the other two; that was, he told me, due to the light Muscovado sugar he used. It had slices of apple inside and on top and it was very spicy and solid, more like a Christmas cake than a sponge. Generally more in your face than the other two. They were all very good, but if I had to plump for a favourite, Sgt Bun would get my vote, in a three-way photo finish.

Because nobody was sharing recipes, I sought the advice of my aunt, who's lived in Dorset for decades. She gave me this version, which she'd made successfully many times.

Brenda's Apple Cake

Makes 1 x 20cm cake

125g unsalted butter
125g caster sugar
2 medium eggs
125g self-raising flour
1 tsp baking powder
a few drops of vanilla essence
2 large cooking apples, peeled, cored, halved and sliced
2 dessertspoons caster sugar and 1 dessertspoon ground cinnamon, mixed

1. Preheat the oven to 180°C/350°F/gas mark 4. Grease and line a 20cm diameter round cake tin.
2. In a large bowl, cream the butter and sugar together until white. Beat in the eggs alternately with the sifted dry ingredients, then add the vanilla essence.
3. Pour the mixture into the prepared tin. Arrange the peeled apple slices on their edges, like arches, thickly on top. Sprinkle liberally with the cinnamon and sugar mixture.
4. Bake in the preheated oven for 50 minutes. Serve warm with whipped cream as a dessert or cold with afternoon tea.

Where there are apples there must also be cider, and if you travel through Devon, Dorset and Somerset, or indeed Shropshire, Hereford and Norfolk, you'll find no shortage of recipes for Cider Cake. The interesting thing about Cider Cake lies in the chemistry: acidic cider and alkaline bicarbonate of soda react together to produce a fizziness that aerates the cake. Particularly useful if you have a shortage of eggs, apparently.

If you're the right age you might think this is nostalgic: a friend who was doing O levels around 1960 said, 'We did that at school; they couldn't afford chemicals.' And if, by the way, you are short of eggs in winter and want to make puddings or pancakes, Maria Rundell, writing in the 19th century, had another intriguing suggestion – use snow:

> *Two large spoonfuls will supply the place of one egg, and the article it is used in will be equally good. This is a useful piece of information, especially as snow often falls at the season when eggs are dearest ... The snow may be taken up from any clean spot before it is wanted, and will not lose its virtue, though the sooner it is used the better.*

I confess I haven't tried this, because I got so caught up in speculating about snow losing its virtue that I ran out of time.

Reverting to Cider Cake, this is a Dorset version, but I've seen a Devon one which has no orange or candied peel; a Somerset one which replaces the cinnamon with nutmeg; and a Herefordshire Apple Cider Cake with Bramley apples, raisins, sultanas, honey and mixed spice (made by Cariad Cakes of Leintwardine, whose wares I had discovered in Ludlow, and decidedly moreish). Basically, as long as you put cider in it, you seem to be able to do what you like.

Dorset Cider Cake

Makes 1 x 20cm cake

350g plain flour
1 tsp ground cinnamon
1 tsp each of baking powder and bicarbonate of soda
225g unsalted butter
110g granulated sugar
finely grated rind of 1 orange
3 medium eggs
170ml cider
1 x 5cm piece candied peel, cut into strips

1 Preheat the oven to 160°C/325°F/gas mark 3. Lightly grease a 20cm diameter round cake tin.

2 Sift the dry ingredients together into a large bowl. In a separate bowl, cream the butter and sugar together until soft, then add the orange rind. Beat in the eggs one at a time, adding a tablespoon of the flour mixture with each egg, then stir in the rest of the flour. Pour the cider in slowly, beating constantly with a spoon.

3 When all the ingredients are combined and the batter is smooth, spoon it into the prepared tin and arrange strips of peel on the top.

4 Bake in the preheated oven for 1¼ –1½ hours until risen and golden. Cool in the tin for half an hour before removing to a wire rack. Serve cold or still slightly warm, cut into wedges.

By any standards (unless you are terminally allergic to fun), the Dorset Knob Throwing and Frome Valley Food Fest was a resounding success. The village has a population of 509, according to the 2011 census; they must all have been there – and then some. The previous year's event had attracted over 5,000 people and by the time I left, just before noon, to catch a train back to London, the place was heaving and cars were being directed into the overflow car park. It was a great day out for family and dogs. There were *lots* of dogs and my last thought as I left was, 'I hope they keep them clear of the ferrets.'

11

Sussex and Kent

Tasty Tales and Gypsy Tarts

With ten days to fill before the next fixed point in my diary, I decided to explore closer to home. The late great Keith Waterhouse once wrote that Brighton 'always looks as though it were helping the police with their enquiries'. I have no idea what he meant, but I had stumbled upon a mystery that perhaps it could help to solve. The internet told me of a thing called Brighton Buttons: two bits of shortbread-type biscuit containing orange rind and sandwiched together with apricot jam. Looked nice. But could I find a place in Brighton that sold them? Not on the web I couldn't. So I set off in search.

Brighton is really more smoothie and panini than tea and cake, but I did find two olde worlde tea shoppes. The first was called, for no apparent reason, The Mock Turtle – perhaps it served *beau–ootiful soo–ooup* in the evening – and it was as near to being the perfect 'time has stood still here' tea shop as I had met in a while. On the wall just inside the door was a panel of old-fashioned brass light switches; the paintwork was vaguely distressed in two tones of grey-turquoise (more attractive than it sounds); the furniture was beaten-up old wood; the crockery inevitably but fittingly blue and white.

As I went in I almost fell over a table laden with the day's cakes – Lemon Drizzle, fudge-iced Date and Walnut, Somerset Apple, scones, flapjacks, brownies – all baked in the bakery upstairs. But no

Buttons. I asked the girl if they did any Sussex specialities and she didn't think there was such a thing. What the hell, I had a scone with cream and jam.

And very gorgeous it was. The tea came with a strainer; the plate had a doily on it. A doily! When did you last see a doily? The cream (certainly clotted; probably Cornish) and jam came in pretty little dishes that you would love to slip into your handbag and take home with you. The scone was warm, crumbly and huge.

When it was time for the bill I noticed that the retro look extended to the till, one of those sit-up-and-beg types where you really had to bash on the keys in order to make anything happen. 'We had such trouble with the electronic one,' said the girl, and I wanted to believe her.

Five minutes' walk across the Steyne from The Mock Turtle was the wonderfully over-the-top Tea Cosy. Its theme is royalty, and as I walked in I thought I might have blundered into an idiosyncratic local museum by mistake. This feeling was enhanced by the fact that I was the only person there. (The Tea Cosy doesn't open until midday and I was there at five past; by the time I left the joint was jumpin' thanks to a group of girls wearing shocking-pink feather boas – it was Friday and the hen weekend had started bang on time.) There was a gallery-sized portrait of Queen Victoria on the back wall, a life-sized cut-out of Queen Elizabeth II against a side wall, a framed cutting from a 1953 edition of the *Daily Mirror* reporting the death of Queen Mary. Bizarrely, in a glass case there was a large replica of a clown – exactly the sort of clown that people who are scared of clowns are scared of, with a rictus grin and alarming feet. There were also reproductions of Union Flags in abundance, including on the front of the menu. Finally, unobtrusively, high up on one wall, there was a photograph of John Inman. I didn't ask.

The tea room was divided into two rooms, front and back, and a sort of landing (from which stairs went down to the kitchen) in between. There, there was a sofa, complete with Union Flag cushion.

I felt obliged to ask permission to sit on it – it might have been part of the exhibit – but the friendly woman in charge assured me I was welcome.

The royal theme extended to the food: 'Prince Harry's tea' turned out to be a boiled egg with soldiers; 'Princess Margaret's low tea' was tea with a slice of cake; 'Beatrice and Eugenie's tea' a cupcake with hot chocolate, cream and marshmallows. There were many more, from Prince Albert to Charles and Camilla.

My hostess had never heard of Brighton Buttons, though she was aware of an apple-based Sussex Pudding, rather like an Eve's Pudding. 'Google it,' I suggested. 'You'll find a recipe. It might be nice to revive it.' She seemed to like the idea, said she'd get her daughter on to it and went to fetch my tea. It came in a pot with a cosy. Hand-knitted, I would guess, in an array of colourful stripes from which red, white and blue were strangely absent. A trick missed? Or merely recognition that there comes a point where even excess can go too far?

Having finished my tea (just the drink, for once) and with time to kill, I looked in the Pavilion gift shop. If I ever run a debating society, I'm going to suggest that 'this House believes that Brighton Pavilion is the most vulgar building ever conceived', but the gift shop was surprisingly and genuinely tasteful. It had beautiful monogrammed cotton handkerchief sachets, an ideal gift for anyone with aspirations of becoming a maiden aunt. It sold a 'rich fruit cake' of no specific provenance and chocolate made in Dorchester ('the home of great British chocolates' – another revelation), but nothing Sussexy. As I headed back towards the station, cafés (not tea shops, and certainly not tea shoppes) seemed to alternate with establishments offering counselling and non-surgical face lifts. There was a New York-style deli selling hot salt beef and pickle on a bagel; the appropriately named Utopia Café, which clearly realised that heaven is Chocolate-Fudge-Cake-shaped; and a market stall whose soda bread looked to die for but whose cake department offered nothing closer to home than a *pain au chocolat* or an apple Danish. Finally I passed an anonymous-looking building whose foundation stone proclaimed itself to have been laid on 24 June 1987 by the Marquess of Abergavenny, Lord Lieutenant of East Sussex.

OK, I thought, *nothing* in this part of the world is local. Not even the personal representative of the monarch. Time to move on.

On the train, an ad for quidco.com (whatever that is) invited me to 'get paid to terminate alien killer zombies'. I'd felt fairly smug about travelling the country eating cake to earn a crust, as it were, but now I was rather deflated: terminating alien killer zombies was undeniably going one better.

As for the Brighton Buttons, I was just going to have to make some myself. Or go back to the Tea Cosy another time and see if they featured as 'Prince George's tea'. Here's a recipe that produces something quite tasty.

Brighton Buttons

Makes about 10 'sandwiches'

125g unsalted butter
30g icing sugar, sifted, plus extra for sprinkling
125g plain flour
finely grated rind of 2 oranges
about 4 tbsp apricot jam

1. Preheat the oven to 180°C/350°F/gas mark 4. Thoroughly grease a large baking sheet.

2. In a large bowl, cream the butter and 30g icing sugar together until light and fluffy. Stir in the flour and beat in the grated orange rind.

3. Put the mixture into a forcing bag fitted with a large plain tube and pipe on to the baking sheet in small rounds. Alternatively, place dessertspoons of the mixture on the

baking sheet. Allow enough space between them for them to spread slightly. You should have about 20.

4 Bake in the preheated oven for 10–15 minutes, until very lightly golden. Remove from the oven and allow the buttons to cool for a minute before removing from the baking sheet with a palette knife. Allow to finish cooling on a wire rack.

5 When cold, sandwich the buttons together with a little apricot jam and sprinkle with icing sugar.

A footnote to my trip to Brighton. I was later browsing through a 1980s cookery book and found recipes for both Brighton Rocks and Brighton Buns. The former didn't claim to be anything other than a rock cake with a punning name aimed at tourists and Graham Greene fans. But when I googled 'Brighton Buns', I found an antique dealer's website and an article by one Nicholas A. Brawer that began:

> *From approximately 1735 through 1925, explorers, travellers, military officers, and European Royalty all employed a distinctive type of folding candlestick on their journeys. Perhaps because of their resemblance when packed for travel to a now-forgotten English pastry, these candlesticks are colloquially and affectionately referred to today as 'Brighton Buns'.*

Clearly the buns are due for a revival, if only so that we can eat them by candlelight next time we go travelling through Bohemia or Byzantium.

Brighton Buns

Makes 12–16

110g unsalted butter
110g granulated sugar
1 medium egg, beaten
225g plain flour
about 1 tbsp blanched almonds, coarsely chopped
50g ground almonds
a few drops of almond extract
whole almonds, for decorating (optional)

1. Preheat the oven to 220°C/425°F/gas mark 7. Grease a large baking sheet.
2. In a large bowl, cream the butter and sugar together until pale and fluffy, then add the beaten egg. Sift the flour into the mixture, then fold in the almonds and almond extract.
3. Using a dessertspoon, make into rocky heaps on the prepared baking sheet. Top each bun with a whole almond if you like.
4. Bake in the preheated oven for about 15 minutes until the buns are a warm golden brown.

Note: The original recipe for these buns contains bitter almonds, but these are hard to come by: in their raw state they contain prussic acid, which has tended to put people off. The above is a safer alternative.

A short trip along the South Coast took me away from prussic acid and into something altogether healthier: fruit with (nearly) everything. Kent isn't called the Garden of England for nothing: the Romans introduced cherries, there are apple orchards everywhere, damsons grow wild and hops – once reviled as a pernicious weed – were first imported in the 16th century.

Hop-picking has long been a source of work for itinerant labourers, students and anyone wanting to get out of London in August or September, and the traditional Kentish Hopping Cakes or Oast Cakes, similar to Welsh Cakes, were cooked on the temporary stoves the pickers brought with them. They were made and eaten to celebrate the end of the harvest, though nowadays you could cook them any time you liked, using a griddle or a heavy-based frying pan. You might miss out on the *Darling Buds of May* feel, but the result would be much the same. Try them, some say, lightly dredged with sugar or spread with cherry jam.

Confusingly, the traditional Hop-pickers' Cake was something completely different – a spicy fruit loaf containing treacle and beer. This wasn't something you could knock up yourself after a hard day in the fields; it required up to an hour and a half in the oven, so is more likely to have been handed out to the workers during a break, like the Fourses Cake I was to discover in Suffolk.

Another Kent speciality from the days of a rural economy was the Flead Cake. This was made in the autumn, when the smallholder's pig was killed and butchered (taking advantage of the onset of cold weather in pre-refrigeration days). Flead is the fat that lines the abdominal wall around the animal's kidneys and it is from this, according to my 1980s book, that the best lard is obtained. The same book told me that 'flead is not now easy to obtain, but suet may be used as a substitute'. The recipe had no redeeming features such as dried fruit, peel or spice – it was an utterly plain Lardy Cake, with far too much anatomical information. My instinct said, 'Let's not go there.'

Sadly, another promisingly named discovery, Kentish Twice Laid, turned out to be a sort of fish cake with hard-boiled eggs.

Having arrived by train to spend a day in eastern Kent, I put myself into the care – and the van – of local food expert Mo Joslin. Mo's book *Kentish Fare Recipes* contains a delicious-sounding recipe for Cherry Batter Pudding and another (get thee behind me, Satan) for Cherry Butterscotch Profiteroles. It's odd that with all this at its back, one of the county's proudest culinary boasts should be a tart based round sugar and evaporated milk.

Mo is a Geordie by birth, a Woman of Kent by long adoption, and she told me the story of Kentish Gypsy Tart. I remember being fed it at school in Bromley, Kent, in the 1970s but, fresh from a childhood in the Colonies, I had no idea it wasn't commonplace. (I learned later – courtesy of Frankie Boyle and Dara O Briain on a repeat of *Mock the Week* – that schoolchildren in Scotland and Ireland also took their lunch to school, so you didn't have to come from as far afield as New Zealand to be out of your depth in the world of school dinners.) Gypsy Tart wasn't anything special – a sort of chewy-pastried, miserly-fillinged treacle tart – but then nothing about our school dinners was special. However, I soon discovered that, insofar as I had thought about it at all, I had been maligning it all these years.

Legend has it that a dinner lady, sometime after World War II, discovered herself with a surplus of sugar and evaporated milk and created this dish to avoid waste. The flaw in this story, of course, is that immediately after the war no one had a surplus of sugar, which remained rationed until 1953. But if you allow the dish to have appeared a bit later in the 1950s, the recipe becomes plausible enough, though the name remains a mystery. The Wikipedia version of the legend gets round this by abandoning plausibility altogether: it tells of a lady in the early part of the 20th century who created a confection to feed undernourished gypsy children. This seems to me to be in the same category as the tale that links Somerset Easter Cakes to the Monmouth

Rebellion. Why should such a benevolent person have nothing to hand but pie crust, evaporated milk and sugar? Don't tell me she didn't have an apple tree in the garden.

Mo's story has the appealing addendum that when Gypsy Tart was served in schools it was always accompanied by a slice or two of apple, to stop the sugar rotting the children's teeth during double maths in the afternoon. That may have been true in the fruit-rich Kent countryside; it certainly wasn't in my suburban grammar. Our teeth were left to fend for themselves until we got home. Her book gives a recipe for a single 20cm tart (serves six), but she took me to meet Jeff Vane of Vanes Bakery in Dover, where they sold individual tartlets. These were completely delicious for those with a sweet enough tooth.

Vanes is the sort of little corner bakery you tend to imagine doesn't exist any more. It began life as Jeff's grandfather's business and has been on the same premises for 80 years. Granddad's speciality was designing the plaques that used to go on wedding cakes: the wall of the shop boasted a magnificent framed art deco certificate awarded to Vanes by the Universal Cookery and Food Associations' Exhibition at Olympia, 1928, for General Excellence in Confectionery. It was signed by six of the great and the good of the culinary world, including, as a member of the Awards Committee, Auguste Escoffier – perhaps past his prime by this time, but still one of the great names in any cookery Hall of Fame. If he'd signed a certificate for my grandfather, I'd have it framed and on the wall for all to see too.

Mo's recipe for Gypsy Tart has you put the filling into a raw pastry case and bake it in a slow oven (150°C/300°F/gas mark 2) for about 45 minutes, but Jeff bakes his pastry blind and cooks the filling for only about five minutes. This means that the filling is only just set, and that's the way I prefer it, though it needs to be in the oven a little longer if you are making a single large tart. Whichever way you do it, it works best if the evaporated milk has been in the fridge for two days or more.

Gypsy Tart

Makes 1 x 20cm tart, to serve 6–8

For the pastry
150g plain flour
75g unsalted butter
a little cold water, to mix

For the filling
300g evaporated milk, well chilled
300g soft brown sugar

1 Preheat the oven to 180°C/350°F/gas mark 4, and put a baking sheet in to warm.

2 For the pastry, put the flour in a large bowl, and rub the fat into it until the mixture is the consistency of fine breadcrumbs. Add only enough cold water to make a dough.

3 Roll out the dough to about 5mm thickness and use it to line a 20cm diameter metal flan tin. Prick the base all over with a fork, then line with foil and fill the foil with baking beans. Put the baking tin on the warmed baking sheet and bake the pastry blind in the preheated oven for about 15 minutes. Remove the beans and foil and return the pastry to the oven for another 5 minutes to dry out the base.

4 Meanwhile, beat the evaporated milk until it begins to thicken – about 3–4 minutes with an electric whisk, 10–15 minutes with a hand-held one. Gradually add the sugar and continue beating until the mixture is thick and creamy. Don't skimp on this stage or the filling will be flat and school-dinnery.

5 Pour the mixture into the prepared pastry case and return to the oven for about 10 minutes. The top should be lightly

browned but still slightly tacky (it will continue to set as it cools).

6 Remove the tart from the oven and allow to cool completely in the tin. Serve with crème fraîche or natural yoghurt – it really doesn't need anything sweeter. Or remember the post-war schoolchildren and serve with slices of Cox's apple.

Serendipity and a friend's birthday took me a few weeks later to Rocksalt, a smart new fish restaurant in Folkestone run by Mark Sargeant, former Head Chef at Gordon Ramsay at Claridge's and now very much a star in his own right. With wall-to-ceiling windows, it has stunning views of the harbour and the menu says that as much as possible of its fish is bought from the local Folkestone Trawler Company. Certainly my smoked coley was as fresh and delicious as any fish I had tasted anywhere. But what really excited me was that the desserts included Kentish Gypsy Tart. The moment I saw it I decided to skip a starter to make sure I had room.

It came as a sliver of a larger whole – my guess was that a full pie would serve 16 or even 24 – but was so rich that you would be hard put to manage a more substantial slice. Our hugely obliging waitress scuttled back and forth to the kitchen three times to check the answers to my questions with the chef and, yes, the pastry was baked blind, so the filling itself wasn't in the oven for long. It was served with a dollop – if that is the word for something so elegant – of thick double cream, flavoured with zest of lemon and lemon juice, which is a brilliant accompaniment to something so sweet. She also endorsed the story about the dinner lady and the limited ingredients, but not the one about the gypsies.

Back in Dover, Jeff Vane's other speciality was the Kentish Huffkin. He described it as a 'soft batch roll' which would be not much different from any other soft roll if it weren't for the distinctive thumbprint in each one. Tradition has it that the baker's wife was in a mood (or huff) about something, went into her husband's bakery and pushed her finger into every loaf that was waiting to be baked. 'Sell those if you can!' she challenged, and of course he did and they became a great success. In fact, Jeff said, *huff* is an old word for dough, but that's the sort of inconvenient fact that needs to be ignored in order to enjoy the story.

Mo's Kentish Huffkins

Makes about 18

675g strong plain flour
2 x 7g sachets fast-action dried yeast
2 tsp fine salt
510ml warm water
2 tbsp vegetable oil
55g unsalted butter, lard or margarine

1 In a large bowl, mix together the flour, yeast and salt. Make a well in the middle and pour in the water and oil. Incorporate the flour into the liquid to form a dough, then turn out on to a lightly floured surface.

2 Knead well for 10 minutes, then return to the bowl and cover with a damp cloth. Leave in a warm place until doubled in size – about 40 minutes. Meanwhile, flour 2 baking sheets.

3 Knead the dough again on a lightly floured surface, and this time knead in the fat until fully incorporated. Shape into about 18 rounds, position on the prepared baking sheets, and allow to prove again for 30 minutes.

4 Preheat the oven to 220°C/425°F/gas mark 7.

5 Make a deep thumb mark in the centre of each roll. Bake in the preheated oven for 10 minutes, then turn the rolls over and cook for a further 10 minutes. When you take them out of the oven, wrap them in a warm tea-towel to keep them soft as they cool.

6 Serve simply split and buttered, or treat them like any other bread roll. Alternatively, fill the thumbprint with a dollop of cream or jam or, as you're in Kent, cherries.

Twenty minutes' drive from Dover is Sandwich, a truly lovely little town that had never crossed my path before (as it were). In medieval times, Sandwich was one of the most important ports in England, but the harbour began silting up after a 'Great Storm' in 1287, then suffered again around 1500 and the town's trading has never been the same since. It's now about 3km inland, but it is still officially one of the Cinque Ports, which meant in the old days that it was exempt from tolls and customs duties, had freedom to trade and could hold its own courts. Nowadays some would say it doesn't mean anything much, except that the Cinque Ports Barons get good seats in Westminster Abbey for a Coronation.

On the evening of the day I visited, a number of local businessfolk were due to attend a meeting to organise resistance to the proposal that a major supermarket should start up in the market place. This would be a terrible shame, because what Sandwich needed was not an in-town supermarket but more places like Rose's Fine Foods, which had proudly opened its doors six weeks before my visit. It's the spiritual descendant of Rose's Tea Warehouse and General Supply Stores, founded on this site in the 1880s. The original Rose's sold everything from tea, groceries, provisions and 'patent medicines at lowest prices' to cutlery, perambulators, china, glass and earthenware. I'm quoting from an 1890s advertisement, so it wasn't me who put 'perambulators' into that list in such a random way.

Rose's remained in the family until Frank Rose died in 1987. Subsequently the building became a 'collectables' shop, then a bookshop, then was empty until a couple of years ago when Chris Howard came along. Revitalising Rose's was a long, slow process because the building is listed, which meant dealing not only with health and safety, environmental health and the like, but with English Heritage as well. However much hassle it was, though, the result was worth it. The counters are the original mahogany, the chest freezers are 18th-century effect, the smaller drawers that would once have stored tea now hold packets of meringues and the whole effect is of stepping back in time. High above the meringue drawers a mahogany wall clock is stopped at just after ten past three. Somehow a rumour circulated that it had stopped at the moment Frank collapsed and was never started again. 'It spread like wildfire,' Chris said. 'But the truth is you need a long ladder to wind it and they probably couldn't be bothered.'

Working alongside Chris were Clare Woods, in charge of food ordering, and Jim Marshall, PR and marketing. Between them they were determined to live up to their website's claim that Rose's was 'a magnificent shopping experience only matched by the finer emporiums of London'. I thought it was, though I was disappointed that they had sold out of both Gypsy Tarts and Huffkins. Even at this early stage they were building up a loyal clientele who snapped up this sort of delicacy.

What they did have – in addition to scores of teas and coffees, jars of Mo's preserves, delicious local cheeses, local cider and apple juice – were cobnuts. You can eat this cultivated variety of the hazelnut as a snack or you can use them in cakes and biscuits. Basically you can substitute them for hazelnuts in more or less anything; Mo makes Cobnut Biscuits flavoured with nutmeg, and my researches unearthed several recipes for Cobnut Cake, flavoured with ginger.

Kentish Cobnut Cake

Makes 1 loaf cake

225g self-raising flour
1 rounded tsp ground ginger
110g unsalted butter, at room temperature
110g soft brown sugar
50g Kentish cobnuts, roasted, peeled and chopped
1 large egg, beaten

1. Preheat the oven to 180°C/350°F/gas mark 4. Grease a 900g loaf tin.
2. Sift the flour and ginger together into a large bowl, then rub in the butter until the mixture resembles coarse breadcrumbs. Add the sugar and nuts and mix well, then stir in the beaten egg. Don't worry if it looks a bit dry – it's meant to be, to give the cake its crumbly texture.
3. Turn the mixture into the prepared tin and press gently with a fork to make sure it spreads into all the corners of the tin.
4. Bake in the preheated oven for about 30 minutes, until a skewer inserted into the centre comes out clean, then cool in the tin. To serve, cut into slices.

Customers are welcome to sit in Rose's and have a sandwich with their tea or coffee. I wasn't going to mention sandwiches because a) they aren't cakes or biscuits and b) they are named not after the town but after the Fourth Earl of Sandwich, an 18th-century aristocrat who was so obsessed with gambling that he had a meat-and-bread snack brought to him at the gaming table rather than take a break for food. Then I read the Sandwich town website (endearingly named open-sandwich.co.uk)

and learned that the first Earl was due to take the title Earl of Portsmouth, but changed his mind before the die was cast. Had he stuck to his original plan, and had his great-grandson still turned out to be an inveterate gambler, we might all have been eating cucumber portsmouths when our formidable aunts came to tea.

Not all of Kent is ancient seaside towns. Orpington, once you're away from the one-size-fits-all high street, is comfortable suburbia. Mock Tudor, stucco and brick – not all of them on the same house – and the sort of place where people give their homes recherché names. At one point I counted eight in a row, two of which were on plaques so small and highly decorated that they weren't readable from the pavement; this must have been really irritating for first-time visitors and the postman, as the houses didn't appear to have numbers. I also passed a Toyota people-carrier whose registration, F12Y UP, was cunningly arranged to read FRY UP and I wondered casually how much they had paid for this. And why.

I was heading for Rolands Bakery, situated in a parade of shops opposite a pleasant little green a couple of kilometres from the centre of town. Like every other English village green this one had a pub; as befitted Orpington's most famous export, it was called the Buff. The sign showed a handsome, rich russet-coloured rooster, obviously a Buff Orpington, but as the word 'Welcome' was prominently displayed under the fascia board I wondered how much mileage they got out of telling punters that they were welcome in the Buff.

I pondered this as I sat gazing out of Rolands' window, addressing a sizeable piece of Kentish Bramley Apple Cake. It was a slightly surprising mixture of cake, pie and pudding, flavoured with cinnamon and with apple slices decorating the top. They offered it with custard; I wasn't sure that's what I wanted at 11 o'clock in the morning, but I could see that if the cake were warm it would be a great combination. The texture was both solid and yielding: it was substantial and filling, and not just because of the generous portion; but it was also soft and spongy because, after all, it was a cake. The apples hadn't been mushed up so that all they contributed was moisture; they were there in slices, firm and tangy. Having looked at my plate and thought, 'Good grief, I'll never get through all that', I found I had no trouble at all.

Recipe? Closely guarded secret. Get yourself to Orpington and try it there. Or have a go at these typically Kentish scones instead.

Mo's Apple and Cheese Scones

Makes about 14

350g wholemeal flour
a pinch of fine salt
75g unsalted butter
1 tbsp baking powder
75g granulated sugar
55g strong cheese, grated
1 large cooking apple, peeled, cored and grated
about 150ml buttermilk
a little milk, for glazing

1 Preheat the oven to 200°C/400°F/gas mark 6. Grease a baking sheet.

2 Put the flour and salt together in a large bowl and rub in the butter until the mixture resembles coarse breadcrumbs. Add the remaining dry ingredients, the cheese and the apple and mix well. Stir in enough buttermilk to mix to a stiff, dry dough.

3 Roll out on a lightly floured surface to about 3cm thick and cut into about 14 x 7cm rounds. Place close together on the baking sheet and brush with a little milk.

4 Bake in the preheated oven for about 15 minutes, until brown. Remove from the oven and cover with a damp cloth for 10 minutes, to make the scones steam and keep them soft. Then remove the scones from the baking sheet and put on a wire rack to cool. Serve buttered.

Note: If you can't find buttermilk, simply add 1 tablespoon lemon juice to the same amount of milk and leave for 30 minutes before using.

12

London – and a Cambridge Detour

'Even of Chelsea Buns there are Counterfeits'

IT HAD PROVED SURPRISINGLY DIFFICULT TO FIND CAKES SPECIFIC TO LONDON. Perhaps the capital has been a cosmopolitan city for so long that French, Jewish and Greek specialities have taken over whatever we once had. So there might have been a spark of desperation in my journeying to North London to see what I could find.

Tottenham High Road and the northern extension that leads into Edmonton and becomes Fore Street are unprepossessing places, peopled largely, on a grey Tuesday morning, by disaffected-looking youths in hoodies. But many of the shops (and one or two boarded-up buildings) boasted the logo of 'I ♥ Tottenham', a campaign started by Haringey Council after the riots of summer 2011 in order to boost civic pride. Among other things, the campaign asks you to support local traders.

So I did. I went into Greggs the Bakers in Fore Street and bought a slab of Tottenham Cake. Greggs may be a chain based in the Northeast, with over 1,500 outlets scattered nationwide, but they were the only people I'd found who sold this local delicacy. (To their credit, Greggs do a number of local delicacies. They sold me Lardy Cake in Yeovil and Yorkshire Curd Tart in York, and would have sold me Aberdeen Butteries in Aberdeen if I'd got to them earlier.)

Background information on Tottenham Cake came from the website of the local Quakers, or Society of Friends, and quoted the autobiography of Lord (Ted) Willis, Haringey-born playwright, creator of *Dixon of Dock Green* and later a Labour peer. Writing in the late 1960s about his childhood just after World War I, he told us:

> *... a peculiar local invention was Tottenham Cake. It consisted of a scone-like base covered with lurid pink icing. It was baked in long flat trays, then cut into cubes, which retailed for a penny each. Luckily the cake was not always cut evenly or the icing uniformly spread, and the smaller defective pieces were sold off at half price.*
>
> *In 1901 it was given away free to local children to celebrate the Spurs' first victory in the FA Cup Final.*

The Society of Friends website continued:

> *Henry Chalkley, the baker, was a Friend. The tradition of a Tottenham cake is continued today at Tottenham Friends Meetings. Now baked by Peter Brown, the pink icing is usually achieved by using mulberries off the tree in the burial ground.*

Peter Brown and the tradition seem to be no longer with us, and whether or not Greggs use mulberries from the tree in the burial ground for the icing I can't tell you. But it is certainly still pink, the base more a heavy sponge than a scone, and just the sort of thing to keep you going on a gloomy mid-morning.

Tottenham Cake

Makes 1 cake

150g self-raising flour
1 tsp baking powder
finely grated zest of ½ lemon
125g unsalted butter or margarine
125g granulated sugar
2 large eggs
2 tbsp milk

For the icing
125g icing sugar, sifted
1 tbsp mulberry juice
1 tbsp water or lemon juice
desiccated coconut, for sprinkling (optional)

1. Preheat the oven to 180°C/350°F/gas mark 4. Grease and line a rectangular baking tin about 22 x 15cm.

2. Sift the flour and baking powder together into a large bowl, then stir in the lemon zest. In another large bowl, beat the fat and sugar together until pale and creamy, then add the eggs, one at a time, beating thoroughly to combine after each addition. Slowly add the flour to the creamed mixture, stirring well. Finally fold in the milk (do not beat at this stage or the cake will not rise).

3. Turn the batter into the prepared tin and smooth the top with a palette knife. Bake in the preheated oven for 20–25 minutes, or until a skewer inserted into the centre of the cake comes out clean. Allow to cool in the tin for 15 minutes, then turn out on to a wire rack to cool completely.

4. Meanwhile, sift the icing sugar into a bowl, then add the mulberry juice and enough water or lemon juice to produce a runny, spreadable consistency. Once the cake is completely cold, spread the icing over it quite thickly, then sprinkle with coconut if desired. Allow the icing to harden, then cut the cake into squares. (This is a fairly solid cake, so you may like to make the squares smaller than usual.) It will keep for over a week in an airtight container.

Note: If you don't have access to mulberries, try raspberry or blackberry juice instead.

Still eager to support local traders and conscious that the bakery I'd just patronised didn't really count, I ventured off the High Road into Lordship Lane, to a café called Marmalade, which was surprisingly delightful given its location. Its card billed it as a 'home-made food café', but it looked like the sort of tea room you would find in a small market town. It didn't sell Tottenham Cake, but it did a mean Victoria Sponge. (I use 'mean' here in the sense of 'memorably excellent'; there was nothing mean about the portion size.)

The café itself was tiny, perhaps six tables, and I seemed to be the only non-regular there. Just as I was going up to the counter to pay, a man came in with a pretty blonde toddling daughter who was greeted by name and with delight by the young woman serving me. The proud father came up with his phone and showed her a recent photo.

'Oh, Chloe,' she said to the child, 'you look like a model.'

'Takes after her grandmother,' explained the father. 'My mum. She was one of the top catwalk models.'

I stopped pretending I wasn't listening.

'Worked for Dior and that lot,' he went on. 'Her claim to fame was that she went out with Robert Mitchum.'

The young woman – Eastern European, I guessed, and apparently not a lover of classic Hollywood – tried to look impressed but failed. It was left to me to say, 'Wow!' The proud father seemed pleased. And I was glad I'd come to Tottenham. Chloe's dad's story deserved an appreciative audience and I liked the idea that this unlovely suburb had sufficient self-esteem to have its own cake. As it happens, several months later Tottenham Cake featured in an episode of *The Great British Bake Off*, so perhaps it is in for a revival.

Rather more famous than Tottenham Cake, and much more widely available, is the Chelsea Bun. This sticky, spirally fruit bun was immensely popular in fashionable parts of Georgian London; the queues outside The Original Chelsea Bun-House were known to elicit complaints from the neighbours. Two of the King Georges – II and III – not to mention the former's wife, Queen Caroline, who journeyed there by boat along the Thames, were habitués, though history doesn't tell us whether or not Their Majesties were expected to join the queue.

The Bun-House was situated just off what is now Pimlico Road – not quite Chelsea, but near enough for all but the most pedantic. The little street still called Bunhouse Place is today not much more than a mews, one side devoted to the delivery entrances of the shops on the main road, the other to a posh housing estate – which is, of course, the only sort of housing estate you are likely to find around here. There's no sign of the bakery now – no lingering aroma of fermenting yeast or fresh-baked bread. Hardly surprising, perhaps, as it was demolished in 1839, but you'd think they might have put up a plaque.

Chelsea Buns were famous enough to make their mark with contemporary commentators. One of them, the antiquarian Daniel Lysons – writing in 1795, George III's time – thought the buns were important enough to feature in his topographic treatise *The Environs of London*. Having been talking about Chelsea industries, including porcelain, stained paper and 'the manufacture of painted silk, &c. for furniture of rooms', he went on to say:

> *The manufacture of Chelsea bunns should not be omitted, having been so long noted, and carried on upon the same spot for more than 100 years. The Bunn-house is situated in the parish of St. George, Hanover-square, which extends over a considerable part of the village.*

'The village', of course, meant Chelsea. Those were the days.

In *A Morning's Walk from London to Kew* (1817), the author and publisher Sir Richard Phillips turned a corner in the course of his perambulations and:

> *Before me appeared the shop so famed for Chelsea buns, which for above thirty years I have never passed without filling my pockets. In the original of these shops – for even of Chelsea buns there are counterfeits – are preserved mementoes of domestic events in the first half of the past century ... These buns have afforded a competency, and even wealth, to four generations of the same family; and it is singular that their delicate flavour, lightness, and richness, have never been successfully imitated.*

At some point in its history, the bun shop was run by a Captain Bun; he and his neighbour, Mr Soot the chimney sweep, are credited with having invented the card game 'Happy Families'.

No, they aren't. I made that up. Captain Bun was a nickname given to a member of the Hand family (the one that owned the shop for four generations) when he joined the Staffordshire Militia in the 1770s.

Fashions change, of course. The popularity of buns waned as the 19th century progressed and the London gentry turned their attention elsewhere. As I mentioned in the Introduction, a light afternoon tea became the in thing. Queen Victoria favoured what came to be known as the Victoria Sponge with her tea, sparking a trend. But this all raised an interesting question:

why should the most famous Chelsea Buns in England now be baked and sold in Cambridge?

There was only one way to find out. I made a day trip to Cambridge to meet Alison Wright, who, with her husband, the food writer Tim Hayward, took over the legendary Fitzbillies bakery and café in 2011. Alison's background is in marketing and advertising, and she recognised a great brand when she saw it. The shop front still boasted the art deco script that has a unique place in the hearts of Cambridge students and academics past and present. Although Alison and Tim had turned Fitzbillies into what she called 'a very different beast', making better use of space and producing an enterprise they believed could be successful today, they had no intention of discarding the heritage – or the Chelsea Buns.

In answer to my question, Alison told me that, in the days before the ubiquitous Chinese takeaway or kebab house, there used to be bun shops all around the country. They seem to have flourished particularly in university towns, where a large population of hungry young men (and in due course hungry young women, too) found buns a handy pick-me-up after rowing or a cheap way of catering if someone was coming to tea. At one time in Cambridge a number of bakers sold sticky buns of different sorts, but Fitzbillies was the one that survived. It called its offering Chelsea Buns because – well, presumably because they were sufficiently like the original for this to be a reasonable thing to do, and because they too knew a good brand when they saw it.

Founded in 1922 by the brothers Ernest and Arthur Mason, using their demob money after World War I, Fitzbillies started life as a small shop; in its early days it was famous more for its cake than for its buns. Its speciality was a fatless sponge cake flavoured with tangerine; Alison and Tim were offered the recipe when they took over, but felt it 'wouldn't accord with modern tastes'. I've tried fatless sponges and can confirm that this is an understatement. Nevertheless, it was quite the thing for tea for the 1930s academics: a menu from 1938 or 1939, displayed on the café wall today, offers Special Fitzbillie Sponge for either 1/6 or 2/9 (7½p or just under 14p in today's money). It's not clear when Chelsea Buns became the house speciality, but they are there on that same menu, 1½d each (not much more than ½p).

A Mr WG Day took the shop over in 1951 and, while hip Londoners were discovering the delights of espresso bars and the much derided 'frothy coffee', the bun held its appeal in Cambridge. Jane Grigson, writing about the wartime food deprivations that persisted into the 1950s, recalled:

> *… the most anxious queues I had ever joined were outside Fitzbillies in Cambridge. No undergraduate tea party was complete without their Chelsea Buns, syrupy, well spiced, licentious and exceptional during these years of ersatz cakes and shortages.*

Alison also told a story about Soviet dissidents who apparently came to Cambridge in the 1950s, passed Fitzbillies and exclaimed, 'They have food queues here too!' What they'd have thought if they had realised that the shop was selling licentious buns is anyone's guess.

When I visited, two long-standing members of staff were still on Alison and Tim's payroll: Gill Abbs, head baker, had been with Fitzbillies since the early 1980s and Tom Whitehead since the 1960s. Tom learned the recipe for Chelsea Buns from Mr Day, so could guarantee that it hadn't changed since; Alison saw no reason to suppose it had changed much since 1922. There's obviously a gap in the history between the demise of the Chelsea Bun-House and the birth of Fitzbillies, but – unless someone turns up an even older recipe from somewhere – this is as near to 'original' as you are going to get.

One of the things that differentiates the Chelsea Bun from other similar buns is its stickiness. Fitzbillies achieves this thanks to a bespoke syrup from a specialist supplier, Ragus (whose name is indeed 'sugar' spelled backwards – well spotted). Ragus have been in the business since Victorian times and their antecedents invented golden syrup.

A by-product of the sugar-cane refining process that used to go to waste, it became, thanks to Ragus, something for which every crumpet-eater has been immensely grateful ever since. What Fitzbillies use is a sort of golden syrup, Alison said, but a bit more treacly. You can't buy it in the supermarket, but it certainly makes Fitzbillies' Chelsea Buns very sticky indeed.

Two other things differentiate Chelsea Buns from others of their ilk: their squareness and their spiraliness. You achieve the spirals by rolling the dough out very thinly, rolling it up like a Swiss roll and cutting it into slices. Then, with the cut sides top and bottom so that the spirals are on display, place them in a tray to 'prove'. And here is the clever bit. Position the slices about 2.5cm apart, so that when they prove and increase in volume they will butt up to each other and, lo and behold, end up square.

Alison didn't believe that a genuine Chelsea Bun could be produced on a domestic scale. Her staff never make a tray of fewer than 40, she said; if you make a smaller batch of dough it doesn't work, and if you make a full batch but bake them in smaller quantities they come out different. She also said that success lay in the thinness and softness of the dough, which gave the buns lots of layers, and this couldn't be achieved without professional equipment. But, as Sir Richard Phillips remarked almost 200 years ago, 'even of Chelsea buns there are counterfeits'. At the time of my visit a Fitzbillies' Chelsea Bun was £1.80. You could buy two for £2.50 from a very tempting bread stall in the market a few minutes' walk away; a single bun in Waitrose for 89p; and four rather smaller ones in a packet in Sainsbury's for £1.20. But they wouldn't be – quite – the real thing.

This recipe is, therefore, by definition not quite the real thing, but it comes from a book published about the time Fitzbillies was first opening its doors.

Chelsea Buns

Makes 12

275g plain flour
1 heaped tsp fast-action dried yeast
75g unsalted butter
85g caster sugar
150ml milk, warmed to blood heat
2 large eggs, beaten
60g currants
1–2 tsp mixed spice

For the glaze
2 tbsp granulated sugar
2 tbsp water

1 Sift the flour into a warm bowl and add the yeast. Rub in half the butter until the mixture resembles fine breadcrumbs, then add half the caster sugar. Make a well in the centre. Add the milk to the beaten eggs and pour this mixture into the well in the flour. Mix thoroughly to combine (it will be too damp to knead), then cover and leave in a warm place for about 1½ hours, until doubled in size.

2 Turn the dough on to a lightly floured surface, knead lightly and roll out to about a 30cm square. Spread with the rest of the butter and sprinkle with half the remaining caster sugar. Fold in half, then roll out again thinly so that one side is about 48cm long and the other at least that wide. The thinner you can roll it and the wider it is, the more spirals you will have in the finished buns.

3 Sprinkle with the remaining sugar, the currants and the mixed spice. Using your hands and starting from the 48cm side, carefully roll up like a Swiss roll, then cut into 12 slices, each about 4cm thick.

4 Thoroughly grease a warmed baking tin of about 25 x 30cm, and place the buns in it, cut side downwards. They should fit fairly snugly: they will increase in size as they prove and should end up butting up against each other. Leave to prove for 15–20 minutes.

5 Meanwhile, preheat the oven to 190°C/375°F/gas mark 5.

6 Bake the buns in the preheated oven for about 20 minutes until golden brown.

7 For the glaze, heat the water and sugar in a small saucepan. Stir until the sugar has dissolved, then reduce the heat to a simmer and continue stirring for 2–3 minutes. Remove the buns from the oven and spread with the glaze, then transfer them carefully to a wire rack and allow to cool before separating. These buns are best eaten within a day of baking, but they freeze well.

As I wandered the streets after leaving Fitzbillies, it occurred to me that Cambridge was all architecture and bicycles. Chapels and gorgeous colleges everywhere. Until you got into the shopping centre, which had the same shops as every other city in England, you couldn't move for academe.

There were building works in Benet Street, where a hoarding told me about the project and assured me that shops were open as usual. It spelled the name – not once but four times – Bene't Street. I made a note of this as being a particularly odd misuse of an apostrophe, but when I met up with friends later and remarked on it, they said, 'Oh yes, it's short for "St Benedict".' So the apostrophe wasn't misplaced at all – it was just the most assiduous piece of pedantry I'd ever seen. Well, this was Cambridge.

Back in London after my visit to Fitzbillies, I found myself in the King's Road, in the heart of Chelsea. I was about to walk past a recently opened branch of the artisan bakery Gail's when something in the window stopped me in my tracks. Chelsea Buns. As at Fitzbillies, I found them a tiny bit too sweet and sticky, but if sweet and sticky are your things, they were wonderful. Gail's also sold me the best *pain au raisin* (and I count myself as something of an expert here) that I had had for a long time. More importantly, so far as I knew they were the only 'artisans' selling Chelsea Buns in Chelsea. Welcome home, historic local bun.

13

East Anglia

An Ancient Blessing and a New Creation

NEVER BEEN TO HARWICH? Never heard of Kitchels? Me neither. Those were two good reasons for making the trip. When I found out that each year, on the third Thursday in May, they elected a new mayor and celebrated the occasion by throwing Kitchels out of the Council Chamber window to the crowds below – well, that was a date in my diary months in advance.

Kitchels were once known as God's Kitchels and the Suffolk tradition was that they were given by godparents to godchildren who visited around Christmas time to ask for a blessing. For many years the mayoral election took place in late December, so it was a good time for the new mayor to shower symbolic blessings on his flock, and the custom continued even after the election date was moved to May in 1949.

The cake itself dates back at least to the 14th century, when it is mentioned in *The Canterbury Tales*. Traditional recipes show the Kitchel as a form of mince pie – a spicy, curranty mixture sealed inside pastry. The main differences are that it requires puff pastry rather than short, and that you bake it as one large pasty and cut it into squares.

Harwich Kitchels

Makes 20–25 squares

450g puff pastry
caster sugar, for sprinkling

For the filling
60g unsalted butter
225g currants
85g chopped mixed peel
60g ground almonds
½ tsp ground cinnamon
1 tsp freshly grated nutmeg

1. Preheat the oven to 230°C/450°F/gas mark 8. Line a baking sheet with baking paper.
2. For the filling, melt the butter in a saucepan and remove from the heat. Add the currants, peel, ground almonds and spices and mix well.
3. Divide the pastry in half and roll both pieces out on a lightly floured surface to a thin square shape. Put one of these pieces on the baking sheet. Moisten the edges with water and spread the currant mixture over the pastry, avoiding the edges. Cover with the remaining piece of pastry and press the edges well together to seal. Using a sharp knife, mark the top of the pastry into 20–25 sections, being careful not to cut right through to the filling.
4. Bake in the preheated oven for 20 minutes until the pastry is puffed up and golden. Sprinkle with caster sugar and cut into sections while still warm.

That isn't what they make today, but it took me a while to find that out.

To reach Harwich Town by train from London you pass first through Harwich International, where you can, if the mood takes you, catch a ferry to the Hook of Holland; then through Dovercourt, a small seaside town which appears in the Domesday Book, was once a spa and is where the TV series *Hi-de-Hi!* was filmed. (If those were my three claims to fame, I am reasonably clear in my mind which one I would keep quiet about.) Only then do you come to the port of Harwich.

Practically the first thing you see as you come out of the station is an impressively tall brick structure called the High Lighthouse. I'd have thought this was tautological (or at least a statement of the obvious) until I read the label and discovered that there was a Low Lighthouse on the other side of the green. At one time they worked in tandem. Shows what I know about maritime history.

By the time I left Harwich a few hours later I knew a lot more about maritime history, because the place is blessed with a very active Heritage Society and there is a Maritime Heritage Trail littered with informative plaques. Harwich boasts, for example, Britain's only surviving treadwheel crane, about which I can tell you nothing except that it was worked by two men walking inside the inner of two wheels and sounded too dangerous for my liking.

In fact, everywhere I went in Harwich there were plaques. I hadn't been sure what to expect of the Kitchel-throwing ceremony, so I arrived early and had plenty of time to wander around. There was good stuff about building up the beach to form a 'soft defence' against erosion by the sea, and about the plants and animals that were colonising the emerging dunes. There was a restaurant named after Samuel Pepys, who became the local MP after he stopped keeping a diary, and a pub where Nelson and Lady Hamilton were said to have stayed. Harwich is also the home of the *Mayflower*, on which the Pilgrim Fathers sailed to America. (There's argument about this, but the locals claim she was built here, whatever happened to her later.) And there was the

Electric Palace Cinema, the oldest unaltered purpose-built cinema in the country; it dated from 1911 and had signs over the entrance doors, showing how those who had paid sixpence were segregated from those who had paid a shilling, like the boys' and girls' entrances in old schools. All in all, Harwich was a very pleasant place to amble on a sunny day.

But there didn't seem to be anyone about. A few dog-walkers, a few builders and that was it. I was disappointed to find that the Guildhall was on a narrow street rather than a large market square – for reasons I can't justify, even to myself, I'd been visualising Brussels. A further plaque told me that the Guildhall was built in 1769 on the site of 'The Bear', where the council had met since 1673. Also, happily, a sign in the window confirmed that the meeting to elect the mayor and other officials was taking place today at 11 o'clock – any minute now. There were people going into the building, so I took another leisurely stroll round the block and hoped for the best.

Proving that optimism is always a good policy, the best was precisely what I got. By the time I'd completed my circuit it was nearing half-past eleven and there were a few friendly folk hanging about, including a photographer from the local paper. They assured me that I was in the right place, that in due course the officials would emerge and proceed to the church (a distance of perhaps 50 metres), that I was welcome to attend the church service and that the Kitchel-throwing would take place after that.

Within a very few minutes, that was what happened. An official in a red coat and tricorne hat was one of the first to appear and various dignitaries, both clerical and secular and all sumptuously clad, soon followed.

You couldn't describe the church as packed, but most clergymen nowadays would be pleased to see this turnout on a Sunday, never mind a Thursday lunchtime. Lots of schoolkids in uniform had been brought along; the officials took up a good few pews; and then there was a smattering of random visitors like me. The reading, appropriately enough for what was to follow, was about the feeding of the 5,000 and we sang, to the rousing tune of *Jerusalem*, a hymn written by a local councillor about Harwich surviving resolutely against the wrath of flood and war. In due course the dignitaries proceeded out again and the rest of us hung about in the street, waiting for the fun to start. The number of children seemed to have swelled considerably; some of them had come armed with supermarket carrier bags, either to help them catch the Kitchels or to stash away as many as they could lay their paws on. Probably both.

Then, not many minutes later, everything I'd heard turned out to be true. After an announcement from the town crier that really did begin 'Hear ye, hear ye', the new mayor and mayoress appeared at one first-floor window, two other officials at the other, and started pelting us with buns. Each one hygienically wrapped, just in case you were worrying. The kids scrabbled about, gathering up as much loot as they could; women behind me turned out to be better catchers than I was (no surprise there, remembering the frequent humiliations of my school softball days); and after about ten minutes and perhaps 200 buns I was beginning to despair. Then one landed on the bonnet of a parked car next to me and I was able to make an undignified grab. I didn't want to deprive anyone – and goodness knows I didn't want to appear greedy – but I did feel it was incumbent on me to taste the thing.

The Harwich Kitchel is no longer remotely mince-pie-like; it's a soft roll of the kind you might wrap round a hotdog at a funfair, only it's sweet and spicy and has currants in it. It was very fresh and pleasantly chewy. Kitchels, I learned (this town was *full* of friendly, informative people), used to be made in Harwich by a baker called Humphrey's, but I'd already walked past its empty premises; they were now produced, to the same recipe, in Dovercourt, not much more than a kilometre's stroll away. My informant warned me that it was up the hill, but this was Essex – Snowdon it was not.

Unlike Harwich, Dovercourt had a normal-looking high street with shops in it; one of these was a bakery called Suncrust, which did indeed make Harwich Kitchels. There was a basket of them on the counter, but it seemed to me that Suncrust were missing an opportunity: there was no sign saying 'local speciality' or 'today only'. Because 'today only' was when you could buy them – they made them for this ceremony, but not all year round, and the two women I spoke to didn't appear to know (or care) much about what was going on.

It seemed a shame. I bought a custard tart and left.

In September, by the way, Harwich hosts a sausage-throwing competition when local butchers make sausages of different kinds which are available to sample in three of the town's many pubs. I may have to go back.

Essex may be revelling in this splendid ritual, but the rest of East Anglia is surprisingly barren when it comes to traditional baking. There was no shortage of recipes; what seemed to be lacking were bakers keeping them alive. Of the recipes I found online, I particularly liked two names. Brotherly Love turned out to be a Lardy Cake similar to those I'd found further west, but minus the fruit. I have no idea why it was so called, though one site did suggest it was traditionally eaten at Easter – a time when families got together and forgot their differences over a particularly gooey piece of cake, perhaps?

The other name that took my fancy did have a satisfactory explanation: Suffolk Fourses Cake, a hearty concoction once baked at harvest time, was served at four o'clock to workers in the fields. By that time they were doubtless glad of it, and of the beer or cider that was handed out with it.

Suffolk Fourses Cake

Makes 2 x 450g loaf cakes

1 x 7g sachet fast-action dried yeast
2 tsp granulated sugar
450ml warm water
675g strong plain flour
½ tsp fine salt
2 tsp mixed spice
175g lard or unsalted butter, softened
175g currants

1. Preheat the oven to 200°C/400°F/gas mark 6. Grease 2 x 450g loaf tins.
2. Sift the dry ingredients including the dried yeast into a bowl, then rub in the lard or butter until the mixture resembles fine breadcrumbs. Add the fresh yeast mixture and the remaining water. Mix well to form a smooth dough.
3. Knead the dough thoroughly on a lightly floured surface, and leave in a warm place to rise until it has doubled in size – about 40 minutes. Knock it back by giving it a few firm punches to get rid of any air pockets, then knead in the currants.
4. Shape the dough into 2 loaves and put into the prepared tins. Leave to prove for about half an hour.
5. Bake in the preheated oven for 45 minutes, then leave in the tin to cool a little before turning out on to a wire rack to become cold. Serve in slices, with butter. The second loaf will freeze if you don't want to eat both of them at once.

Nobody seemed to be making either of these cakes, but I persisted. On the One Suffolk website I found a recipe for Newmarket Cake, which contained chocolate and almonds – the richer ingredients perhaps reflecting the fact that the Newmarket racehorse owners were in a different economic league from their agriculturally labouring neighbours. There are precious few regional specialities containing chocolate, so even though this one isn't *very* chocolaty, I thought it was worth sneaking it in.

Newmarket Cake

Makes 1 x 20cm cake

225g unsalted butter, at room temperature
225g granulated sugar
225g plain flour
2 tsp baking powder
125g chocolate, grated (milk or plain, to taste)
4 large eggs, separated
100g blanched almonds, finely chopped
about 100ml very strong black coffee, cooled

1. Preheat the oven to 180°C/350°F/gas mark 4. Grease a deep, 20cm diameter round loose-bottomed cake tin and line with baking paper.
2. In a large bowl cream the butter and sugar together until pale and fluffy. In a separate bowl, sieve the flour and baking powder together, then stir in the grated chocolate.
3. Whisk the egg yolks. Then, using a large metal spoon, gradually add the dry ingredients to the butter and sugar, alternating with the whisked egg yolks. The mixture will appear very stiff at this stage but persevere.

4 In a scrupulously clean bowl, whisk the egg whites until they form soft peaks. Add a large tablespoon of the whisked egg whites to the mixture and stir vigorously to loosen. Then gradually and carefully fold in the remainder of the egg whites, alternating with the chopped almonds and coffee.

5 Spoon this rich mixture into the cake tin and level the top. Place on the middle rack of the preheated oven and cook for 60–75 minutes until the top is slightly browned and the centre is firm and springy to the touch. Remove from the oven and allow to cool slightly before removing from the tin and leaving to become completely cold on a wire rack.

Having made it myself, I can promise you that this is delicious, but I scoured Newmarket without being able to find it. It's difficult to find anything in Newmarket that isn't connected with racing.

That said, the National Horseracing Museum on the high street turned out to be worth a visit. I have no strong views on seeing the racing colours Frankie Dettori wore on the famous day in 1996 when he won his 'magnificent seven' at Ascot, but I was suitably struck by the lofty Regency-style Subscription Rooms in which, in the days before bookies came into being, aristocratic punters threw absurd sums of money around. I was also impressed by the candelabrum presented to Admiral Rous in 1866: it's over a metre high and topped with a silver effigy of the Admiral, who, in addition to serving with distinction in the Royal Navy and travelling as far afield as Labrador and St Helena, was steward of the Jockey Club for over 25 years. As with Mary, Queen of Scots' alleged involvement with shortbread, you wonder where he found the time. Certainly there was no suggestion that he ever sat down at four o'clock to regale himself with chocolate and almond cake.

Later in the year I went with my sister, who lives nearby, to Newmarket Races on an evening when the racing was followed by a

Meatloaf concert. Now there is a man you would think had a hearty appetite – and indeed there was no shortage of food on offer. We ate generous portions of fish and chips, but no cake.

I had better luck with another prosperous part of the county, Southwold, where the local Butter Buns are still made by Mills & Sons, the butcher's in the market place. 'Monday, Wednesday and Friday: they usually come out of the oven about 10 o'clock,' I was told, evoking visions of eager housewives with net bags and headscarves, In fact, Southwold is much more up-market than that, with nine separate 'greens' scattered about the town, an impressive 15th-century church and rows of colourfully painted beach huts, which the Southwold website describes as 'iconic'. Not a word I would normally associate with beach huts, but these – like the rest of the town – are rather smart. As for the buns, I did have to join a queue to buy them, but there wasn't a headscarf in sight. They were worth both the trip and the wait: they were soft, vanilla-y and glazed with honey.

But Southwold was the only success story in an otherwise fruitless search. In fact, unless you're in Southwold on a Monday, Wednesday or Friday morning, the thing to do in Suffolk is forget the traditional stuff. Instead, go for tea in one of the alluring tea shops with which the county abounds, which is what my sister and I did the next available Saturday afternoon.

These tea shops tend to be in the affluent villages that grew up in the days when wool was something that made you rich rather than requiring a special programme on the washing machine. As a result the villages have disproportionately large churches, known as 'wool churches', with impressively chunky towers. Those who know about this sort of thing will tell you that the style is called Perpendicular, but if I tell you it's chunky I hope you'll know what I mean.

If you can go to only one Suffolk village, go to Lavenham. It's lovely. Its church may be Perpendicular, but the rest of it certainly isn't. Munnings Emporium and Tea Room is housed in a building called the Crooked House and it offered a useful fact sheet that explained the village history. Apparently when the wool trade collapsed, Lavenham went from being ultra-rich to extremely poor. There was no money to update houses, so it stayed in a time warp, the most original medieval village in the country. The Crooked House was built by a wealthy cloth merchant around 1395; it's on a rather token hill, but the wood has tended to lean in a downhill direction and the house has been crooked for about 500 years. The effect is enhanced, if you look at it from the street, by the fact that the house on the downhill side of it seems to have been tucked into its armpit, as it were: the two nestle together in a way that obviously works for them but that I can't see a building-society surveyor thinking much of. The Crooked House claims to be the crookedest building in Lavenham, but there are a number of others – including the gloriously rambling Swan Inn – that run it close.

It may be, as Denis Thatcher is said to have maintained, never too early for a gin and tonic, but there are times when it is too early for afternoon tea and this was one of them. So we moved on to Clare, where the 13th-century priory is impressive, but the really fun thing is the pargeting.

Never heard of it? Neither had I.

It's decorated plasterwork, once a widespread local craft. In the 17th century, old timber-framed houses were frequently plastered or re-plastered to keep out the draughts that inevitably crept in as the timbers moved and shrank. In Clare, some bright spark thought, 'We could liven this up a bit' and, while the plaster was still damp, ran something like a comb over it to create shells, herringbone and other such patterns. It's subtle and unobtrusive, because it's all in the same colour and material as the background, but it gives the place a certain *je ne sais quoi*. And, best of all, the people who did it were called Pargetter, like poor Nigel who fell screaming from the roof in *The Archers* a few years ago, or Pargeter, like Edith, better known as Ellis Peters of the Brother Cadfael chronicles fame. It had never occurred to me to wonder about the origin of this name, but I was – as ever when I add a new piece of trivia to my store – very happy to have learned it.

If there is a nice tea shop in Clare we didn't notice it, which is why teatime found us in Long Melford. It's perhaps not as picturesque as either Lavenham or Clare, but the harshest critic would have to admit that it is long enough to justify its name and its church is reckoned one of the finest in the area. Not only that but, after trying one in Brighton, I had set my heart on having another cream tea outside Devon and Cornwall – just for comparison purposes, of course. Tiffins Tea Emporium in Long Melford sold me a very fine one. The jam, although not home-made, was a well-respected brand from an adjacent county and the clotted cream turned out to be Rodda's of Cornwall. (Where had I been all my life that I had never heard of this stuff?) My sister was enthusiastic about the Carrot Cake and there was also a splendidly red-looking Red Velvet Cake. Both of these are American recipes, but we made a note to come back some time when eating anything other than local specialities (or cream teas for comparison purposes) wouldn't make me feel I was straying from some self-imposed straight and narrow.

There was one East Anglian speciality I was still trying to track down, though: Norfolk Vinegar Cake. Young assistants in delis and bakeries tended to look blank when I asked for it, perhaps because when they were doing science at school they did it with proper chemicals and didn't learn about the aerating effect of acid/alkali reactions. They didn't know, either, that once the cake was baked the vinegar lost much of its acidity and provided what I had read somewhere described as 'just a hint of tartness'.

I was about to give up on this particular quest when I discovered Shire Foods of Norfolk. They're based in Downham Market, a town worth visiting for its clock tower alone: it dates from 1878, when it cost the substantial sum of £450, and in its early days its dials were lit by gas – quite a talking point at a time when many houses were still using candles. Pat Gould of Shire Foods described his company as packers, bakers and fine food wholesalers; one of its brands is the Real Norfolk Cake Company.

There's a tendency all over England, it seems to me, to stick the name of the county at the beginning of a cake's name and hope to appeal to those looking for local and traditional products. This was particularly prevalent in Norfolk. I'd found, from another manufacturer, a Norfolk Cherry & Coconut Cake and a Norfolk Banana & Pineapple Cake, both featuring ingredients not widely grown in the county. I have nothing against this (after all, I'd recently eaten a Cornish-and-Essex cream tea in Suffolk; who was I to claim a moral high ground?). It just wasn't what I was looking for.

So I was delighted when Pat told me that he had wanted to produce a traditional Norfolk product and, failing to find anyone who could make it for him, had resurrected an old recipe and done it himself. Like all his cakes, it used British sugar and a rapeseed oil from Cambridgeshire; it was rich and fruity and you'd never know it had vinegar in it.

I liked Pat Gould's attitude: he also made a tasty Real Norfolk Plum Cake that actually contained plums, the only one I'd found anywhere in the country that did. As far back as the 16th century, 'plum' has been used in culinary contexts to mean 'currants or raisins', which of course are dried grapes and are what most other so-called Plum Cakes contain. The OED's best guess is that such things as plum porridge, plum pudding and plum bread were originally made with prunes – dried plums – and retained their name when currants and raisins became widely available and were substituted for the original ingredient.

Norfolk Vinegar Cake

Makes 1 x 23cm cake

450g plain flour
225g unsalted butter
225g granulated sugar
225g each of raisins and sultanas
1 tsp bicarbonate of soda
275ml milk
2 tbsp cider vinegar

1. Preheat the oven to 180°C/350°F/gas mark 4. Grease and line a 23cm diameter round cake tin.
2. Place the flour in a large bowl. Rub the butter into the flour until the mixture resembles fine breadcrumbs. Stir in the sugar and the fruit.
3. Mix the bicarbonate of soda with a tablespoon of the milk. Pour the rest of the milk into a large jug, add the cider vinegar and stir in the bicarb mix (it will froth). Add to the cake mixture and stir well without beating.
4. Spoon the mixture into the tin and bake in the preheated oven for 30 minutes. Then turn the oven down to 150°C/300°F/gas mark 2 and continue to bake for another hour or so until a warm skewer inserted into the middle comes out clean. If the cake appears to be browning too quickly, cover loosely with kitchen foil.
5. Remove from the oven, place the tin on a wire rack and allow the cake to cool in the tin before turning out.

Vinegar Cake uses cider vinegar and East Anglia is famous for its apples and its cider, but I was surprised to discover that this hasn't always been so. To absorb some East Anglian atmosphere I'd been reading Ronald Blythe's *Akenfield: Portrait of an English Village*. Published in the late 1960s, it's an oral history of a Suffolk village and it told me it was only 100 years earlier that new owners of the land had switched from cereals and roots to orchards and planted many thousands of apple, plum and pear trees.

Apples may have been a comparative novelty, but the diary of the Akenfield fruit harvest named 13 commercial varieties, including Worcester Pearmain, Laxton's Superb, William Crump and Cox's Orange Pippin. Then came a list of 'East Anglian apples, some of which can be found in the old gardens in the village but which aren't grown commercially':

> *Lady Henniker, Norfolk Beauty, Norfolk Royal, Green Roland, Histon Favourite, St Edmund's Russet, Doctor Harvey (the great winter apple from Norfolk), Sandringham, Sturmer Pippin, Lord Stradbroke, D'Arcy Spice and Costard (not an East Anglian apple but familiar throughout Britain. There are records to show that it was being sold at Oxford in 1296. The original costermonger was a seller of Costard apples.)*

Reading *Akenfield* had, just from this brief extract, proved an excellent investment of time: I hadn't known that was why costermongers were called costermongers and I promptly put it next after pargeters on the list of useless things I'm really pleased to have found out. I also hadn't heard of half those varieties of apples. Who was Lady Henniker? Who was William Crump? Is Laxton's Superb any more superb than any of the others? I had no idea, but it would be a rich vein of speculation when I was next staring out of a train window.

As it happens, I found myself doing precisely that a day or two later on a train to Norwich. Lured there by its apples, I was going to talk to a man mysteriously named Grimsby, who ran a company called Pye Baker of Norwich.

Although Norwich has a sizeable and buzzing market, the high spot of food shopping is the Colman's Mustard Shop and Museum, situated in the splendidly OTT Arts and Crafts-style Royal Arcade. This was designed in 1899 by an architect called George Skipper, of whom John Betjeman made the grandiose claim that 'he is to Norwich rather what Gaudí was to Barcelona'. Skipper was also responsible for a number of Norwich's impressive buildings, including the Jarrold department store and what is now the headquarters of Aviva, formerly the Norwich Union. Good on you, George.

Colman's itself dates from 1814, when a flour miller named Jeremiah Colman took an existing mustard-manufacturing business, made it his own and subsequently acquired a Royal Warrant from Queen Victoria. The shop had been there only since 1973, but had been carefully designed and decorated to feel much older. Unsurprisingly, most of what it sold was mustard, but it also offered Ninhams Traditional Cake Mixes and Scone Mixes, some of which contained Colman's Mustard, and the company's unique Colman's Mustard Chocolate Bar. The website even had a recipe for Orange-Spiced Chocolate Cookies, containing both mustard powder and mustard-flavoured chocolate, as well as spice (in the form of cinnamon) and orange (in the form of orange zest and Grand Marnier). Question: is the delectability of Grand Marnier sufficient to counterbalance the slight weirdness of putting mustard in chocolate cookies?

Question two: who'd have thought that wandering into a mustard shop would spark a conversation about cake?

A couple of kilometres down the Aylsham Road, an unremarkable-looking industrial estate was home to Pye Baker of Norwich. The real name of the man I was meeting was John Watt, but he described himself as 'affectionately known as Grimsby', because that's where he came from. He had mates called Wigan and Barnsley and we agreed it was just as well he didn't know anyone from Welwyn Garden City – or, I thought afterwards, Ugley, Nasty or Crackpot. He was also a self-confessed food-history geek and told me that Norwich had one of the oldest market charters of any city in England, granted by Henry II in 1158. Under its provisions the local baker had to make a 'Yarmouth Pye' every year as a levy to the king. Grimsby's research had so far failed to discover what a Yarmouth Pie was; his best guess, given that Yarmouth was a fishing port, was that it was something along the lines of a Stargazey Pie, based on the local herrings. But he liked the old-fashioned spelling and used it when he set up Pye Baker in 2008. Shortly afterwards, hearing himself described as 'Pye Baker of Norwich' at a local farmers' market, he decided that had a ring to it and changed the company's name accordingly.

Pye Baker's primary business is artisan breads and Grimsby waxed eloquent on the virtues of good local ingredients – butter in cakes, rapeseed oil grown a few kilometres away for all but his Italian-style breads, which of course required olive oil. 'If you're going to make something traditional, make it traditional,' he said. He won't use margarine and his stomach turns at the mention of trans fats and their contribution to the obesity epidemic. Having recently lost some 30 kilos himself, he could afford to make pronouncements about self-control and I was inclined to take his point when he said, 'If I want to promote people getting fat, it's going to be from something really tasty.' Reverting to geek mode, he quoted the great 19th-century chef Antonin Carême saying to his illustrious but gluttonous client, the future King George IV, 'It's my job to tempt your appetite, it's yours to control it.'

All I could say in response was that in the course of this project I'd found that if I had two afternoon teas on the same day, it was easier to be modest about dinner. However true this may be, I'm not sure it has much to do with self-control.

We could clearly have gone on gossiping all afternoon, but Grimsby had four farmers' markets to prepare for and I was there to talk about the Norfolk Apple Bun – a special bun he had created in honour of the county.

'We have a lot of customers in North Norfolk,' he explained, 'and North Norfolk is sometimes known as Chelsea-on-Sea' (because of the many well-heeled Londoners who've moved themselves and their culinary tastes there). When he was contemplating developing a new product he thought, 'What's Chelsea famous for? The Chelsea Bun. What does Norfolk have an abundance of? Apples. Put the two together and you have the Norfolk Apple Bun.'

He's a man who likes to laugh, and he laughed quite a lot at this.

When we went through to the bakery, I found that the bun did indeed look like a Chelsea Bun, although it wasn't as shiny – it had the same swirliness, but less of the syrup. The style of baking differed, too: the pieces of dough were placed far enough apart on the baking tray that they didn't run into each other and have to be torn apart. 'The buns just touch, so that they come out as their own individual thing,' Grimsby explained. They were obviously hand-made: they all looked more or less alike, but there were slight variations in the pattern of the currants or the placing of the spiral. When I looked at six side by side, that asymmetry was really appealing: Grimsby's aim was 'a form of consistency, but with an individuality'.

He'd recently invested in a BDM – a bun divider mould. Apart from a heavy-duty mixer it was the only piece of machinery in the bakery. But he used it only for cutting up the dough: his team still took the buns out of the machine, knocked them back to get rid of any air pockets and rolled them out again by hand. The BDM could save a lot more labour if they let it, but that would lose the hand-made look.

The buns' key ingredients are currants, butter and 'a smidgen' of sugar in an enriched dough, along with lots of grated apple. The addition of apples has three benefits, Grimsby explained: 'One, the flavour's really nice; two, it's a bit of a novelty; and three, it's one of your five a day.'

I had a feeling this might be pushing it, but before I could say so he added, 'If you can slip in an apple while you're having a nice sticky bun, then all the better.' I thought fleetingly of a Terry's Chocolate Orange and found it hard to disagree.

'Also,' he went on, 'the whole idea of linking something to its roots is quite old. Look at the Chelsea Bun. It's 200 years old. Calling it "Chelsea" was a way of saying, "This is local. This is what we're about." It's purely marketing.'

Being local, as I'd already learned, was very important to Pye Baker. From the Mrs Temple's Cheese company in North Norfolk they bought not only cheese but whey, 'which is a by-product for her, but we use it in Irish soda bread'. Grimsby also told me – and this may have been the geek in him peeking out again – that in Ireland, back in the day, a farmer's wife would use either buttermilk or whey for her soda bread, depending on what else was going on: on the days you made butter, you produced buttermilk; on cheese days you produced whey. The soda bread must have had a slightly different taste, but that was less important than the fact that nothing went to waste.

As far as Grimsby was concerned, waste in a kitchen was a by-product of bad management. 'If I have breadcrumbs left over, I'll pop them into a treacle tart.' (It sounded very good, his treacle tart – it contained golden syrup, eggs, lemon zest and brown butter, and was cooked until it was just set, like a custard.) 'If I have food left at the end of the day at a farmers' market, I'll give it away. I'd rather do that than throw it away. It's a crying shame that people's hard work should end up in the bin.'

Before I left, he promised to look at his recipe for Norfolk Apple Buns and send me a version that could be made on a small scale at home. He was proud of his creation and wanted other people to try it. Sure enough, two days and, from his point of view, four busy farmers' markets later, there it was.

The Pye Baker of Norwich's Norfolk Apple Buns

Makes 12–16

For the dough

600g strong organic white flour
60g caster sugar
15g fine sea salt
18g fresh yeast or 1 x 7g sachet fast-action dried yeast
60g unsalted butter
125ml each of water and milk
2 free-range medium eggs

For the filling

300g grated Cox's apple, unpeeled but cored
a squeeze of lemon juice
180g caster sugar
240g currants
¼ tsp ground cinnamon
50g unsalted butter, softened

For the glaze

the juice of the apples from the filling (see method)
50g caster sugar
a good pinch of ground cinnamon

1 For the dough, measure the flour, sugar and salt into a large mixing bowl, along with the dried yeast, then rub in the butter until the mixture resembles fine breadcrumbs. In another bowl, whisk the water, milk and eggs – along with the fresh yeast if you are using it –

then pour into the flour mixture and mix to a sticky dough. Knead for 10 minutes. Don't add more flour. Just leave the bowl covered for 1 hour.

2 To make the filling, put the grated apple in a strainer over a large bowl and squeeze some lemon juice over it. Rub this into the apple and leave to drain for 15 minutes. Then squeeze the apple to remove as much of the juice as you can (pressing it in your hands works best).

3 Put the dry apple in a bowl and add the sugar, currants and cinnamon. Mix this to a paste with the softened butter and set aside.

4 To make the glaze, measure the apple juice, top it up to 50ml with water and put this in a pan. Mix the sugar and cinnamon and add to the juice. Bring to the boil, simmer for 1 minute, then take off the heat and allow to cool.

5 Lightly flour your worktop. Knead the dough for 10 seconds, cover, leave for 15 minutes and then roll out into a rectangle. Spread the apple filling over this and roll up tightly. Slice the roll into 2.5cm rounds and put these on a baking sheet lined with baking paper, cut side upwards and about 2.5cm apart. Leave covered in a warm place until risen (about 45–60 minutes).

6 Preheat the oven to 190°C/375°F/gas mark 5.

7 Bake the buns in the preheated oven for 20–25 minutes. Remove from the oven and brush with the cinnamon-flavoured glaze. Allow to cool, then enjoy.

I should mention that I enjoyed them very much: not as sweet as the traditional Chelsea Bun, soft, flavoursome and obviously – with all that apple – good for me. It was yet another day when I could go easy on dinner.

As a footnote, Pye Baker also made quite the fattest Eccles Cake I'd ever seen. 'What I like about an Eccles Cake is the filling,' said Grimsby, 'so this is 90 per cent filling.' The puff pastry ('all butter,' he emphasised) was so thin that I could see the fruit through it. I made my farewells and left before he could tell me it was one of my five a day.

14

Around the Midlands

'Just Don't Call Them Eccles Cakes'

At Euston, the ticket collector greeted me with, 'Hello, flower, how are you today?' I was reminded of a university friend from Cheshire who used this endearment and I told the man that no one had called me flower for a very long time. He replied, 'I'll make it up to you, princess.'

The much younger woman next to me, who'd given her ticket to the other collector, objected that no one had called *her* flower or princess.

'Oh, I'm sorry, flower,' said my man.

'Too late now,' she said cheerfully, as if telling this friendly stranger that he had ruined her day had in fact made her day.

From Euston I was heading for Coventry, my starting point for a brief foray into the Midlands. Having discovered the concept of Godcakes when I was in Harwich, I'd been reading up about them in Florence White's *Good Things in England* and now knew that they were a tradition in Coventry too.

Across the country there are many variations on the theme of what Florence calls 'fruit and pastry baking' and much of the variation is down to shape. What sets the Coventry Godcake apart is the fact that it's triangular – an isosceles triangle, to be precise. In Suffolk, as I'd seen, the Kitchel is torpedo-shaped; Eccles and Chorley Cakes are round; in a day or two I would be going to Banbury, whose cakes are oval. In addition to differing in shape, some of these are made with puff pastry, others with short. It's all to do with people in different places evolving slightly different versions of the same thing which, in the days before mass communication and travel, remained largely undiscovered by the outside world.

Florence White had also told me that Godcakes had been on display at the first exhibition of the English Folk Cookery Association, held in January 1931; they were made by a Mr R H Buckingham of Coventry from whom, she said, 'they can always be obtained'. Apparently they were becoming hard to find even then. However, I'd read that they'd recently had a revival and was on my way to meet the woman responsible.

Lots of Coventry is a bit gloomy – you walk into town from the station past a succession of charity shops and betting shops; the only half-timbered building in evidence in the centre is a Wetherspoon's pub; and the first large shop you come to is Primark. The only cheery thing was the statue of Lady Godiva on her horse in the centre of the newly pedestrianised Broadgate.

Tennyson once missed a train out of Coventry, so to pass the time in pre-crossword days he wrote a poem about the city's most famous daughter, who had ridden naked through the streets in protest against her husband's harsh taxes. A few lines of the poem appear on the base of the statue:

Then she rode forth, clothed on with chastity:
The deep air listen'd round her as she rode,
And all the low wind hardly breathed for fear.

Noble words about a noble gesture. Or so I might have thought had I not found myself humming the 1960s pop song, recorded by Peter and Gordon, that was also a tribute to Lady Godiva. Their heroine was a stripper and the song mentioned 'her long blonde hair, falling down across her arms, hiding all the lady's charms'. Sir William Reid Dick's sculpture in Broadgate, on the other hand, has draped the hair very carefully so as to *display* the lady's charms. So much for being clothed on with chastity. This Godiva is a very sexy lady and, although she is riding side saddle, as ladies always did, she'd have looked more demure if she'd thought to keep her knees together. There's a newsagent just across the way called Peeping Tom, and frankly I'm not surprised. I wonder if they pedestrianised Broadgate because cars kept crashing into her.

Moving on from naked women, if you want to be a tourist in Coventry, the place to go is the Transport Museum. Celebrating the fact that Coventry was the birthplace of the British cycle and motor industry, it has a fantastic collection of all sorts of vehicles, including those gorgeous cars with running boards that look black in old films but in real life turn out to be in rich colours such as burgundy or royal blue. Signs said, 'Please do not touch the vehicles', 'Please do not climb on this vehicle'. Well, obviously they didn't want school parties clambering all over everything, but I was on my own, I'd wiped my feet when I came in and those running boards were just *made* to be climbed on. Didn't they want me to enjoy myself?

Apparently not. Instead, feeling as if I'd been told off without doing anything wrong, I concentrated on the ads. There was a re-creation of a shopping street with lots of pre-war advertisements, and they were fun. A poster promoting Hercules cycles showed the mythical hero, scantily clad in a loincloth, muscles bulging, lion skin draped casually around his shoulders. He bore a massive club in one hand and was effortlessly lifting a bicycle above his head with the other. Was the point that the bike was incredibly lightweight? Or that it had been made by superhumanly strong people? Or should be ridden only by demigods? I have no idea.

A highlight among the cars: Queen Mary's Daimler, faithfully restored to the condition it was in when it was delivered to Her Majesty as a Silver Jubilee present in 1935; it was finished in its 'original livery of royal claret and black with a vermilion coach line'. Somehow managing to look like a chunky 1935 car and yet be limo-length, it was undeniably splendid and had a running board I longed to climb on. However, although there wasn't specifically a sign telling me not to, I'd got the message by now.

In another part of the museum I learned that driving tests didn't become compulsory until 1935, which meant that for about the first half-century in the life of the automobile you applied for a licence only if you felt like it. Scary. Time for a cup of tea? I thought so.

Tea, and a little something to go with it, was, of course, the reason I was there. At the time of my visit Esquires Coffee House in the Transport Museum was the only place in the city where you could buy a Coventry Godcake. The independent bakery that used to make them went out of business several decades ago; they then weren't available commercially until very recently, when Leigh Waite of The Heritage Cake Company came along.

Don't mention Eccles Cakes in front of Leigh. She'll sigh. Too many people assume that's what her Godcakes are. (She doesn't care for the expression 'glorified mince pie' either, although there's no denying that the filling of the Godcake resembles Christmas mince.) But do ask her about the triangular shape. It's pre-Reformation symbolism, she'll tell you, and it's likely that the Godcake dates back to the late medieval/early Tudor period – say 1500, for the sake of argument. As in Harwich, they were given, along with a blessing, by godparents to godchildren at New Year. The three corners of the triangle represent the Holy Trinity and the fact that there are three knife slashes in the top of the cake is no coincidence. Another part of the tradition says that, on receiving the cake, the child should bite the corners off one at a time and recite, 'God the Father, God the Son and God the Holy Spirit'.

The revival of the Godcake was something of a happy accident. Leigh is a qualified Blue Badge tourist guide and used to work in the Coventry Guildhall, where she met and learned a lot from local historian David McGrory. One day and 'quite randomly', as she put it, he gave her a recipe – for Coventry Godcakes. Probably about 200 years old, it had been handed down through the generations of a local family and had come to light as part of a local history project in nearby Walsgrave. Leigh told me she had been an enthusiastic amateur cook ever since she was big enough to hold a wooden spoon, so making Godcakes seemed like an obvious contribution to Coventry's planned Heritage Weekend.

They were a great success, but that might have been the end of the matter had Leigh not been approached by the Transport Museum, who were interested in featuring local foods. So, pleasingly, the triangular cakes turned into a business through the efforts of a triangle of people: Leigh herself, the museum's marketing manager Stephanie Brown and Steve Prime, franchise holder of Esquires. A display card on the counter explained the cake's background and tourists loved them, Steve said. Once they'd stopped asking for Eccles Cakes, that is.

Going back to the history, the wealthier you were the bigger the cake you could afford. (Leigh's cakes have a base of 16cm and a height of 8cm. Application of Pythagoras' Theorem tells me that the shorter sides are therefore just over 11cm, but I'd eaten mine before it occurred to me to measure them.) Records are sparse until the mid-19th century, when an 1856 edition of *Notes & Queries* recorded the New Year cake-giving tradition and said that there were 'halfpenny ones cried through the streets and others of much greater price, even, it is said, to the value of a pound, used by the upper classes'. Shades of 'One a penny, two a penny, Hot Cross Buns'. And the connection doesn't stop there: just as Godcakes were associated with New Year, so Hot Cross Buns are connected with Easter and the concept of its being a blessing to have one, and bad luck not to, applies to both. Superstition or a bun-maker's marketing ploy, who can tell?

Splashing out £1 on a cake must have been really showing off in the 1850s: it was a week's wages for a shopkeeper or clerk. I wondered if the buns being sold 'two a penny' were smaller than the 'one a penny' ones; or were they just yesterday's stock being flogged off cheap? Come to that, if you bought your bun rather than being given it as a blessing by your godparents, did it count?

Elisabeth Ayrton, in *The Cookery of England* (1974), quotes an 18th-century manuscript found in Reading Museum, which has this to add to the story:

> *The earliest mince pies were boat shaped, with flattened lids, to represent cradles. In the Reformation they were forbidden, as they were thought Popish since they represented the cradle of the Christ Child, and the spices of the filling the gifts of the Three Kings.*

Mincemeat as we know it seems to have evolved as a way of spicing up meat dishes; the recipe in the Reading manuscript contains both tongue and beef suet, plus copious quantities of currants, apples, wine and spices. By the time Mrs Beeton came along 100 years later, the meat was sometimes dropped but the suet was still very much in evidence. Florence White describes a filling for a pasty she ate as a child (in the 1860s or '70s, perhaps a decade after Mrs Beeton was writing) made with scraps of lard, brown sugar, currants, nutmeg or cinnamon and sometimes a little chopped apple.

The published recipes I'd found for Godcakes didn't specify the ingredients of the mincemeat, but Leigh was adamant that it was the key. For her the single most important ingredient was an absent one: surprisingly, in light of the above, she shunned suet and concentrated on fruit, butter and spices. She glazed the pastry with milk, not egg white as some people do, and pressed the cakes face down into golden caster sugar (which spreads more easily than granulated) before baking to give them a crunchy top.

Steve Prime was keen to move away from the generic style of most modern coffee shops and stock more individual things, more local products with stories behind them; Leigh was the ideal person for him to turn to, because that was what she wanted to do too. At the time we spoke she was working on Walton Ginger Cake from Walton Hall near Stratford-upon-Avon, famous for its dark, sticky top ('Rather good with a fine cup of coffee'). Legend has it that it was made on the Walton estate, where the local lord discovered it, liked it and asked his wife to re-create the recipe. Walton Hall is a hotel and spa these days, and if they have any sense they'll have a Ginger Cake on their menu and a display card telling visitors all about it.

Also on Leigh's list were another Coventry special, Corporation Custard; Warwickshire Honey Scones, sweetened with local honey and perhaps – in a break from tradition – just a *tiny* bit of sugar to give a more modern taste; Warwickshire Shy Cake, a plain cake flavoured with lemon and ginger; and Bosworth Jumbles, about which I was very excited because I couldn't find anyone who sold them and I was planning to visit the Bosworth Battlefield Heritage Centre and see what I could find out about them.

What I especially liked about talking to Leigh and Steve was that they were both interested in things that would be a source of local pride – and they were both young. This wasn't about reminiscing that things were better in their day. Leigh reckoned she was bringing back a tradition, promoting good old-fashioned cooking from scratch, supporting other local traders and doing something that could bring in the visitors and be a boost to the local economy.

Not only that, but she had a very good line to help promote her wares. David McCrory had said after a taste test: 'With cake, sometimes you're a bit bored by the time you get to the end of it, but with a Godcake you've just got going.'

Leigh's recipe is, she says, 'the most accurate and reliable version that we have' and she isn't sharing it with anyone yet. But this one will give you a reasonable idea. Some versions add the zest of 2–3 lemons to the mincemeat, but Leigh says this isn't authentic. Up to you.

Coventry Godcakes

Makes 12

375g puff pastry
milk and golden caster sugar, to glaze

For the mincemeat
75g unsalted butter
20g granulated sugar
40g currants
¼ tsp freshly grated nutmeg
⅛ tsp ground allspice
1 tbsp rum or brandy

1. Preheat the oven to 220°C/425°F/gas mark 7. Grease a baking sheet.
2. First make the mincemeat by mixing the butter and sugar thoroughly together in a suitably sized bowl. Add the currants, spices and rum or brandy. Suspend the bowl over a pan of simmering water for a few minutes to heat it through, then allow to cool before using.
3. On a lightly floured surface, roll out the puff pastry thinly. Cut into 10cm squares and place a generous dessertspoon of mincemeat towards one corner of each square, so that it covers a little under half the pastry and leaves a triangular area with no filling at all. Moisten the edges of the square with water, fold over along the diagonal to make a triangle and press the edges together to seal. Brush the tops with a little milk.

4 Sprinkle the caster sugar on a flattish plate and press one side of each cake into it to give an even covering. With a sharp knife, make three parallel slits in the sugary side of each triangle.

5 Place on the prepared baking sheet, sugar side up, and bake in the preheated oven for 10–15 minutes, until risen and golden brown. Cool on a wire rack and eat fresh.

One of the happiest aspects of my cake travels had been the opportunity to visit friends scattered round the country and, more often than not, to take advantage of their good nature and their cars. That's how I came to be at the Bosworth Battlefield Heritage Centre and Country Park on the Sunday after my visit to Coventry. The Heritage Centre's exhibition pre-dated the furore about discovering Richard III's remains under a Leicester car park – much of their enthusiasm centred on the archaeological evidence which, a few years earlier, had finally confirmed the exact site of the Battle of Bosworth Field. That's where, on 22 August 1485, Richard lost his life and throne to the man who became Henry VII.

One feature of the exhibition was a video of someone purporting to be the 'barber surgeon' on the battlefield. After a gruesome description of how he took arrowheads out of wounds, he recommended a poultice of barley, turpentine and honey to keep the wound clean. As so often with recipes involving strange combinations, I wondered what they had tried and rejected before settling on that.

The centre's management had done a good job, outside as well as in. You could, if you chose, treat the park as nothing more than a place to stroll with children and dogs, but scattered along its paths were boards topped with warriors' helmets, giving snippets of information to those who cared to know. One of them described the power of the longbow – still very much in evidence at Bosworth –

and said, 'Look to your right, to the white fence. A good archer could have hit you from there.' The white fence was a surprising distance away and, although there was no sign of a longbowman pointing his weapon at us, we instinctively moved a few steps further up the hill, out of range.

A war memorial in the form of a sundial talked us through the day of the battle. Engraved in its metal surrounds, at the point where the dial's shadow would fall at eight o'clock in the morning, were the words, 'Early in the morning men prepare their souls and their equipment for the forthcoming battle. Sounds of stone on blades and murmured Latin prayers are soon drowned out by the din of the drums calling the men to muster.' At noon: 'Bodies strew the field, blood soaks the ground.' Then by three in the afternoon it was all over: 'The last of the Plantagenet kings, slung naked across a horse. A victor leads his tired army to Leicester and a day's deeds are recounted.'

A thousand men killed in not much more than six hours in the course of a war that waged on and off for 30 years. The final statistics must have been appalling.

I'm not sure if one of the dead was Richard III's chef. The exhibition reminded us that 'an army marches on its stomach', though it was a few centuries later that Napoleon (or possibly Frederick the Great) came up with that line; both armies would have had cooks and bakers in their retinue. But legend has it that the recipe for Bosworth Jumbles fell out of a chef's pocket and was gathered up by – goodness knows whom. Anyway, it was preserved for posterity.

This is, to say the least of it, odd, for a number of reasons. For a start, the first record of jumbles (sometimes spelled jumbals or jumballs) I can find is dated 1596. Then, there seems to be no suggestion that they were specific to this part of the world; the name was a generic one for biscuits that were twisted into a knot. Not to mention that the battlefield must have been carnage: who in the world was wasting time picking up pieces of paper? And, with the greatest possible respect, they're only biscuits – if it had been a chef's signature method of stuffing a partridge inside a duck and then putting them inside a swan, that might have been worth salvaging.

But let's not be cynical. I'd come armed with Leigh Waite's email address to pass on to the right person in the café, but sadly the only real disappointment about Bosworth Heritage Centre was the catering. We were served run-of-the-mill paninis and tea in paper cups by girls who couldn't have been less interested, and I couldn't see that a conversation about why they didn't sell Bosworth Jumbles was going to get very far. In due course I had a go at making my own and hoped that Leigh would show more entrepreneurial spirit than I had.

Bosworth Jumbles

Makes about 30

150g slightly salted butter (or unsalted butter plus a pinch of salt)
150g caster sugar
1 medium egg
275g plain flour
1–2 tsp finely grated lemon rind, to taste
50g ground almonds
a little icing sugar, for dusting

1. Preheat the oven to 180°C/350°F/gas mark 4. Grease a baking sheet.

2. In a large bowl, cream the butter and sugar together until soft and fluffy, and then work in all the remaining ingredients, apart from the icing sugar. The mixture will be stiffish.

3. Roll the mixture into several long sausage shapes and break these into smaller pieces, about 8cm in length. Form these into S shapes and place on the greased baking sheet.

4 Bake in the preheated oven for about 15 minutes, until golden. Dust with icing sugar, then lift carefully off the baking sheet and cool on a wire rack. Store overnight in an airtight tin to allow the flavours to develop.

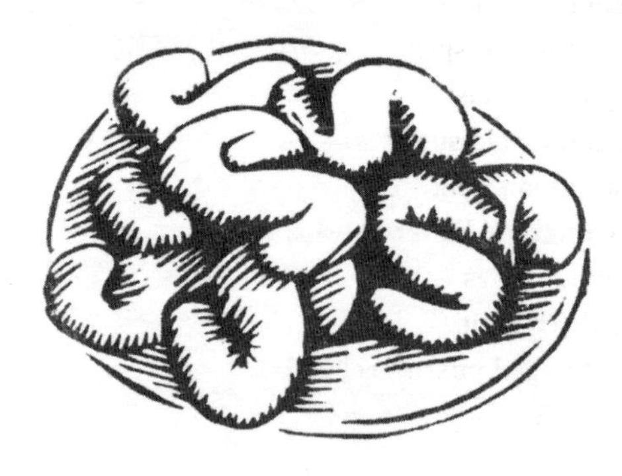

Handing out cakes on feast days wasn't unique to Coventry. In St Albans they used to make Pope Lady Cakes on New Year's Day or Lady Day (25 March, the day the Virgin Mary is supposed to have conceived Christ). The tradition has died out now, but the Pitt Rivers Museum in Oxford has two examples. Sadly these aren't on display, but there is an image on the museum's website, catalogue number 1913.52.2. Go to 'Explore' at the top of the home page, then search the Online Database Collection. They are worth it. They are seriously cute dough figures – asymmetrical and three-dimensional, with currant eyes and broad grins made from notches in the dough. The contrast with the anodyne, flat, coloured-icing decoration of the standard gingerbread man could hardly be greater. These little guys (14.5cm high) are alive, well and want to tell you about a funny thing that happened to them on the way to the museum. They make you smile just looking at their picture, which is quite an achievement for a lump of dough.

Pope Lady Cakes

Makes about 12

450g strong plain flour
½ tsp fine salt
2–3 tsp mixed spice
1 tsp dried yeast
75g granulated sugar
about 130ml milk
110g unsalted butter
2 medium eggs
175g dried fruit
50g chopped mixed peel
24 currants

For the glaze
3 tbsp milk
2 tbsp granulated sugar

1 If you have a bread-making machine, put the yeast, flour, sugar, butter, salt, spice, eggs and milk into the pan in that order, and select the basic dough programme. Then, when the programme is complete, go to step 4.

2 If you are making the cakes by hand, sift the flour, salt and spice together into a large bowl. In a small jug, combine the yeast with 1 teaspoon of the sugar and 1 tablespoon of the milk. Leave to froth.

3 Rub the butter into the flour until the mixture resembles fine breadcrumbs. Pour in the frothy yeast and beaten eggs, with enough of the remaining milk to make a dough. Beat and knead well until the dough is smooth and the basin and your hands are clean. Cover with a tea-towel and leave in a warm place for a couple of hours until the dough has doubled in size.

4 Preheat the oven to 230°C/450°F/gas mark 8 and grease 2 baking sheets.

5 Knead the remaining sugar and the fruit and peel into the dough, and work again until smooth. Divide into 12 equal pieces, then shape into roughly human form, using a small piece of dough for each head and fashioning arms and legs from the main piece. Use currants to represent the eyes. Place on the greased baking sheets, about 7.5cm apart, and leave for about 20 minutes to rise until doubled in size again.

6 Put the baking sheets into the preheated oven and bake for about 15 minutes. Meanwhile, make a sugar glaze by heating the milk and stirring in the granulated sugar until it has dissolved. Remove the cakes from the oven and, while they are still hot, brush with the glaze. Return to the oven for 3 minutes. Serve as fresh as possible, ideally warm from the oven.

It's usually assumed that Pope Lady Cakes are meant to represent the Virgin Mary and the Christ Child, though some people trace their origins back to pre-Christian times and the pagan fertility goddess Eostre, from whom the word Easter derives. Some also, in an attempt to explain the name, allege an association with Pope Joan, the only female pope. Joan, according to one version of her story, was born in England in the ninth century, fell in love with a monk, disguised herself as a man and fled to Athens with him. When he died she moved to Rome, joined the priesthood, became a cardinal and eventually Pope John VIII. Unfortunately, there's no evidence that Joan existed or that Pope John VIII was other than the man he appeared to be.

Pope Lady Cakes may also have been the precursors of Hot Cross Buns, which St Albans Cathedral and Abbey Church claims to have invented. A monk called Thomas Rocliffe, working in the abbey refectory in 1381, developed a recipe for a spicy fruit bun with a cross cut in the top; he distributed these to the poor on Good Friday, along with the customary basin of sack. (One source says soup. Perhaps it depended on the weather.) They became known as Father Rocliffe's Buns or Alban Buns. The abbey revived them during Lent 2013 and they were very like a modern Hot Cross Bun.

You might have noticed that there's some confusion of legends here, as there often is when pagan traditions bang up against Christian ones. There is even the suggestion that the cross is a pre-Christian symbol, its four points representing the four seasons or the four phases of the moon. It can all get hideously complicated, but I don't care. The Pitt Rivers figures are cute.

Wherever they came from, spicy buns were only for special occasions. A decree from the time of Elizabeth I specifically forbade bakers to 'make, utter or sell by Retail, within or without their Houses, unto any of the Queen's Subject, any Spice Cakes, Buns, Bisket, or other Spice Bread, (being Bread out of Size, and not by Law allowed) except it be at Burials, or upon Friday before Easter, or at Christmas; upon pain of Forfeiture of all such Spice Bread to the Poor'. A bit drastic, but in those days the powers that be didn't want the rest of the population getting above themselves.

People getting above themselves – or certainly a little out of control – seemed to be a risk when we got to the ancient market town of Rothwell in Northamptonshire the next day. Northamptonshire is an undersung county, I always think, and it has a number of traditional recipes, so it was good to discover that Rothwell was keeping one of them alive. Rowell (as it is generally pronounced and sometimes spelled) has a market charter dating back to 1204, the reign of King John. This makes it not as old as Norwich, but older than quite a few others. The King's 'beloved and faithful Richard, Earl of Clare and his heirs' were granted the right to hold a fair for five days each year, around the Feast of the Holy Trinity.

Holy Trinity falls eight weeks after Easter and on the occasion of our visit it coincided with the late May bank holiday.

A further charter, granted by James I in 1614, permitted the sale of 'all manner of cattle, merchandise and other stuff'. It is this charter that is ceremonially read at the start of the fair each year by the town's bailiff, who rides round the town on horseback and proclaims it a total of nine times. There were men carrying halberds, local dignitaries wearing the heavy metal chains of office, a brass band: so far, so traditional, even if one of the readings was outside the Co-op, a venue whose historical significance escaped us. But by lunchtime most of what was on sale was beer, with the odd burger and swirl of candy floss thrown in. In the 21st century the fair was of the dodgems-and-things-that-swirl-you-round-and-round variety, with a *lot* of pounding music and boozy revelry.

It was a shame, because Rothwell is a lovely little town with a handsome church said to be 'easily the longest in the county'. This was a claim I'd never heard before. Are there other counties with several long churches where the privilege of being dubbed the longest is hotly disputed? The church also boasted, if that's the word, a remarkable 'bone crypt' containing the remains of some 1,500 people. The story goes that these were discovered by a gravedigger working in the church 'many years ago'. The poor soul slipped, fell 4 metres in the pitch dark, landed in this mass of bones and – understandably – lost his mind from the shock.

Back on Market Hill, where the fair was happening, the shops were almost all closed, but a notice in the window of the Heritage Centre explained why we had come. At the end of the week the Rothwell Fair Curd Tart Competition was to be judged. Entry forms cost 50p, the first prize was £20 and the notice advised that entrants might vary the recipe as they wished, though I assumed this didn't mean that you could enter a Chocolate Fudge Cake and expect to win. In any case, it was just as well I wasn't going to be there on the day of judgement – I'd been present on two occasions recently when throwing food about had been the order of the day, and if Rothwell got rowdy when Curd Tarts were around I didn't want to be there.

Curd Tarts – also known as Cheesecakes – aren't unique to Northamptonshire; they are part of the ancient and widespread tradition of ensuring that as little food as possible went to waste. Just as Eccles Cakes used up scraps of pastry and Lardy Cakes developed where the butchering of pigs yielded plenty of lard, so Curd Tarts were a way of using the solid, curdled part of sour milk – the result of separating the fats in the milk from the liquid whey. A Yorkshire friend whose mother used to make these in the 1950s recalled that they disappeared once the family acquired a fridge. But they seem to be making a resurgence – they are now widely available in Yorkshire (where the same friend says she hadn't seen them for years until recently) and I subsequently bought one in Derbyshire.

Traditional English Cheesecakes are nothing like the creamy, fruity concoctions on a digestive-biscuit base that most of us would think of as a cheesecake today. Instead, they have a pastry case (usually short, sometimes puff), with a filling based on curds and dried fruit. At their simplest they are flavoured with nothing more than nutmeg or allspice, but some contain lemon juice and lemon rind and my Derbyshire purchase had raspberry purée.

Texture varies, too: the proportion of egg yolk to egg white is never the same from one recipe to another; one Yorkshire version contained no solids except the curds themselves, so the result was custardy, whereas the Derbyshire version had ground rice, making it quite solid (though this was softened by a generous quantity of sultanas). Jane Grigson, brought up in the northeast, included breadcrumbs, as did a recipe I found from Lincolnshire and another from Leicestershire. This last used puff pastry and added a dash of rum or brandy. I was beginning to see that the Rothwell Heritage Centre's permission to adapt the recipe in any way you saw fit was not as cavalier as it sounded.

Thinking about it, it's not surprising that Curd Tarts or Cheesecakes should have been made in all sorts of ways. As with all those variations on 'fruit and pastry', the question 'What shall we do with that sour milk?' was likely to produce any number of similar but subtly different answers in any number of places. Also, it would have been an entirely domestic question, asked by housewives and housekeepers, so there would have been no need to come up with a generic answer and proclaim that yours was the original. Most recipes – bearing in mind all the variations just mentioned – resemble that given for Yorkshire Curd Tart on page 303, but I thought I'd also include this richer, Leicestershire version with its addition of cream and alcohol.

Leicestershire Curd Tarts

Makes 18

225g puff pastry

For the filling

1 litre milk plus 2 tsp lemon juice, or 250g cottage cheese
100g granulated sugar
100g unsalted butter, softened
50g fine fresh breadcrumbs
2 medium eggs, lightly beaten
180g sultanas and currants, mixed
½ tsp freshly grated nutmeg
½ tsp finely grated lemon rind
a dash of rum or brandy
2 tbsp double cream

1 If you are making the curds yourself, heat the milk until it is tepid, then add the lemon juice. Leave to cool and form

curds. When the mixture is firm, strain it through butter muslin to separate the curds from the whey and leave to strain overnight.

2 Preheat the oven to 220°C/425°F/gas mark 7. Roll the pastry out thinly and cut it into 18 x 8cm rounds. Use these rounds to line 18 deep patty pans. Prick the bottoms with a fork. Chill the pastry cases until you are ready to fill them.

3 Turn the contents of the butter muslin into a bowl, soften with a fork, then beat in the butter. (Or sieve the cottage cheese into a bowl, then beat in the butter.) Add all the remaining ingredients. Don't worry if the mixture seems runny – it is meant to be. Pour the curd mixture into the pastry cases.

4 Bake in the preheated oven for 10–15 minutes, then turn the oven down to 160°C/325°F/gas mark 3 and continue to bake for a further 10–15 minutes, until the pastry is golden and the filling is set.

Also traditional to Northamptonshire, though I couldn't find anyone who made it, is the Seblet Cake. As I had seen in Suffolk, there were plenty of cakes associated with the harvest, but this one is connected with the sowing season. In the days when wheat was sown by hand, a seblet was a basket used for carrying the seeds and the Seblet Cake was handed out to the labourers once the job was done. The OED records the word as being used specifically in Northamptonshire in the 1630s. A century later, Jethro Tull came along and changed the face of seed-planting for ever. So perhaps we can blame him for the demise of the Seblet Cake: with the invention of the horse-drawn seed drill, it was the horse rather than the farm labourers who needed a reward at the end of the day.

Northamptonshire Seblet Cake

Serves 8

175g unsalted butter
175g caster sugar
3 large eggs
110g plain flour
110g self-raising flour
2 tsp caraway seeds
about 15ml milk

1 Preheat the oven to 180°C/350°C/gas mark 4. Grease and line the bases of 8 x 10cm diameter patty tins or 1 x 18cm diameter round cake tin.

2 In a large bowl, cream the butter and sugar until light and fluffy, then gradually beat in the eggs. Sift the flour into the mixture, and fold in together with the caraway seeds. Add only enough milk to give a soft mixture.

3 Pour this mixture into the tin(s) and bake in the preheated oven until firm to the touch, about 50 minutes for a large cake, 35 minutes for individual ones. Eat fresh.

Like Cheesecakes, Seed Cakes such as this were made all over the country. The traditional flavouring was caraway, but that must just have been because it was readily available. I find it hard to believe that people actually liked it, particularly in the quantities in which they used it. Florence White quotes an 1852 recipe for 'a rich seed cake' which has over *two tablespoons* of caraway seeds to 125g each of flour and butter. By way of comparison, Nigel Slater has a recipe for a similar-sized cake (which he admittedly describes as 'light and understated') with a mere teaspoon of caraway. He adds the further warning: 'Cast aside all thoughts of generosity or the more the merrier. A pleasing seed cake is about how few seeds you add rather than how many … Caraway seeds are particularly pervasive, and too many will introduce a medicinal, musty quality to your baking.'

Today, you can find recipes on the internet containing poppy seeds, sesame seeds and others, but a traditional, old-fashioned Seed Cake is still caraway, caraway and caraway. Florence White helpfully suggests that if you don't like seeds, you can substitute caraway essence; but nowadays that seems to be available only as an essential oil (it's said to be good for the digestion and to relieve flatulence). If you want the caraway taste without the seeds, go for Kümmel liqueur. Or do what I do – forget the caraway altogether and make something nicer.

With nowhere open to buy cake in Rothwell because of the fair (though the Little Blue Owl Cake Company shop looked as if it would be worth a visit next time we were passing through), it was time to move on, in search of a bit of calm and, inevitably, a cup of tea. A few kilometres down a back road we found an Elizabethan folly called Rushton Triangular Lodge. Now in the care of English Heritage, it had a tiny shop where they sold good-looking lemon curd, but sadly neither tea nor Curd Tarts.

The lodge was, however, well worth the detour. It is, as its name suggests, a triangular building – triangular in floor plan, that is; its wall rise up at right angles to the ground in the conventional way. It was built by a local Catholic grandee called Thomas Tresham, whose coat of arms features a group of trefoils; this is a pun on the family name, which can, at a pinch, be interpreted to mean 'I am three'. The building is heavily adorned with symbolism connected to the Holy Trinity – just like the Godcakes made not so very far away in Coventry. I liked the idea that my cake search in the Midlands was coming full circle, even though it was all about triangles.

So that I could complete my circuit of 'don't call them glorified mince pies', my friend kindly dropped me back at Coventry Station the next morning. From there I took a train to Banbury.

These days lots of people haven't heard of Banbury Cakes. What they know about Banbury is that you ride a cock horse to its cross. The nursery rhyme goes back to at least the 18th century and some say further, identifying the 'fine lady upon a white horse' as Elizabeth I. But the present cross is neo-Gothic and commemorates the marriage of Queen Victoria's daughter Victoria to Prince Friedrich Wilhelm of Prussia. Three earlier crosses – the High Cross or Market Cross, the Bread Cross and the White Cross – were all destroyed in 1600 by powerful local Puritans who objected to their fancy design and their associations with Catholicism. It was one in the eye for them, I couldn't help feeling, that the 19th-century replacement should be so shamelessly ornate.

It's possible that the recipe for Banbury Cakes was brought to England by Crusaders in the 12th century – a similar type of cake is known to have existed in Syria at that time, and the Crusaders would have been able to acquire dried fruit and spices at a reasonable price. A more recent theory is that it owes its origins to a Jewish settlement in Banbury that pre-dated the Crusades and survived Edward I's expelling the Jews from England in 1290. According to some, the Eccles Cake, the Chorley Cake and Scotland's Black Bun are all spinoffs of the Banbury original (though funnily enough I hadn't heard anyone mention that up North).

As to the recipe itself, there's some confusion, because a completely different sort of Banbury Cake appears in Gervase Markham's *The English Huswife*, published in 1615. The book's subtitle is nothing if not flamboyant: *Containing the Inward and Outward Virtues Which Ought to Be in a Complete Woman*. I hadn't realised that the ability to make Banbury Cakes was a virtue without which no woman was complete, and the thought briefly made me feel rather inadequate, but I got over it.

Gervase's Banbury Cake is what's called a double-dough bun, with fruit and spices mixed into one batch of dough and then covered by a very thin outside layer of plain dough. So when you slice into it, you have a pale outer casing and a rich brown interior, but it's all bun, not a pastry case with a fruity filling.

The Puritans suppressed this, for the usual 'connected with Catholicism and jollification' reasons. They were truly not a bundle of laughs.

Gervase Markham, on the other hand, must have been rather fun. He was also an expert (or, I suspect, self-styled expert) on horses and horsemanship and produced a book called *Markham's Method or Epitome Wherein [Is] Shewed His Approved Remedies for All Diseases Whatsoever Incident to Horses, and They Are Almost 300 All Cured*; later in life he turned his attention to archery and came up with *The Art of Archerie, Shewing how it is most necessary in these times for this Kingdom, both in Peace and War, and how it may be done without Charge to the Country, Trouble to the People, or any Hindrance to Necessary Occasions. Also, of the Discipline, the Postures, and whatsoever else is necessary for the attaining to the Art.* Be grateful you weren't the designer trying to fit all that text on the book jacket.

Banbury Cakes are also mentioned in Ben Jonson's comedy *Bartholomew Fair*, first performed in 1614, in which a baker from Banbury makes cakes that are 'serv'd to Bridals, may-poles, Morrises, and such profane Feasts and Meetings'. No wonder the Puritans banned them.

Credit for reviving the Banbury Cake is given to a woman called Betty White in the late 18th century; thereafter they became so popular that, with the arrival of the railways, people came to Banbury by the trainload to sample them. An 1852 *Directory of Oxfordshire* mentions that 'what is termed the original cake shop in Parson's Street' sold 'in 1840 no fewer than 139,500 of the two-penny cakes; and in the month of August … on an average 5,400 weekly …' To save you doing the sums, this means that output nearly doubled during the summer holidays – not bad when you consider how far from the seaside Banbury is.

That 'original shop' and bakery in Parson's Street had been on the same site since at least 1550; Philip Brown's family became connected with them in 1818. Philip is now the proprietor of Brown's Original Banbury Cakes and the only person who knows the original recipe. When I met him, in the elegant lounge of Whately Hall hotel, he acknowledged that there had been many recipes over the centuries, some, like Gervase Markham's, involving yeast, some not, but the one he used had remained substantially the same since the 16th and 17th centuries.

Sadly, the building in Parson's Street fell into disrepair and was demolished in 1969. Philip now makes the cakes by hand from his home in Hook Norton, a village about 16km away that you'll have heard of if you are a local or a beer drinker. This fact enables someone else to say with perfect truth that they are the only people in Banbury making their own Banbury Cakes, but that's a geographical quibble. Brown's Original Banbury Cakes are something special.

That was certainly the opinion of June Irani, a former Banbury café owner who now works as a distributor of high-quality aloe vera products. I'd spoken to her on the phone a few weeks earlier. 'Banbury Cakes have been cheapened,' she told me. 'You can buy them all over the place and people think they're just like an Eccles Cake. That's because they're not made to the traditional recipe. Brown's version may be more expensive, but it's the best. It's the Rolls-Royce of Banbury Cakes.'

A Brown's Banbury Cake later won plaudits from that renowned connoisseur, my godson. He approved both the lemony tang and the sugariness. But then he can do ten laps of the car park to work off the excess energy; people would stare if I tried to do that.

This recipe may not be the Rolls-Royce, but I'll vouch for its being, say, the Mini Cooper or perhaps the MGB GT.

Banbury Cakes

Makes about 10

350g puff pastry
beaten egg white and caster sugar, for topping

For the filling
55g unsalted butter, melted
juice of ½ lemon
225g mixed currants and chopped mixed peel
110g demerara sugar
1 level tsp mixed spice

1 Preheat the oven to 220°C/425°F/gas mark 7. Lightly grease a baking sheet.

2 For the filling, mix the melted butter, lemon juice, currants, peel, sugar and spice together in a bowl.

3 On a lightly floured surface, roll out the pastry thinly and, using a large biscuit cutter or a saucer, cut out 10 circles. Place a dessertspoon of mixture diagonally across each one. Dampen the edges of the circles and draw up into the centre. Seal well, then turn over and press down on each one very gently with a rolling pin to flatten them slightly into a rough oval shape.

4 With a sharp knife, make 3 diagonal cuts across the top of each cake. Brush with the beaten egg white and sprinkle with sugar. Place on the prepared baking sheet and bake in the preheated oven for 15–20 minutes, until golden. Remove from the oven and cool on a wire rack. The cakes keep well in an airtight container, but are best served slightly warm: reheat gently in the oven or microwave.

For Philip, both the business and its history were clearly labours of love. In addition to a silhouette of Betty White dated around 1770 (which makes it one of the earliest silhouettes ever made, anywhere), he showed me photos of the ancient beehive ovens built into the wall in Parson's Street, still in use in his father's time; the old bakehouse that was converted into a tea room in the 1890s; and the horse-drawn cart 'that fell apart on Hightown Road just before the war'. He also told me, rather sadly, that he didn't sell nearly as many Banbury Cakes as he used to and that, although he had 'made provision', there wasn't anyone in the family likely to take over the business when he was gone.

One of the places the cakes *were* available was the local museum café. They sat proudly on a plate on the counter-top, separated from the more commonplace fare below. There was even a notice about them and their history. The young man behind the counter remembered that his nan used to buy Banbury Cakes for his grandfather as a treat when they were younger. Then, for a few decades, it seems, 'Banbury Cakes went very quiet.' He was pleased that there was a revival of interest: 'After all,' he said, 'they're part of who we are.' A heartening sentiment, I thought, coming from someone who hadn't even begun to worry about turning 30.

15

Beds to Lincs

Old Clangers and Recent Revivals

I WAS HOME FROM BANBURY just long enough to empty my suitcase into the washing machine, take the contents out again and put them back in the case. Then it was off to King's Cross for the last leg of my journey.

I took a slowish train to Peterborough because I wanted to visit somewhere else along the way. The route first took me through a number of drab dormitory towns, probably all charming but not at their best viewed from the train. I wasn't tempted to stop at any of them; I had eating to do and a destination to do it in.

Sandy is home to the Royal Society for the Protection of Birds and, perhaps less famously, the Bedfordshire Clanger. Gunns Bakery on the Market Square has been making this strange pasty for 50 years, and they do it in Biggleswade and Bedford too. I call it strange because it is the two-course meal in one that I'd been asking about in Cornwall: an oblong suet pastry case containing chopped gammon at one end and a spicy, chunky apple sauce at the other. The story is that the Clanger was originally eaten by farm labourers, who for hundreds of years took it to work with them and ate it cold at lunchtime. Then in the 19th century, when women were increasingly employed outside the home, the pasty could be left simmering at home, ready to be eaten hot in the evening. It may sound odd, but in fact it is quite a tasty thing and the savoury and sweet ends are perfectly compatible; there's no need to keep them apart and meticulously eat the one before the other. It's no weirder than pork with apple sauce. Or at least no weirder than pork with apple sauce *en croûte*.

Gunns is an unpretentious café – the sort of place where they serve tea with the bag still in the mug – but it was doing a roaring trade at half-past 11 on a mid-week morning and everyone was very friendly. The woman who cleared away my plate admitted she'd never tasted a Clanger herself (and they have a vegetarian option, so that couldn't be the reason). Perhaps it was because she was of an age to have watched *The Clangers* on TV as a child and couldn't separate the pasty in her mind from the family of knitted, pink mouse-like creatures who conversed in whistles.

Sandy is another rather drab town (though to be fair it was a decidedly drab day – I don't suppose even Florence or Vancouver would have looked its best), with more than its share of premises to let. But it had a butcher's, a clockmaker's and a specialist sweet shop offering – somewhat belatedly, or perhaps they just hadn't taken down the sign – bespoke Easter eggs. It also had a rather charming church, St Swithun's, set squatly on a surprisingly large floor area. It looked much like many another parish church, but as if some gigantic hand (God's, in a clumsy Friday-afternoon moment?) had pressed down on it and murmured 'Oops' when it didn't bounce back.

Opposite the church was a tandoori restaurant called the Gandhi, which struck me as unusual until I read the small print: it was the Gandhi in Sandy. Ha ha. Between there and the station – a walk of all of three minutes – I passed a fish and chip shop called the Town Fryer and a hairdresser's called Trim and Proper. I suppose a place that is almost universally known as Sandy Beds is entitled to make a speciality of bad puns.

But why is the local foodstuff called a Clanger? When I looked it up in the OED all it could tell me was that a clanger was 'a mistake, esp. one that attracts attention; a social *faux pas*'. One of the examples it gave was this joyous quotation from the *Daily Mail* of 3

February 1959: 'He wore medals – and a carnation. He said: "I have boobed dreadfully, old boy. Apparently a carnation with gongs is a terrible clanger."'

This brought me no nearer knowing the answer to my question, but I was delighted to have read it. If ever I'm awarded a DBE, I'll know not to wear a carnation with it.

Peterborough, just over half an hour farther on from Sandy, is an obvious place to start exploring the East Midlands. It's also, as even the locals agree, a place you want to leave as soon as possible, so that's what I did. I spent the night a few kilometres away, at the home of a friend who said her car would love a longer run than it usually got pottering into town and back. She was very happy to drive me round Rutland and Lincolnshire and deposit me at Grantham, the next stop up the main East Coast line, at the end of the day.

Our first port of call the following morning was Oakham, county town of Rutland, the smallest county in England. Oakham is itself no smaller than many other market towns (and despite its market-town charm, it hasn't resisted the temptation to have a Chinese takeaway called Wok This Way), but Rutland is immensely proud of its smallness. It spent 20 years or so as part of Leicestershire, but has been officially independent again since 1997; its motto is *Multum in Parvo* ('much in little') and it even boasts its own dwarf. On one of the older houses is a plaque announcing this as the home of Sir Jeffrey Hudson (1619–82), the 'smallest man from the smallest county in England'. He certainly was small – he was a favourite of Charles I's queen, Henrietta Maria, and a portrait of the two by Van Dyck shows a 14-year-old Jeffrey coming no higher than Her Majesty's hip. Almost every mother I know complained that her sons were towering above her at that age.

Oakham also has one of the smallest castles in England. That claim is slightly cheating, though, because, although it's billed as a castle, all that remains is the Great Hall. Built in the late 12th century, it is, according to those in the know, one of our finest surviving examples of secular architecture of the period. It survived when all around it had disappeared because it was used as a courtroom, with inquisitions and assizes held here until very recently. (A daunting thought. I would have liked to believe that we stopped having inquisitions longer ago than 'very recently'.)

The hall is tall, vaulted, majestic, making you feel you should speak in hushed tones, as if you were in a cathedral. But here's a funny thing: the walls are covered in horseshoes. An old custom decrees that every peer on first setting foot in the town must present a horseshoe to be hung inside the castle. There are horseshoes donated by umpteen members of present and past royal families, as well as lesser aristocrats. The oldest survivor is a gift from King Edward IV after his victory in the battle of nearby Losecoat Field in 1470, but the tradition apparently dates back even further than that.

Funnier still, they are all hung – to my way of thinking – upside down. However, the enthusiastic young man in charge presented me with a cutting from the *Rutland Times*, which explained (with surprising force) that those of us who have always thought you hang a horseshoe open side up to prevent the good luck falling out have got it completely wrong. You hang them the other way up to prevent the Devil making his nest in the bottom. Obvious, really. Fancy no one outside Rutland having thought of that.

Enough history; on to the cakes. As we headed back to the Market Square we passed the Butter Cross. It wasn't substantially different from any I'd seen in other old towns, except that it boasted stocks with five leg holes. My friend speculated that there might once have been a local ne'er-do-well who had only one leg and who got into trouble so often it was worth building special stocks to accommodate him.

It was market day and a stall sold us a Lincolnshire Plum Bread made by Modens of Spilsby. Because it was from Lincolnshire rather than

Rutland, there was no need for it to be small. Instead, it was a good, chunky fruit loaf weighing 400g. Like most other Plum Breads it didn't contain plums, but was 27 per cent sultanas and 13 per cent raisins – and big, juicy sultanas and raisins at that. The package suggested you ate it sliced, spread with butter and alongside your favourite cheese, so I made a note to myself to try it that way.

Lincolnshire Plum Bread

Makes 1 loaf cake

55g each of currants, raisins and sultanas
225g strong white flour
1 tsp fine salt
1 x 7g sachet fast-action dried yeast
85g granulated sugar
1 tsp mixed spice
55g lard
30g chopped mixed peel
1 medium egg, beaten
about 100ml milk, at room temperature

1. Soak the dried fruit in plenty of cold water for about an hour to plump it up, then drain in a colander.
2. Put the flour, salt, yeast, sugar and spice in a large bowl. Rub in the lard until the mixture resembles fine breadcrumbs, then mix in the drained fruit and the peel. Add the egg and just enough milk to make a soft dough. Knead well, then cover with a tea-towel and leave to rise in a warm place for about 3 hours.
3. Grease and line a 450g loaf tin, tip the dough into it and leave to rise again for about 40 minutes.
4. Preheat the oven to 190°C/375°F/gas mark 5.

5 When the dough is ready, bake in the preheated oven for 50–60 minutes, until a skewer inserted into the centre comes out clean. Leave to cool a little in the tin, before turning out on to a wire rack. Cut in slices to serve.

Rutland does have a culinary speciality, but we were out of season for it: it's a Valentine's Day tradition called Rutland Plum Shuttles. These are rich, yeasty currant buns made in the shape of the shuttles used by weavers in the nearby Vale of Belvoir.

Rutland Plum Shuttles

Makes 12–15

330g plain flour
55g unsalted butter
55g caster sugar
55g currants
25g chopped mixed peel
about 150ml milk
6g dried yeast

1 Sift the flour into a warmed bowl. Rub in the butter until the mixture resembles fine breadcrumbs.

Add the sugar, currants and peel and mix well.

2 Warm a little of the milk until it is tepid and whisk the dried yeast into it. Stir the yeasty liquid into the flour mixture, adding just enough of the remaining milk to make a soft dough. Knead well, then cover with a tea-towel and leave to rise in a warm place for about 1 hour, until doubled in size.

3 Turn the dough on to a lightly floured surface and knead until smooth. Divide into small pieces and shape into ovals about the size of a sausage, with slightly pointed ends.

4 Place on a greased baking sheet, and leave in a warm place to rise again for about 20 minutes.

5 Meanwhile, preheat the oven to 220°C/425°F/gas mark 7. When the shuttles are ready, bake in the preheated oven for 15–20 minutes until golden. Eat warm, with butter.

Oakham's Castle Cottage Café had been recommended as the best in town and although on the day of our visit it wasn't offering anything local, it did do a spectacularly good scone with cream and jam, a subject on which I was beginning to lay claim to expertise. The cream was nicely clotted and the scones enormous, irregular in shape and a perfect combination of crumbliness and doughiness. I stuck to tea but my friend succumbed to one of the simpler offerings in a flamboyant range of hot chocolates; she resisted the Ultimate Eton Mess Hot Chocolate, with cream, strawberries and meringue bits, because, as we agreed, you have to draw the line somewhere.

A few minutes' walk away in Gaol Street, the multi-award-winning Hambleton Bakery offered an amazing array of bread, including various sourdoughs, a 'Campagne' Bloomer and a Date and Walnut Loaf; they were also obviously proud of their latest speciality, a Rutland Pippin. It was a pasty in the shape of an apple: 'a crusty dough encasing Lincolnshire sausage meat, ham hock and Stilton cheese, topped off with hand-made Bramley apple purée'. Technically outside the scope of this book, but we bought a couple anyway and were not disappointed. Hambleton also have a splendid deli-cum-grocer's across the street, where I bought a Little Lincoln Imp cheese to eat with my Plum Bread. It turned out to be an excellent choice.

The real goal of the day's trip was Grantham, and from Oakham it was perfectly sensible to go via Melton Mowbray. Their famous – and now Protected Geographical Indication – pies are sold in Ye Olde Pork Pie Shoppe, but so, to my surprise and delight, was Melton's contribution to the world of teatime self-indulgence, the Melton Hunt Cake. Both pie and cake are made by Dickinson & Morris, who have been on these premises in one incarnation or another since 1851. They claim to have invented the cake in 1854 'to accompany the stirrup cup at local hunts' and still use the original recipe, including 'sultanas and currants which have been steeped in Caribbean rum for 48 hours, Muscovado sugar, butter, fresh free-range eggs, cherries and almonds'. So it's a rich and alcoholic fruit cake, available in several sizes: I bought one of the smaller ones, 240g, about 8cm square and 4cm high, which looked as if it would comfortably serve three or four, but I could have gone for an individual serving or the full-sized cake. There was also an iced and marzipanned version, for those who wanted to get into the Christmas spirit at the beginning of June. The recipe is – of course – a closely guarded secret, but try your favourite Christmas cake recipe, soak the fruit in rum and see what happens.

The reason I was surprised was that I'd thought the cake was served only to those who had proved their mettle with the hunt. I was glad to find that I was allowed to eat it without having contributed to the demise of a local fox.

A stirrup cup was a cup of wine or other warming drink handed to someone who was already on horseback, ready to depart on a journey or go home after the hunt. One blog I came across suggested that the cake was moist enough to be eaten without a drink at all, or was possibly best accompanied by a decent sherry or port. When it had rum in it already? And you had a horse to control? That's the sort of mixing-your-drinks stupidity I grew out of when I was a student, and that even the discreetly veiled ladies of Market Drayton might have frowned upon. I planned to have mine with a cup of tea, and possibly with the Lincoln Imp cheese too.

As it transpired, I ate it a few weeks later in the course of a long, hot walk, and it was very sustaining. Lush, fruity and with just enough of a kick to encourage you to keep putting one foot in front of the other without inducing an undignified stagger.

We couldn't leave a historic market town without a bit of history, so we observed that Melton had a pub called the Anne of Cleves, which had had an interesting career. Originally a Cluniac monastery, in 1538 it came into the possession of Henry VIII's Chancellor, Thomas Cromwell, of *Wolf Hall* fame. After Cromwell's downfall it was given to Henry's fourth wife, Anne of Cleves (along with Richmond Palace, Hever Castle in Kent and various other properties) as part of her divorce settlement. Assuming that the marriage was, as most people believe, unconsummated, there can have been few women in history who did so well out of not having sex.

In Grantham, we had an appointment with Alastair Hawken, who had revived another old tradition – the Grantham Gingerbread. He explained how he felt our regional differences had been diluted, 'now that we can get from London to Grantham in hours instead of days'.

'It's a bit like dialects,' he said. 'I grew up in a village 30km south of Grantham and there were people there, of the older generation, who had never left the village. They'd never been to Grantham, never mind London or anywhere else. But now you fly the nest much younger and you fly a lot further. I think it's same with our recipe heritage – we're so much more global than we used to be. We seem to have embraced other people's cuisines far more than they have embraced ours, so over the last two or three generations ours has tended to suffer.'

Alastair went on to tell me that there used to be a number of bakeries in Grantham that produced the local gingerbread until the big supermarkets arrived and changed everyone's shopping habits. The last bakery making Grantham Gingerbread closed down about

30 years ago. 'Mrs Brown wasn't going to the bakery every Friday for bread and buying a bag of gingerbread while she was there. But I think there's a resurgence of interest in shopping locally and buying local things; and it's important that we bring these things back while we still can – not out of panic, not because we have to, but because we want to.'

Having been born in Grantham makes Alastair a 'Grantham Gingerbread' – that's how engrained the biscuits once were in the local culture (the football team is called the Gingerbreads too). In the late 1990s, he was working in London and looking for a change when, as he put it, 'the cappuccino spaceship was landing' – and it set the entrepreneurial aspect of his brain in motion. The coffee shop revolution seemed to be confined to the area within the M25 and Alastair still had connections with Grantham, where rents and rates were appreciably cheaper; he decided to try his luck there. 'If it was going to go wrong, it would go wrong on an affordable basis,' was his reasoning. The result was Panini, the café on Westgate which he set up to sell, as the name suggests, panini. And cappuccinos. Both of which were quite a novelty in Grantham in 2000. A few years later his ideas for expansion into larger cities fell foul of the higher rents, so it was time to look for other opportunities.

Then in 2010 came the cuts, and the council withdrew funding from Grantham Museum. Alastair, as a prominent member of the local business community, organised a group to run it privately and looked for ways to help it make money. The museum, he told us, had 20,000 visitors a year. 'If we sold a packet of Grantham Gingerbread to half of those people, at a profit of £1 a time – that's £10,000 in the till. Grantham Gingerbread is part of our heritage – we should be flogging it.'

The problem was, no one was making the gingerbread and neither of the two surviving local bakers was interested. So Alastair, good entrepreneur that he is, decided to do it himself. Well, he had a food business already – why not?

There followed 15 months of 'playing': trying to understand what the original recipe was and seeing how close they could get to it; testing products on focus groups among the older generation who remembered the real thing; and finally coming up with something they thought was authentic – and that Grantham could be proud of. Being proud of themselves is not something the people of Grantham tend towards. They couldn't even decide whether or not they wanted a statue of their most famous daughter, Margaret Thatcher, in the town. Alastair's attitude was, love her or hate her, she was a significant historical figure. Promote her, promote Grantham, promote the gingerbread.

So what is Grantham Gingerbread? Well, although I'd had my share of gingerbread over the past few weeks, this was completely different from anything else I'd tasted. I know I said that about Grasmere Gingerbread, but this was different again. An individual biscuit weighs 12g and is a bite-sized dome shape. But it's not the soft texture of the traditional gingerbread man and it doesn't contain treacle, so it isn't chewy like Parkin. It's crunchy, with cracks across the top like an amaretto biscuit (and indeed a Cornish Fairing) and a slightly hollow, slightly honeycomby centre. The taste is a ginger tang rather than an overpoweringly ginger hit. *Particularly* nice dunked in tea.

As part of his 'promote Grantham, promote gingerbread' approach, Alastair had taken great care with the packaging, too. It's an eye-catching box illustrated with gingerbread men, the history of the Grantham Gingerbread and fun facts about Grantham (and who would have thought there would be so many of those?). Many people are aware that it is the place where Margaret Thatcher was born and Isaac Newton went to school; railway enthusiasts will know that 'The Mallard set the world speed record for a steam train at Grantham, reaching 126mph on 3 July 1938'. But how about 'The spire of St Wulfram's Church was once the tallest building in England' or 'The claw track used by modern-day bulldozers was first developed by Grantham company Hornsby in 1905'?

(Mr Hornsby, by the way, sold his invention to an American company called Caterpillar, hence the change of name.)

It must have been working. At the time of our conversation, only nine months since the packaging had been delivered, Alastair had sold about 500,000 biscuits in packets of 15 – well over 30,000 packets – to National Trust properties, delis and farm shops around the country.

For the time being all the cooking was done on the premises, in the kitchen above the shop, which was not much bigger than my kitchen at home, though rather more industrially equipped. On Sundays – the only day Panini didn't open – a contingent of local teenagers came in and rolled balls of dough. As we spoke, Alastair was rolling dough in his fingers, weighing each ball on a domestic-looking kitchen scale – it was a labour-intensive business.

The raising agents are important, he told us: they use both baking soda and baking powder for complicated chemical reasons that boil down to 'the dough has to do a lot of work once it goes into the oven'. It has to rise and then fall down at the edges to produce a dome shape. The baking soda also helps to create the honeycomb texture.

With only one egg and 225g butter to 450g each of flour and sugar, it's quite a dry dough, which can cause production problems: ideally it needs to be around 22–25°C to be workable and it will suffer from glutenisation if it isn't in the oven within half an hour of the dry ingredients being mixed with the wet ones. And glutenisation is bad because ...? Basically it will make a dry dough even drier and affect the overall appearance.

The other key aspect of the appearance is the colour – it needs to be very pale. This means it has to be baked in a very slow oven, because anything over 130°C will caramelise the sugar and produce that lovely, rich colour that you get with – well, caramel, for example – but isn't what Grantham Gingerbread is about. Alastair had, over the last few years, learned much more about biscuit baking than he'd ever realised there was to learn, and had often sat in the kitchen in the small hours of the morning thinking,

'I must be bonkers. William Eggleston must be up there laughing his socks off. Or tearing his hair out.'

William Eggleston was the creator of this legendary biscuit, in the days when Grantham was a regular stopping place for the coaches on the Great North Road. While the horses were being changed at the George Hotel, passengers and drivers would refresh themselves with a hard, flat biscuit called the Grantham Whetstone. This was one of the earliest forms of biscuit ever offered for sale anywhere and a convenient, if not madly exciting, food for travellers to carry with them. The story goes that one day in 1740, William, the baker, mistook one ingredient for another and accidentally created the Grantham Gingerbread. I tried to press for more on this: did he put in ginger instead of cinnamon, say? No one seems to know; Alastair had compared the ingredients in the two recipes and found it difficult to imagine how a simple mistake could have produced one instead of the other. He'd be the first to admit it could be nothing more than a good story, but if nothing else it makes it plausible to claim that Grantham Gingerbread was the first sweet biscuit sold in Britain. That's if you assume the ones in Aberffraw, which are probably 500 years older, were handed out for nothing.

For Alastair, one of the nicest parts of the whole Grantham Gingerbread experience had been receiving a visit from an elderly man called John Oldham, who promptly pointed out a spelling mistake on the package (the first print run had Egglestone, with a superfluous e). Mr Oldham knew this because William Eggleston had been his great-great-great-uncle. All his family, from William down to himself and his own children, had been local bakers, so he was able to produce family recipe books and to confirm that the recipe Alastair was using was the same as the one he had. A real eureka moment.

Doing it all by hand obviously limits production numbers – despite the expertise of the Sunday morning teenagers – and Alastair's investigations into ways of upping his output had not uncovered any biscuit-making machine that created a ball, of any size. Yes, there were metal cutters and extruding tubes and various other things that could produce biscuity shapes, but nothing the right size and shape for his purposes. He'd researched in all sorts of places, looking at machines used in Poland for producing meatballs, in Italy for gnocchi and even as far afield as Taiwan for he couldn't remember what. A machine used in India for making the sweets called *rasgulla* came close, but he couldn't get funding to import it.

So what did he do? He found a machine used for making fish bait. The balls known as boilies, made from meal worms and similar delicacies, which fishermen put on the end of a barb to attract unsuspecting carp, were exactly the same size as Grantham Gingerbreads, and a man called Mark in that well-known fishing port of Birmingham made machines to produce them. The machine – which was on the bench in front of us but very much in the prototype stage as far as Alastair was concerned – looked like an oversized toasted-sandwich maker, with a dozen or so blades on the inside surfaces, top and bottom. Using the sort of gun that might have been intended to pipe grouting round a bath tub, he extruded five ropes of dough into it, closed the lid, rubbed it back and forth a bit and hey presto, 70 perfect balls of Grantham Gingerbread dough. The problem was that 70 wasn't enough – Alastair wanted a larger gun (he was looking at the kind used for filling sausages) and a larger ball-making machine so that he could produce 1,200 Gingerbreads at a time.

He was aware that his kitchen was set up to produce cappuccinos and panini, not to be a biscuit factory, so he was looking at opening an industrial unit in town and quadrupling production to 12,000 biscuits a week. He also realised that the recipe was never intended for use on a mass scale. The trick, he said, was to walk before you tried to run and to know your product so well that you could cope with the hurdles you were bound to come up against. He wanted to run a profitable business, but he still desperately wanted to be authentic, to respect the heritage, to do it *right*.

At this point in the conversation, the timer went off and Alastair's demonstration batch came out of the oven. The crackle on the top, produced by the raising agents, was perfect. And, fresh out of the oven, they were delicious.

Alastair had started by saying that if he gave me the recipe he couldn't allow me to leave the building. But when he looked at the two conflicting versions I had brought with me, he decided that if I was going to publish a recipe it had to be the right one. Otherwise people would be cooking either something that wasn't very good or something that wasn't the real Grantham Gingerbread. He saw himself not as the owner of the recipe but as its custodian, so it was, to use his words, 'only fair and true' that I should put in the real thing.

So that's what I've done (see next page). Thank you, Alastair. The quantity may seem a lot, but they're only little and they keep well in an airtight tin. He doesn't recommend freezing the raw dough and baking only half a quantity at a time – it doesn't work. Make the lot, invite some friends round for a cup of tea and encourage them to dunk.

We left Alastair with this passing thought. A small market town in Lincolnshire that few people outside the UK have heard of has produced one of our greatest scientists, some pioneers of steam railway, our first female prime minister – and gingerbread. Alastair, entrepreneurial to the last, expressed the opinion that gingerbread was probably Grantham's most significant achievement. My friend and I raised quizzical eyebrows. Well, OK, we compromised – gingerbread and gravity.

Grantham Gingerbread

Makes 30–35

225g salted butter
450g caster sugar
1 medium egg
450g plain flour
2 tsp ground ginger
1½ tsp bicarbonate of soda
1 tsp baking powder

1 Preheat the oven to 130°C/250°F/gas mark ½. Grease several baking sheets.

2 In a large bowl, cream the butter and sugar together until light and fluffy, then gradually beat in the egg. In a separate bowl sift the flour, ginger, bicarbonate of soda and baking powder together, then stir into the butter mixture to form a fairly firm dough.

3 Roll into 30–35 balls the size of a walnut and place well apart on the prepared baking sheets.

4 Bake towards the top of the preheated oven for 40–45 minutes until crisp and very lightly browned (you'll probably have to do this in 2–3 batches). Allow to cool for 10 minutes before transferring to a wire rack.

16

Yorkshire

Lots of Curds and a Little Chocolate

I'D SAVED YORKSHIRE UNTIL THIS LATE STAGE because the annual Tastes of Yorkshire Food & Drink Family Festival took place on Ripon racecourse on a Saturday in early June and struck me as the sort of event I should visit. So, true to form, I invited myself to stay with a friend who lives in York and suggested she might like to come.

But first I had a Friday afternoon to spend in the city, and that could mean only one thing: Bettys.

In a country that has its fair share of swanky places to have tea, Bettys Café Tea Rooms on St Helen's Square stand out: they are quite simply magnificent. The founder, a Swiss named Frederick Belmont, opened his first shop in Harrogate in 1919, then went on the maiden voyage of the *Queen Mary* in 1936. On his return, he commissioned the ship's designers to use their brilliance to create a shop for him in York. The result is a place you'd happily take royalty to tea – possibly Queen Mary herself, or perhaps Hollywood royalty such as Joan Crawford or Vivien Leigh.

In their absence I decided to go to the smaller branch in Stonegate, where the tea room is up a winding staircase from the shop. As I came in, I overheard a couple asking for a Bakewell Tart. The young man told them, absolutely courteously, that Bettys stocked only Yorkshire and Swiss products. After the couple had gone, I noticed a plate of Eccles Cakes on the counter and wondered what inspired this proudly Yorkshire and Swiss firm to ban a Derbyshire product but make an exception for, of all things, a Lancastrian one.

The purpose of coming to Bettys, however, was not to embarrass pleasant young shop assistants but to try one of their famous Fat Rascals™. They're oversized scones, really, flavoured with currants and citrus peel, but they're scones of a particularly endearing quality, because they're decorated with glacé cherries and almonds to give them the appearance of a face. A flyer advertising 30 years of Fat Rascals shows a box of four, standing up so that only the cherry eyes appear over the rim: it demands the caption 'Wot, no clotted cream?'

In 1983, looking for a Yorkshire speciality that could become uniquely theirs, Bettys chefs discovered the Turf Cake, which shepherds used to cook in a covered pan over a peat fire. They tweaked the traditional recipe and the Fat Rascal was born. It's been their signature dish ever since and they sell well over a quarter of a million a year. They sold one to me, too – warm, lavishly buttered and not only endearing but delicious as well.

A number of other people make a product similar to Fat Rascals, but – out of respect for Bettys – they use a variety of other names. In various parts of Yorkshire I've seen them called Chubby Rogues, Little Tykes and Fat Scamps. A couple of days after my visit to York I found that the deli in Helmsley sold Chubby Hunters. I asked why and the man told me about Bettys having a trade mark. Yes, yes, I said, but why Hunters? It's not a synonym for Rascals. No, he explained patiently, as if talking to an idiot, but it is the name of this shop. I hadn't noticed. I made my purchases as quickly as I could, avoiding further eye contact, and hastened away.

This is a recipe that you can call anything you like in the privacy of your own home.

Chubby Scallywags

Makes 12–15

450g self-raising flour
225g unsalted butter
125g currants
75g chopped mixed peel
2 tsp ground cinnamon
1 tsp freshly grated nutmeg
2 tbsp soft brown sugar
a pinch of fine salt
equal quantities of milk and water to mix
1 medium egg, beaten, to glaze
glacé cherries, halved, and blanched almonds, to decorate

1. Preheat the oven to 220°/425°F/gas mark 7. Grease and line a baking sheet.
2. Put the flour into a large bowl. Rub the butter into the flour until the mixture resembles breadcrumbs. Add the currants, peel, spices, sugar and salt and mix thoroughly. Then add just enough milk and water to make a smooth dough.
3. Roll out to about 12mm thickness and cut into 12–15 rounds about 6cm across. Glaze generously with the beaten egg.
4. Make 'faces' using the cherries for eyes and almonds for the nose and mouth.
5. Place the rounds on the prepared baking sheet, dust with a little caster sugar and bake in the preheated oven for 15 minutes until lightly browned and well risen.

If you aren't a scone person, you could go for Bettys' recently launched Fat Rascal Lolly, a milk chocolate disc on a stick, with dark and white chocolate facial features. It would be quite appropriate, because York's culinary history is much more about chocolate than it is about baking. The home of Rowntree's and Terry's, not to mention Craven the humbug maker, the city has one of England's few chocolate museums. This reawakened a question that had been at the back of my mind for some time: why was everyone who made chocolate a Quaker? Not only those I've mentioned, but Cadbury's in Birmingham and Fry's in Bristol – all 19th-century confectionery companies, all founded and run by Quakers.

The guide who took me round York's Chocolate Story provided the answer. Quakers couldn't become academics, he explained – you weren't allowed into Oxford or Cambridge unless you were C of E. They couldn't become Members of Parliament, because they wouldn't swear an oath of allegiance to anyone but God, and they had similar problems if they wanted to practise law. They couldn't go into the army, because they were pacifists. So really that left business. The attractions of chocolate were that it was warming, enjoyable and, crucially, non-alcoholic. It enabled the socially conscious Quakers to do something useful and profitable, while keeping their workers off the gin.

This snippet came at an early stage in the tour and made me feel I'd had my money's worth before anyone had started handing out samples. If you add that I learned that orange Smarties are special because they're the only ones whose coating is flavoured, and that Terry's Chocolate Orange was nearly never born because the original thought was to make a Chocolate Apple, the trivia addict in me had a very good afternoon. I also tugged a metaphorical forelock at the portrait of George Harris, marketing director of Rowntree's during the 1930s, who developed the Kit Kat. Thank you, George.

There was the opportunity to linger at the end of the tour and create your own chocolate lollipop, but I'd done well on the free samples and I had a home to go to, even if it was someone else's. Next stop: Ripon racecourse.

The Tastes of Yorkshire Festival turned out to be on a smaller scale than the Dorset Knob Throwing of a few weeks before and, although Yorkshire ales and Yorkshire wines were in evidence, it took itself more seriously as a foodie event. The bouncy castle, for instance, was just that – there were children playing on it, rather than adults selling and consuming beer. There was an enthusiastic jazz band, plenty of ice cream sellers and someone doing a brisk trade with a hog roast. A few kids running around, quite a few people with dogs, but not a ferret in sight and, so far as I could see, no plans for anyone to throw anything later in the day. And, despite having struck it lucky with the weather, it wasn't as busy as I would have expected.

There was plenty to keep us amused, though. A programme of cookery demonstrations included one by a jovial young man who did good-looking things with venison and set the smoke alarm off with his caramelised shallots. Nobody seemed too perturbed – we were promised the blaring would stop after two minutes, though it felt more like five, and there was no sign of a fire engine. Was this Yorkshire phlegm, I wondered? I was once at a wedding in Buckinghamshire when the smoke alarm went off; the fire brigade was out in force within moments and stayed long enough not only to ensure that there was no fire but also for the bride to climb on to one of the engines in her long dress and have her photo taken wearing a fireman's helmet. But in Ripon the presenters just spoke a little more loudly and carried on.

The young man was followed by a woman of Italian origin who demonstrated the best ways of making and cooking pasta. Contrary to many people's belief, adding oil to the water isn't the key to stopping pasta sticking when you boil it; rather it's the *amount* of water that makes the difference. 'Here in Yorkshire we've got the best water in the world,' she said in an accent that had no trace of Yorkshire in it, 'so make sure you use plenty of it.' Yorkshire patriotism is notorious, of course; one of the stalls was selling 'bottled beers from God's own county', but I couldn't help feeling that boasting about the quality of the water was going a bit far.

There was, when I went to look for it, no shortage of cake. It was at Tastes of Yorkshire that I had what would be the first of many Yorkshire Curd Tarts. Davill's of Ripon made one that was quite crumbly, with plenty of raisins to stop it being too dry. It was a surprising texture if you weren't used to it, and it might not be everyone's cup of tea (as it were), but I was keeping an open mind.

Davill's also made a Ripon Fruit Bread that was more like a bread than many others I'd tried. Light in both colour and texture, it had a few sultanas and raisins but most of its fruit content was cherry. It was best eaten fresh, and it made a refreshing change from some of the heavier fruit breads I'd had in other parts of the country – there's only so much Christmas cake masquerading as a light snack that a girl can take.

On our way back to York from Ripon, we discovered why Tastes of Yorkshire had been so comparatively underpopulated – or at least so comparatively restrained. It had been competing with the annual Great Knaresborough Bed Race, an attraction of much longer standing and a Mecca for eccentrics from miles around. By the time we got to Knaresborough at around half-past four, the race was over and the crowds were dispersing, though the streets were full of beer drinkers, ice cream eaters and children with painted faces. It all seemed very good humoured; unlike in Rothwell, shops had clearly been open – with the exception of Bojangles hairdresser, which had a notice in the window to the effect that it was closed because it was in the Bed Race. I hoped everyone who would normally have been having highlights done on a Saturday had been out to support them.

The main road had been shut for most of the day as 90 teams of six pushers manipulated a bed and its occupant through the streets of Knaresborough and across the River Nidd. Not just any bed, either: the regulations are most specific. It must not exceed 2 metres in width, 4 metres in length and 3 metres in height, must possess an audible horn or hooter but no means of mechanical propulsion, and must have a built-in buoyancy aid capable of supporting the bed and the passenger for not less than five minutes. It was utter madness, involved the whole community and raised tens of thousands of pounds for charity. All it needed to make it perfect was for someone to organise a cake-throwing competition.

If they did, they could get the cakes from Ye Oldest Chymist Shoppe in England. Although now trading as a sweet shop and tea rooms, this was an apothecary's in 1720 – making it 30 years older than the chemist's I'd visited in Sherborne – and ceased to be a pharmacy as recently as 1997. It sold such potential missiles as fudge and clotted cream toffee, while the Lavender Rooms upstairs offered scones and a Knaresborough Toasted Tea Loaf, served with butter. You could throw any of those quite satisfactorily if you mapped out a suitable course. I made a note to write to the Knaresborough Lions Club, who organise the Bed Race, and suggest it.

Next morning saw me on a train to Darlington and, as this was the nearest I was going to get to the northeast, it was time to contemplate the subject of Stotties. If you watch wildlife programmes on TV, you may be familiar with the sight of gazelles leaping up and down, stiff-legged, to show a predator how fit they are or to warn others of their own species that danger lurks. This is called 'pronking' or 'stotting', and the name of the Stottie Cake apparently comes from the same source: it's said to derive from the practice of bouncing the freshly baked bread to check its texture.

Although it's called a cake, the Stottie is really what's known as a hearth bread, originally baked at the bottom of a coal oven. It can be served as a bread roll, but traditionalists make it dinner-plate size and fill it with – well, anything, really. Like a wrap or a pitta bread, it can go with meat, fish, cheese, salad and, I dare say, chips.

Although this is a northeastern speciality, it has its equivalents elsewhere. A friend who was born in Southport remembers his dad going every morning to the local baker, dog in tow, to collect the six Barm Cakes that were on permanent order for his family. Barm is the foam formed on the top of a fermenting liquor such as beer; it was traditionally scraped off and used to leaven Barm Cakes. This, and the addition of hops, gave them their stronger-than-most-buns taste. Southport is socially a cut above other parts of Lancashire and environs, or would like to think it is, so my friend's family ate them buttered at mealtimes or with a normal sandwich filling such as cheese or ham for lunch or a snack. In down-market Bolton, apparently, they'd have filled them with a pasty; in Wigan it would have been a pie. I'm not sure whether or not to believe this, but I have found images on the web showing a Barm Cake filled with a pie and served with chips (not even a baked bean in sight, never mind a salad garnish – none of your poncy southern five-a-day rubbish here). Smaller than the northeast's Stottie, but much the same thing, it's still made by at least one Manchester-based baker, whose website proudly illustrates it filled with bacon and sausage. It's also widely regarded (in what the locals still call Lancashire) as the *de rigueur* outer coating of what I would call a chip butty and my Southport friend would call a chip barm.

Darlington's real claim to fame is nothing to do with food; it was one end of the world's first steam-worked public railway, the Stockton and Darlington, opened in 1825 (some five years before William Huskisson met his untimely end in Eccles). Needless to say, Darlington has a museum on the subject. Called Head of Steam, it's an appealing 'time's stood still' sort of place packed with locomotives and memorabilia.

I mention it because it was here that I learned that Edward Pease, the railway pioneer and promoter of the Stockton and Darlington line, was a Quaker. Being teetotal and not going into Parliament obviously enabled people to achieve all sorts of greatness.

The reason I was in Darlington was that my friend from the Lake District had kindly offered to drive over and be my chauffeur round North Yorkshire. From the Head of Steam we headed across the northern edge of the moors to Whitby, which was central to my investigation of Yorkshire baking. That's because it's the home of Botham's, craft bakers since 1865, whose range includes Ginger Parkin, Whitby Gingerbread Loaf (subtly different, as I was to discover), Yorkshire Brack and Whitby Lemon Buns.

So there was lots to talk about next day when I met Jo Botham, one of the four great-grandchildren of the founder, Elizabeth Botham, who are now running the company. We sat in the tea room above the shop – quite the largest I've seen, because Elizabeth was a successful and savvy woman who, once her first shop was up and running, took over the two next door and expanded in a big way. There was a photograph of her on the wall. She was round-faced, plump and smiling and my first reaction was 'She looks sweet.' Then I looked again at the mouth and chin and thought, 'You wouldn't have wanted to mess with her.'

Quite right too: she had 14 children and a husband who was, as Jo put it 'a broken man' after he lost his farm so, a bit like Sarah Nelson in Grasmere, she needed to get on and make a living. She started doing extra baking at home and selling her products at the market: an elderly local had recently told Jo that her grandmother remembered Elizabeth walking across the fields with her baskets of bread and pies, all the children tagging along behind her. Clearly a determined woman.

By 1870 Elizabeth had taken a small shop away from the centre of the town; she then moved to the current premises in Skinner Street, renting them from the local brewery, and ran an alehouse at the back while keeping a shop at the front. Before she was finished (in 1902, having been a widow for over 20 years), Elizabeth had married one of her daughters to a local corn merchant – a canny move for a baker wanting a reliable source of flour at a favourable rate. She was able to buy a manor house and farm on the outskirts of town, rent out the farm, entertain her vast family there and allow two of her sons to take over the business – though she didn't look to me like a woman who would readily have taken a back seat.

Jo set a Whitby Gingerbread Loaf and a Ginger Parkin on the table in front of us. I started by asking what the difference was between them, although I could see part of the answer at a glance. The Gingerbread Loaf was a luxuriant orangey gold – the nearest I could find on a Dulux chart was called Moroccan Flame. It was a rich, luscious, alluring colour. By contrast, the Parkin was decidedly brown.

'OK,' said Jo, drawing a deep breath as if the question was more difficult than it sounded. 'Both are made with a high percentage of treacle. Or rather, a special dark golden syrup, which doesn't have the bitterness of molasses but has more depth of flavour than ordinary golden syrup. You can see an infinite number of versions of gingerbread, some of which are biscuits, some of which are cakes. Our Gingerbread Loaf is neither a biscuit nor a cake nor yet a bread. It's somewhere in between. Slice it thinly, butter it and eat it with a farmhouse cheese, that's the traditional way, though I have quite a sweet tooth and I like it with honey.'

The main difference between this and Parkin is that Parkin contains oatmeal. 'It's an ancient product that goes back to the days when Whitby was more of a seafaring port than it is now. Seamen used to take it with them on whaling vessels.' Nowadays lots of people make it, even if they don't take it to sea; Jo told me he had five or six recipes for Parkin, including one called Leeds Parkin, and they were all subtly different.

Here's one based on a recipe in Florence White's *Good Things in England*, which she describes as 'very old'.

Yorkshire Parkin

Makes 10–20, depending on size

300g self-raising flour
110g unsalted butter
300g medium oatmeal
1 tbsp ground ginger
110g soft brown sugar
400g golden syrup
50g black treacle
1 medium egg
2 tbsp milk
1 tsp bicarbonate of soda

1 Preheat the oven to 160°C/325°F/gas mark 3. Grease and line a 25cm square cake tin.

2 Put the flour into a large bowl. Rub the butter into the flour until the mixture resembles fine breadcrumbs, then add the oatmeal, ginger and sugar.

3 In a small pan, melt the treacle and syrup together over a low heat, and add to the mixture. Beat the egg, milk and bicarbonate of soda together in a jug, add to the mixture and mix well.

4 Pour the mixture into the prepared cake tin, and bake in the preheated oven for 1½ hours. Cool in the tin on a wire rack, then turn out and cut into small or large squares – beware, this parkin is quite rich. Store in an airtight container for a few days before eating to allow the flavours to mature.

A couple of weeks later I asked a group of friends to do a tasting test on both Botham's Parkin and their Gingerbread Loaf. There were five of us, three of whom had degrees in biology and were proud of their status as Scientists – obviously ideal people to analyse the diverse qualities of ginger cakes.

We found that, in addition to having a gorgeous colour, the Gingerbread Loaf sliced neatly and looked elegant on the plate. But it really did need the cheese to make it interesting – despite being quite powerfully gingery, it was a bit dull on its own. The Parkin was moister and had more texture; we all liked the 'bite' of the oats and although it was fine with cheese it was also good by itself. One of the group summed it up succinctly: 'It's a friendly cake.'

I was glad I'd put the question to scientists.

The recipes Botham's use didn't all come from Elizabeth: some were introduced by other people who have worked there over the generations. The company has had Swiss bakers and French bakers; a chef who survived the torpedoing of the *Lusitania* during World War I and brought Botham's the recipe for butter cream that they use to this day; and a Danish baker in the late 1960s who gave them his own take on pizzas. 'Our pizzas aren't really like anybody else's,' Jo laughed. 'But they've got a strong local following.'

Danish pizzas in North Yorkshire? I should think people come from far and wide.

As for Brack, they make several kinds, including one containing stem ginger and orange zest, which is very popular in Japan. (And why shouldn't it be?) There's also a Date and Walnut Spelt Brack, spelt being an ancient form of wheat which is now organically grown and stoneground in Yorkshire. It gives, Jo said, 'a lovely, sweet, nutty flavour', which is, of course, enhanced by the walnuts. Not to mention the slice of Wensleydale that is recommended as an accompaniment.

These variations apart, Yorkshire Brack is essentially a type of fruity tea bread made without any added fat. But, Jo added, 'I wouldn't necessarily be leaping at it as a diet food, just because it has no fat in: it's actually quite high in sugar, which is unfortunately the trade-off. It's very moist, very sticky.' Prior to baking, the fruit is soaked in Resolution, Botham's own blend of tea.

It's called Resolution because that was the name of a ship belonging to one of Whitby's famous sons: Captain Cook. He wasn't born there (he came from Marton, inland a bit), but began his seafaring career there as a teenager. The ships that carried him on his famous South Sea voyages – the others were *Endeavour* and *Discovery* – were also fitted out there. There's a statue of him, I discovered later, above the harbour, gazing out to sea, looking suitably steadfast and, unlike Columbus in Barcelona, facing roughly in the direction of his travels.

The town's other famous son is Dracula and he *was* born there, in the sense that Bram Stoker was inspired to write the original book while holidaying in Whitby. Today you can celebrate this fact at the Dracula Experience, where, for the modest sum of £3, you can see Dracula rising from his grave and 'hear his dreadful warning', whatever that may mean. You can see Dracula and his 'voluptuous vampires' and the man who feeds flies to spiders and then eats the spiders. Walking past it later in the day, I decided I could find a better use for three quid.

It may be the connection with Dracula that has inspired England's Goth community to make Whitby the home of a twice-yearly festival. Not only does the town fill with Goths and Goth musicians, it fills with people who have come to watch the Goths, photographers who want to photograph Goths posing in the undeniably Gothic ruins of Whitby Abbey, and people who aren't Goths at all but choose this weekend to parade the streets of Whitby in Victorian costume. It's in honour of this that Botham's have come up their most recent creation – Whitby Goth Cake, billed (in suitably Gothic script) as 'a rich dark chocolate cake with a hint of beetroot, topped with Belgian chocolate butter frosting'. It is *seriously* chocolaty, but so delicious that I had eaten my slice before it occurred to me to experiment with whether or not it could be made to drip gorily from my fangs. Then I remembered that I had left my fangs in my other handbag, so that was the end of that train of thought.

By the way, Whitby is twinned with Anchorage. Not a sign of a Baked Alaska, though.

The one Botham speciality I hadn't yet tried was the Lemon Bun, so, once my friend had finished photographing Whitby's pretty little harbour, we stopped off at Botham's tea rooms in Pickering to try it there.

Jo Botham had told me that you can tell a Whitby local from a stranger by the way they eat the Lemon Bun. Strangers tuck into it, enjoy it and have done with it. Locals know that the thing to do is tear it in half and fold it inside out to make a sort of lemon icing sandwich. I was explaining this to my companion in Pickering; the waitress overheard me and laughed. 'Oh, that's what they say in Whitby,' she said, as if Whitby were in, for example, Transylvania.

It may or may not be what they say in Whitby, but as a piece of gastronomical advice it's spot on. The bun itself is pleasant – soft, squishy, sweet, with a few currants – but without the icing it wouldn't be anything out of the ordinary. Put a generous spreading of soft white lemoniness in there and you have something special. Jo had told me it 'sounds pretty simple, indeed it is pretty simple, but I've never found one the same anywhere else. It's not just like an iced finger, believe me.' I did.

This recipe isn't Botham's, but it will make something along the same lines.

Yorkshire Lemon Buns

Makes 12–16

225g plain flour
a pinch of fine salt
30g unsalted butter
30g granulated sugar
finely grated rind of 1 lemon
7g dried yeast
½ tsp caster sugar
1 medium egg
150ml milk, lukewarm
55g currants

For the icing
225g icing sugar
1 tbsp water
3 tbsp lemon juice

1. Sift the flour and salt together into a large bowl, and rub in the butter until the mixture resembles fine breadcrumbs. Stir in the sugar and lemon rind and make a well in the centre.
2. Mix the yeast with a little of the milk and leave to froth. In a separate bowl beat the egg with the remaining milk, then add both these mixtures to the well in the flour, along with the caster sugar. Mix together well, then stir in the currants.
3. Leave the bowl in a warm place for 20 minutes, then beat the mixture well and leave to rise, covered with a tea-towel, for a further hour.
4. Using floured hands, shape the dough into 12–16 buns and put them on greased baking sheets or into greased patty tins. Leave in a warm place for 20 minutes.

5 Meanwhile, preheat the oven to 180°C/350°F/gas mark 4.

6 Bake the buns in the preheated oven for 20 minutes. Leave to cool thoroughly on a wire rack before icing.

7 To make the icing, sift the icing sugar into a saucepan and add the water and lemon juice. Heat gently until it is just warm and stir until smooth, then allow to cool so that it is tacky rather than runny. Drizzle generously over the buns and leave in a warm place to dry. Eat fresh.

From Pickering, my next stop was Helmsley, where I'd never been before and which shot to the top of my list of prettiest places ever (overtaking Knaresborough, which had held the slot for the past three days). Its spacious market square is surrounded by wisteria-clad pubs, butchers, bakers and – well, no, not candlestick makers, but delis, bookshops and all the good things of life. There's a ruined castle, as there is in much of North Yorkshire (William the Conqueror was busy here, protecting his territory from the Scots), but what really makes Helmsley special is the walled garden attached to the local estate of Duncombe Park. I dare say that tourist operators know about it, because there's plenty of parking space, but if you're on foot and looking to see what the town has to offer it's in a secluded spot behind the castle's visitor centre. To get there you pass a number of craft workshops, including one making walking sticks, shepherds' crooks and wading staffs for anglers, which promptly went on to the list of outstandingly specialist purveyors that I'd started outside Witney's cello shop.

The garden is hidden away, just waiting to be discovered. Dating back to the 18th century and originally planned to produce fruit, vegetables and flowers for the great house, it fell into disrepair in the early 20th century and has been restored only in the last 20 years. It now has espaliered fruit on every wall, a physic garden full of herbs and 'healing' plants, flowers, flowers, flowers and a laburnum arch. North Yorkshire is obviously *the* place for laburnums and we had picked the right time to visit: we saw them everywhere we went, glowing with a natural yellow that put the DayGlo rapeseed fields to shame.

The garden added to its charms by opening at the earlier-than-usual hour of half-past nine in the morning. So not only did we have the place to ourselves – literally the only other people there were the gardeners – but we had time to admire it at our leisure and it was a perfect place to leave my friend and her camera while I went off to my half-past ten appointment to talk about more cake.

Helmsley is the home of Thomas the Baker, one of the many people who make the world a better place by supplying it with Yorkshire Curd Tarts (I'd had several by this time and was a firm fan). The recipe was passed from an older baker to the company's founder, John Thomas, when he started the business in 1981.

In Thomas's reception area there was an array of notices about their keynote products and as I waited to meet Steve Simpson, the bakery manager, I learned that it was a Yorkshire tradition to bake Curd Tarts at sheep-shearing times. 'The work was hot. Curds made from fresh milk have always been regarded as a refreshing food.' In fact, Steve told me, the best curds are made from the 'first milk' taken from the cow after a calf is born. Known technically as colostrum (as it is in human mothers), it's also referred to as beestings or, in Yorkshire, bisnings or bislings. That's nothing to do with bee stings; it's the Old English word for colostrum, and the point is that it is high in antibodies to protect the newborn child or calf against disease. It's also lower in fat and higher in protein than ordinary milk – and it makes great Curd Tarts.

Friends who have a home in Finland came up with a good piece of local colour when I told them about this. Their local restaurant makes a Beestings Pudding, which is a bit like a crème brûlée.

Curds, as I had learned in Northamptonshire, are a by-product of cheese-making and North Yorkshire is very much dairy country. So any excess curds were turned into Curd Tarts. Obviously, when you're producing them on a commercial scale, you can't rely for your most important ingredient on having enough cows giving birth, so these days Thomas's supplier takes fresh milk and adds acetic acid (concentrated vinegar) to curdle it. In the old days it would have been rennet – a substance containing the enzyme rennin, prepared especially from the stomachs of calves – that did the work. These days that's probably considered unsustainable, or not suitable for vegetarians, or perhaps just a bit disgusting, and acetic acid makes an acceptable alternative.

As I'd seen with the Leicestershire Curd Tarts recipe (page 260), it's not difficult to make curds at home: you can either add acetic acid or lemon juice to full-fat milk; or wait for the milk to go off and separate; or at a pinch just use cottage cheese instead. Thomas could make their own on a commercial scale, but it would be wasteful as they have no use for the whey. Instead they buy most of their curds from Yorkshire-based Longley Farm, who make yoghurt, cream, fromage frais and the like, and consume whey in abundance.

In addition to curds, Thomas's version of the tart contains margarine, sugar, egg and currants, but no spices, in a pastry case. The company is part of the reason why Curd Tarts have become ubiquitous in the county: they have 30-plus shops, predominantly in North Yorkshire but stretching as far north as Bishop Auckland and as far south as Pontefract and Wakefield. But it's noticeable, Steve remarked, that Curd Tarts are not as popular 'down there' as they are closer to home. It struck me that this was taking regionality to an extreme, but it must be because the West Riding, as it used to be – parts of South and West Yorkshire as they are now – didn't have the same dairy traditions. Indeed, some of Steve's suppliers have been surprised to hear that the Yorkshire Curd Tart is one of Thomas's most successful products, because those that come from any distance away have literally never heard of it.

Steve admitted that when he first came to work at Thomas 30 years ago he'd never eaten a Curd Tart and didn't think he would like it. He was now a complete convert: 'It's a strange product; when you see the ingredients before it comes together it's not particularly appetising, but the combination is really delicious.'

I asked about the texture, because that was what had struck me as unusual when I first had one. 'It's crumbly – not custard-like. It's not a cake and it's not a custard. It has pieces of curd in it, which are quite moist, and the sugar complements the sourness of the curd. So it all welds together. And our pastry is nice and buttery, and that finishes it off.'

There are many, many recipes for Curd Tarts, but this is the one a Yorkshire friend has been using for years.

Pat's Yorkshire Curd Tart

Makes 1 x 20cm tart

250g shortcrust pastry

For the filling

110g cottage cheese, or the curd drained from 1.2 litres milk soured with lemon juice **(see page 260)**
55g soft unsalted butter or margarine
30g currants
45g caster sugar
1 medium egg
1 tsp finely grated lemon rind
1 tsp lemon juice
a little freshly grated nutmeg

1. Preheat the oven to 190°C/375°F/gas mark 5.
2. Roll out the pastry and use it to line a 20cm diameter round metal pie dish.

3 Sieve the cottage cheese or curd into a bowl, and mix together with the butter or margarine. Add the currants and sugar, then beat in the egg. Add the lemon rind, lemon juice and nutmeg and mix well. Spoon into the pastry case.

4 Bake the tart in the preheated oven for 15 minutes, then turn the oven down to 160°C/325°F/gas mark 3 and continue baking for another 20–25 minutes, until the filling is set. Eat warm or cold.

It would be a crime to be in this part of Yorkshire and not visit Rievaulx Abbey, the gorgeously ruined 12th-century Cistercian abbey tucked into a valley just north of Helmsley.

Starting to research this book a few months earlier, I'd been excited to discover the existence of Yorkshire Moggie or Moggy Cake – a sticky, gingery and treacly concoction, like Yorkshire Parkin without the oats. I'd never heard of it, but I became even more excited when I carried on googling and was referred to a site for Rievaulx. Sadly, the reason for this turned out to be that the site carried an advertisement feature for a publication called *The Cat Guide*; this offered 'a handy selection of food ideas for your cat, cat charities and innovative products to keep your moggy happy'. Equally sadly, when I clicked on the link and found the guide's food pages, there was much worthy talk about essential fatty acids and naturally hypoallergenic diets, but nothing at all about a local cake featuring ginger and treacle.

So, apart from the fact that it is alleged to come from Yorkshire, I know nothing about the origins of Moggy Cake. I have no reason to suppose it has any connection with Rievaulx Abbey. But what the hell; I was there now.

Yorkshire Moggy Cake

Makes 1 x 23cm cake, to serve about 12

450g plain flour
2 tsp baking powder
225g caster sugar
225g black treacle
180g unsalted butter
150ml milk
1 medium egg

1 Preheat the oven to 160°C/325°F/gas mark 3. Grease and line a 23cm diameter round cake tin.

2 Sieve the flour and baking powder into a large bowl and stir in the sugar.

3 Put the treacle, butter and milk in a small pan and heat gently, stirring, until melted. Stir this mixture into the dry ingredients, then beat in the egg.

4 Pour this mixture into the prepared tin and bake in the preheated oven for 1 hour. Leave to cool in the tin slightly before turning out on to a wire rack. Cut into wedges to serve.

To get to the abbey you drive down into a dale and through the tiny village of Rievaulx which, on a pleasant early summer morning, was idyllic, but must be pretty bleak and remote at a less mellow time of year. At its height, the abbey had 600 choir monks – '600 voices raised in the prayer of the Lord', as the information board said – and standing in the nave, of which a substantial shell remains, you can tell that this would have been quite something. Rievaulx grew rich on the proceeds of mining and sheep farming, but only the highest ranking of the abbey's residents would have seen any benefit from this. The monks' food was described as 'scanty' and the audio guide made much of the fact that few of the rooms had fires. It was all part of the discipline, as was sleeping on rush mats and getting up in the middle of the night to say prayers. In the strictest times the monks followed a vegetarian diet; eggs, cheese, chicken and fish were allowed on feast days.

So, I wondered, if they were making cheese, did they make Curd Tarts? There was nothing to tell me, but the detour to visit the abbey wasn't wasted: the tea room sold them. They were noticeably different from Thomas's: undeniably gritty, so much so that they must have had something like ground rice in them to provide the texture. But gritty in a good way.

Sounds a bit weird? Lots of things sounded weird to me before I started this trip. I know better now. Or perhaps I've eaten so many cakes that I simply can't tell any more.

17

Derbyshire

Of Puddings and Tarts

HATHERSAGE IS MY FAVOURITE PLACE in the Peak District, so I decided to stay there and spend time with yet another couple of friends who had placed themselves at my disposal. I took a train from York to Sheffield and changed, an operation that made me take back my snide remarks about Edinburgh Waverley. In Sheffield, platform 2 was adjacent to platform 5, and platform 2A was between 2B and 2C, so it fell down on both the arithmetical and the alphabetical fronts. Plus no one in their right mind would confuse it with Grand Central Station.

One of the reasons I like Hathersage is that Robin Hood's friend and companion John Little – better known as Little John – is buried in the churchyard. It's a particularly neat churchyard, with all the headstones in disciplined rows; Little John's grave is surrounded by a neat cast-iron railing, about knee height, with a neatly clipped yew tree at either end. Lying down to measure myself against it would have made the place look untidy, but at a rough calculation I'd say Little John would have made two of me. Which makes him, at another rough calculation, over 3 metres tall, comfortably more than Goliath's biblical six cubits and a span. I doffed an imaginary cap to him; I didn't want a man of that size thinking I was being disrespectful.

Little John is said to have died in a cottage to the east of the churchyard, now destroyed. These days there is a rather grand house on that plot with, on the morning I visited, a Range Rover parked outside it. I don't know how much money there was in robbing the rich to give to the poor, but Little John would have been doing very nicely if he could have afforded to live there.

Sadly there isn't a Hathersage Cake that I know of and I could see all sorts of arguments against making an extra-long éclair and calling it the Hathersage Little John. But, meandering round the town after my visit to the churchyard, I discovered that the local bakery did sell Derbyshire Oatcakes.

Oatcakes of one sort or another are found all over the North of England and in Scotland, wherever the climate and terrain made it easier to grow oats than wheat. They are most revered in Staffordshire. Stoke City FC has a fanzine called *The Oatcake*, which is deemed (by someone) important enough to have its own page on Wikipedia; they celebrate Oatcake Day in August; and although the last 'hole-in-the-wall' oatcake shop closed in 2012, the cakes are still a staple of Sunday morning breakfast and feature in the names of various tea shops and sandwich bars around the county.

However, for the moment I was in Derbyshire and the oatcakes' packet told me they were made from a traditional recipe, delicious grilled or fried. That's presumably as part of the full English, because they are basically a big, thick pancake and I could see that they would be good with baked beans on top. The girl in the shop also recommended using them as a lunchtime wrap – she liked them with chicken salad. Back home some days later I tried one with a curry and found it a very acceptable substitute for the naan bread I had forgotten to buy.

However, oatcakes weren't the reason for my trip to Derbyshire. I was primarily interested in finding out what I could about the Bakewell Pudding, how it differed from a Bakewell Tart, and why the tart had become ubiquitous while the pudding remained a Bakewell speciality.

But my appointments in Bakewell weren't until the afternoon, so there was opportunity to explore other parts of the county first.

When I had started researching cakes for this book I had come across a labour of love called *Old Derbyshire Desserts*, put together by John Dunstan, a Derbyshire-born pastry chef-cum-guitar enthusiast. It included a Bolsover Cake, which he described as being 'in the fine tradition of recipes from Derbyshire using dried fruits'. Bolsover is no more than 45 minutes' drive from Bakewell and we had several hours to spare, so we decided to check it out.

Bolsover is most famous for its castle, a substantial pile atop a substantial hill; it's a genuine medieval ruin turned into a sumptuous and occasionally erotic *pied-à-terre* by a 17th-century playboy. The kind of attraction every town should have. The locals, by the way, historically pronounce the place's name Bozer; though I imagine a fair amount of boozing also went on in the castle's heyday.

Anyway, John's book told me to be sure to try a slice of Bolsover Cake when I visited the castle. My friends and I discussed phoning and checking that they still served it, to save what some would call a wasted journey; then we decided we had time to spare anyway and didn't bother. With hindsight, it was a brilliant decision.

The castle's café – which was light, spacious, airy and altogether a tempting place to sit and eat cake – offered a Victoria Sponge of a height I had rarely seen (only two layers, but each of them a depth that would have been satisfying on its own) and a Coffee and Walnut Cake ditto. But the lady behind the counter, who had lived in Bolsover all her life, had never heard of its having its own cake. Indeed, she said that when she started to work there she had looked for a local speciality and couldn't find one. Fortunately, I had John's book with me and she copied the recipe down.

When I rang up a couple of months later I found that she had made the cake more than once and that it had been very successful. If my friends and I had been sensible and phoned in advance, this wouldn't have happened. If there's a moral in this story, I'm not sure what it is, but I was – there's no grown-up way of putting it – thrilled to bits.

Bolsover Cake

Makes 1 x 25cm cake

450g plain flour
2 tsp baking powder
350g unsalted butter
225g caster sugar
4 medium eggs, beaten
225g each of raisins and currants
55g chopped mixed peel
a few blanched almonds, chopped
a pinch of freshly grated nutmeg
a pinch of fine salt
100ml sherry

1. Preheat the oven to 160°C/325°F/gas mark 3. Grease and line a 25cm diameter round cake tin.

2. Sift the flour and baking powder together into a large bowl. In a separate bowl cream the butter and sugar together until soft, then add about a quarter of the beaten eggs and a tablespoon of the flour mixture. Mix to combine, then add more eggs and flour and continue until all have been used. Stir in the fruit, peel, almonds, nutmeg and salt. Add the sherry and stir until everything is incorporated.

3. Pour the mixture into the prepared tin and bake in the preheated oven for about 1 hour and 30–40 minutes, or until a skewer inserted into the middle comes out clean. Allow to cool completely in the tin before turning out.

There are those who would look at a map and say that going from Hathersage to Ashbourne via Bolsover was very much taking the long way round – but they are the sort of people who would have rung up in advance to save a wasted journey. Let's ignore them.

Ashbourne may not be the prettiest of Derbyshire's towns, but it had two butchers, a fishmonger, a real bookshop and a number of antique shops, so there was plenty for the discerning to spend their money on. There was also a lovely deli called The Cheddar Gorge, where I bought the product I'd come to Ashbourne to try – Spencers Original Ashbourne Gingerbread. I knew that Spencers still had a bakery there but had closed their shop in 2012, so finding The Cheddar Gorge was a happy accident.

As I had discovered in Market Drayton, gingerbread had been popular across the North of England for centuries before the Napoleonic Wars. So it seems frankly unlikely that a busy market town such as Ashbourne should have had to wait until then to get hold of a recipe, but that's the story. Or perhaps they had one, but decided the French version was better. Either way, between 1803 and 1814, 172 French prisoners of war were billeted there. Whether, as legend has it, the POWs included the personal chef of a captured French general whose recipe for gingerbread was copied and adopted into local culinary tradition is open to question, but whether it's true or false it's given the town a unique product.

Ashbourne Gingerbread is paler than many others: from the knowledge of sugar chemistry I'd gleaned in Grantham, I guessed it was cooked at a low temperature. Spencers' version is a pretty-looking biscuit, about 6cm long and 4cm wide with a slightly rounded top, and because of its colour it looks rather like a shortbread. It tastes a bit like one too: a crumbly, buttery, gingery shortbread. Not in the least bit French, but very pleasant nonetheless. This recipe simply cuts the dough into rounds, but there's nothing to stop you being more adventurous with the shape if you want to. It also gives quite a mild ginger flavour – increase the quantity if you prefer your gingerbread stronger.

Ashbourne Gingerbread

Makes about 16

225g self-raising flour
a pinch of fine salt
2 tsp ground ginger
1 tbsp golden syrup
120g unsalted butter
120g soft brown sugar

1. Preheat the oven to 130°C/250°F/gas mark ½. Grease a baking sheet.
2. Sift the flour, salt and ginger together into a bowl. In another, larger, bowl cream the syrup, butter and sugar together, then stir in the flour mixture.
3. Knead the mixture on a lightly floured surface to make a smooth dough. Roll out to a thickness of about 12mm and cut into 5cm rounds. Place these on the prepared baking sheet.
4. Bake in the preheated oven for about 25 minutes, until very lightly brown. Remove from the baking sheet with a spatula, and cool on a wire rack.

Spencers do still have a shop – in Wirksworth, a town that is only marginally off the route from Ashbourne back to Bakewell and Hathersage. Spencers the Baker was tiny and looked the way bakers' shops used to look before I was born, in films starring, perhaps, Jack Warner or Stanley Holloway. Round the corner was The Old Bakehouse, which was still using the same coke-fired ovens it had been using since the 1890s. A lot of Wirksworth looked as if it hadn't changed lately. It had been worth a little detour.

Bakewell is another place where shoppers can have a good time, so I felt safe to abandon my friends for an hour or so. While they looked for birthday presents, my first stop was the Old Original Bakewell Pudding Shop, where puddings have been made and sold since the 1860s. The story – part told to me by Jemma Beagrie, the shop's business manager, and part gleaned from the website bakewellonline.co.uk, which has a page called 'Putting the Record Straight' – goes that the pudding was created by accident at the Rutland Arms, a hotel that still dominates the Square. A waitress who had been called into the kitchens to help out on a busy night made a mistake: she was supposed to be producing a strawberry tart, but forgot to stir her egg mixture into the pastry and instead spread it on top of the jam in the pastry case. A classic was born.

The landlady of the Rutland, Ann Greaves, was friendly with Mrs Wilson, the wife of the local candle maker, who lived in what is now the Old Original Bakewell Pudding Shop. Mrs Greaves apparently told Mrs Wilson the story of the pudding disaster-turned-triumph and either gave her the recipe or inspired her to have a go at it herself.

This story is disputed by some: food historian Ivan Day has found a recipe dating back to 1835, whereas bakewellonline's account puts the invention in the 1850s. A further story says that Will Hudson, the landlord of the Castle – not the Rutland Arms – gave a copy of the original recipe to his good friend, the baker George Bloomer, in order to 'even things out' in the town. George repaid this generosity by giving Will a loaf of bread every day until he died – a promise he may have regretted, as Will lived to be 88. Be that as it may, Bloomers were still there when I visited, several generations on, selling an Original Bakewell Pudding®.

The question of whose Original was the *most* original was obviously a touchy one round the town, so perhaps it was better not to delve too deeply.

What was not in doubt, however, was that Mrs Wilson set up shop in her own home, a building that was already the better part of

200 years old, and started selling the puddings that made Bakewell famous. As Jemma put it, with a gesture embracing the considerable historical charm of her shop and restaurant, 'That's one thing I can say, when other people say, "We've got this history, we've got that history" – you haven't got the history we've got.'

Until 2011, Jemma's puddings were made on the premises, but the business outgrew the space available. They now have a 'brand-new, spanking, fantastic bakery' on an industrial estate in Bakewell – she was determined not to leave town – and have acquired new modern bread-making kit, but the production method for the puddings hasn't changed: it's still all done by hand to Mrs Wilson's original recipe.

That means a puff pastry base (which not everyone uses), a layer of strawberry jam and a topping of eggs, almonds, sugar and butter. The absence of flour keeps it like a custard rather than a cake mix. 'It does set,' Jemma said, 'but it's a sort of loose filling. Particularly when it's warmed up in the oven, it oozes – it's amazing.'

Having sampled one, albeit cold, I agreed wholeheartedly. The pastry was flaky but not greasy; there was a generous quantity of jam; and the pudding part was delicate, not overpoweringly eggy. I'd done a lot of sampling of sweet things by this stage and had moments of feeling jaundiced (I use that word advisedly), but this definitely won a seal of approval.

Despite her enthusiasm for the pudding, Jemma also sells Bakewell Tarts. I'd have thought that the pudding makers of Bakewell would turn their noses up at the common (I use that word advisedly too) tart, but no: 'You have to maximise what your customers want. Very often people who come here don't know the difference between the two, and what better way to explain than to show them how they both look and how they both taste? It's a great way of converting people. They try the tart and say, "I've had that a million times", whereas the pudding is fresh, unique and completely different.'

Leaving Jemma, I went round the corner to the Original Farmers' Market, where Richard Young has made a study of early Bakewell Pudding recipes. It was he who remarked, with a chuckle in his voice, that 'original' was a popular word in Bakewell. His wife Carolyn had just finished making a batch with a difference, containing fresh lemons and peel. She told me, with understandable pride, that a number of French visitors to her shop had compared it favourably with their home-grown *tarte au citron*. The Youngs had also broken with tradition by using a shortcrust base with a bit of puff round the top, which Richard said was less greasy: 'Puff pastry can be greasy, particularly in a slow oven, because you're not crisping it up.'

The 1835 recipe which Ivan Day had found and which Richard also had in his collection uses puff pastry spread with 'a variety of preserves with strips of candied lemon peel' and a custard made from clarified butter, sugar, ten egg yolks and two egg whites, flavoured with bitter almonds, lemon, nutmeg or cinnamon. 'When cold,' it instructs, 'grate white sugar over pudding.' It's recorded that a Mr Stephen Blair paid £5 for this recipe. Indeed, Richard's researches have turned up the fact that the pudding was openly on sale in the town to anyone who would pay that sum for it. Mr Blair must have been very fond of it, or convinced that he could make money out of it, because £5 was a phenomenal sum in 1835 – a month's wages for the best-paid factory worker. But it's interesting to note that in those early days there was a choice of flavourings. So one pudding could be almondy and another cinnamony, yet both could lay equal claim to being authentic. These were deep waters.

In the 1840s the cookery writer Eliza Acton was rather snooty about Bakewell Pudding, despite the fact that her recipe sounds delicious. (Eliza was anti-cake in general, for very modern-sounding health reasons: she referred to them as 'sweet poisons'; blamed them for more illness 'than would easily be credited by persons who have given no attention to the subject' and included as few in her best-selling *Modern Cookery for Private Families* as she felt her readers would let her get away with.) For Bakewell Pudding she used no pastry; instead, she lined her dish with 'quite an inch-deep layer of several kinds of good preserve mixed together' and a generous quantity of candied citron or orange rind. She then added a dash of liqueur (almond or lemon or other flavouring – more scope for debate) to the custard and complained that the result was 'rich and expensive but not very refined'. Superior, she thought, was the Alderman's Pudding made in the South: it had apricot jam only and no candied peel, so was indeed more 'refined' in the sense of having fewer flavours fighting with each other.

The mystery to me, though, was that Bakewell Pudding was still made almost exclusively in Bakewell. I say 'almost' because I'd seen it in Ashbourne, but that's only 30km away – I'd not noticed it further afield. But Bakewell *Tart* is everywhere. How did that come about?

Richard blamed Mrs Beeton. Her *Book of Household Management*, published in 1861, included a recipe for Bakewell Pudding which she described as 'very rich'. It contained puff pastry, jam and the eggs, sugar and butter that go to make a custard, but she added 1oz (just under 30g) of almonds 'which should be well pounded'. In other words, something similar to modern ground almonds, which would have made the custard more solid.

In 1884 a Derbyshire guidebook mentioned 'Bakewell Pudding, a local delicacy, something between a Maid of Honour and a jam tart'. Many recipes for Maids of Honour contain ground rice, ground almonds or even, in 1892, potatoes. Finally, in a cookbook published in 1917, there came a recipe which was not only called Bakewell Tart but contained both flour and baking powder. It also had 12 drops of lemon essence and no almonds, but the real point is that the moment you added flour (or ground almonds or breadcrumbs), you had a solid, cake-like filling, rather than a custard.

As late as 1954, Dorothy Hartley, author of *Food in England*, wrote – ungrammatically and slightly contentiously – that Bakewell Pudding was sometimes called Bakewell Tarts. But she made a point that neatly sums up the discussion:

> *The whole art is in getting this mixture the right soft consistency. More milk may be added to make the custard softer, or a* few *[her emphasis] fine white breadcrumbs to make it set more steadily, but the result, when carefully baked, should be set, but must be quite soft and creamy.*

As to why Mrs Beeton should have committed or promulgated her sacrilege, Richard could only speculate. 'If you watch modern-day chefs,' he said, 'they're all trying to do one better than the other; they take a recipe and do it their way. Or it may be that people started putting something cheaper in it to make it go further.'

So, for example, someone who didn't care for custard might have thought it would be less gooey if they added ground almonds. Maybe some long-forgotten alderman didn't like raspberry jam and expressed a preference for apricot. Or some over-stretched housewife bulked up the family meal with cheap flour or breadcrumbs. These are guesses, but they're all possibilities.

What it boils down to, Richard went on, is that Bakewell Tart was almost certainly never invented as such. It developed. It evolved. Today it is found sometimes with icing and a cherry, sometimes without. And, as anyone who has tried them both will agree, it has little in common with its custardy ancestor.

Like the Old Original Bakewell Pudding Shop, the Original Farmers' Market sold both. Richard's version was a white-iced, cherry-topped Mr Kipling lookalike, which he described as lovely, moist and hand-made. He wasn't in the least bit snobbish about it. 'To me,' he said, 'a Bakewell Tart is a Bakewell Pudding with flour in it. It's as simple as that.'

So here is a slightly updated version of Mrs Beeton's 'very rich' pudding.

Rich Bakewell Pudding

Serves 4–6

110g puff pastry
200g jam of your choice

For the filling
1 medium egg, plus the yolks of 4 more
110g unsalted butter
175g granulated sugar
30g ground almonds

1 Preheat the oven to 220°C/425°F/gas mark 7.

2 Roll out the pastry on a lightly floured board until thin. Line a 21cm diameter loose-bottomed flan tin with this. Prick the base with a fork, line with greaseproof paper and baking beans and bake blind in the preheated oven for 10 minutes. Then remove the paper and beans and cook for a further 5 minutes. Remove from the oven and reduce the temperature to 180°C/350°F/gas mark 4.

3 Spread a generous layer of jam over the bottom of the pastry base.

4 Put the egg and egg yolks into a bowl and beat well. Melt the butter in a small pan, and add to the eggs along with the sugar and the ground almonds. Beat all together until well mixed, then spoon into the dish over the jam.

5 Bake in the preheated oven for 25 minutes, then reduce the oven heat to 160°C/325°F/gas mark 3 and continue baking for another 30–35 minutes, until the filling is just set. If the top appears to be browning too quickly, cover loosely with foil. The pudding can be served cold but is best warm, with the filling oozing from it.

Another place it would be a crime not to visit while in the area was the glorious, multi-award-winning Chatsworth Farm Shop. Home-produced venison, pheasant, bread, jams, beer, local fruit and veg, hand-made chocolates from Holdsworth's in Bakewell – you could spend a *lot* of money in this place and go home very happy indeed. In the cake and pud line, I noticed the Original Buxton Pudding ('hand-made with love from a secret recipe'), a Moorland Pudding containing Bramley apples and winberries, and a Bakewell Brownie, which was a gooey chocolate concoction with the addition of the traditional Bakewell flavours of almond and raspberry. Frankly, despite the list I have just given, I could have spent a lot of money exclusively on Bakewell Brownies and gone home happy.

I didn't, because we had planned to have dinner in the Scotsman's Pack in Hathersage, a pub I'd always had a lot of time for and which I had just learned was owned by Jemma Beagrie and her husband. It was friendly and hospitable and I liked the fact that one of us could stick to the conventional pub fare of steak and kidney pie and chips while another had the more enterprising vegetarian haggis with orange and whisky sauce. It was also – or so I thought at the time – the very last night of my travels and it was worth indulging ourselves just a little.

I did the railway journey from Sheffield to London many times in my student days, and ever since I have felt nostalgic when I look through the window and see the twisted spire of Chesterfield Parish Church. For once, though, on the day I was heading home, my cake researches over, I didn't hark back fondly to younger and wilder times. Instead, I thought, 'Someone ought to come up with a lopsided cream horn and sell it as Chesterfield Church Cake – they'd make a fortune.'

Epilogue

Pontefract Cakes

WHEN I GOT BACK FROM DERBYSHIRE, I thought I might stay at home for a while. I'd researched (and eaten) enough cakes to last me a lifetime and delved into some fascinating histories. Then I discovered that Pontefract, West Yorkshire, home of the Pontefract or Pomfret Cake, held a Liquorice Festival in the middle of July. I know that Pontefract Cake isn't a cake – it's a medallion of liquorice, about 4cm in diameter and a bit under 1cm deep, traditionally stamped with the distinctive image of the town's ruined castle. But Kendal Mint Cake isn't a cake either and I'd found plenty to interest me there.

Besides, I'd never been to Pontefract.

To get there on a Sunday I had to catch a train to Wakefield and then take a bus, which was pleasantly reminiscent of my trip to Cornwall all those cakes ago. I was also back in friendly, sensibly priced country – 500ml of water cost 70p at Wakefield Bus Station (as opposed to £1.35 at King's Cross); for £4.50 I could travel on any bus I liked all over West Yorkshire for the entire day; the bus driver called me 'love'; and a chirpy man giving way to me in the queue suggested that if there wasn't room for all of us I could sit on his knee. As it happened, the bus wasn't crowded and this kind offer wasn't put to the test.

Central Pontefract is cobbled and has wonderfully evocative street names: Gillygate, Baxtergate, Beastfair, even a narrow lane called Ducks

& Green Pease Row. I had a feeling, looking at its abundance of bookies and tattoo parlours, that on a grey day it would be pretty gloomy and run down. But today the weather was glorious, it was just a week since Andy Murray had won Wimbledon, all of Britain seemed cheerful and Pontefract in particular was *en fête*. Or, if you prefer, heaving. Kids in pushchairs carried ice creams in one hand and Mickey Mouse balloons in the other; there was a mini-funfair, a machine that offered you the chance to hit something with a hammer and ring a bell, two lads on extraordinarily tall stilts, a man in a sparkly pantomime dame costume with a bright pink wig that was Marge Simpson in all but colour – everything you could want on a hot and sunny Sunday afternoon. Not to mention stalls everywhere.

The first one I noticed suggested I might volunteer for the Samaritans; the second that I take an interest in de-polluting our oceans; and the third asked a question to which I hadn't previously given any thought: 'Why not have an owl at your wedding?' This was the local birds of prey centre, offering passers-by, suitably gauntleted, the opportunity to stroke a tawny owl. Ten-year-old boys were queuing round the block.

Tempting though it was to join the queue, I reminded myself firmly why I was here and found the stalls telling me about liquorice. It was introduced into the area *c*.1500 by monks who used it for medicinal purposes: it's said to be good for treating wounds, for asthma, coughs and urinary problems, and for freshening the breath. It's also 50 times sweeter than cane sugar, so was a useful natural sweetener too. By the early 17th century, Pontefract Cakes not unlike the kind you still get today were being sold as medicinal pastilles. By the early 18th century, the mayor had forbidden the sale of liquorice cuttings outside the town, giving Pontefract a monopoly over the plant and its trade. You wouldn't have thought that liquorice was a likely candidate for this sort of protectionism, but apparently so.

Then around 1760 an apothecary called George Dunhill had the bright idea of adding sugar to the medicinal pastille and turning it into a sweet. Confectionery history was made. Dunhill's is now part of the Haribo Group, but their Pontefract Cakes are still made locally. They look much as they have looked for centuries – except that the stamp now includes the words 'Haribo Original'.

Just because black is liquorice's natural colour, that doesn't mean it has to stay that way. One stall was selling 'cables' in I-wouldn't-feed-that-to-my-kids hues: the rhubarb and custard flavour was pink and yellow intertwined; the strawberry was a shocking magenta; and one cable was a bright turquoise that just doesn't exist in the food world. The fact that this was labelled 'Blackcurrent' added to the feeling that you'd get an electric shock if you ate it.

Speaking of electricity, I also learned that the electric cable the James Bond villain Jaws famously bit through in *Moonraker* was in fact made of liquorice. From Pontefract. Was there no end to the plant's uses?

It would seem not: I was delighted to find that Davill's of Ripon, whom I'd encountered at the Tastes of Yorkshire festival a month or so earlier, had risen to the occasion by producing a 'special for the show' Liquorice Cake. It was the sort of enterprise that deserved a Royal Warrant, but as those aren't up to me I did the next best thing and bought one. Two layers of a firm sponge containing Pontefract Cakes, sandwiched together with butter cream, topped with rich chocolate icing and decorated with liquorice allsorts, it survived remarkably well being carted around in a hot carrier bag for several hours and was delicious, if a tad battered, the next day.

Across the main road, away from much of the hubbub, lay Friarwood Valley Gardens, which used to be liquorice fields and are nowadays billed as 'Pontefract's hidden treasure'. There, in the pavilion attached to the bowling green, a kindly lady sold me a cup of tea and a scone for less than £1 and tried to persuade me to stay and play Bagatelle or Beetle. She didn't seem to think that coming all the way from London for a couple of hours to talk to people about liquorice was remotely whimsical – she just wanted me to enjoy myself and, ideally, contribute another 50p to her cause. As I was making my excuses and leaving she said, 'Do come back.' She didn't mean in half an hour to join in the games, she meant to Pontefract, her home, this place she was proud of. Pop in any time.

I don't know when or if that's going to happen, but I shall treasure the thought.

Serendipity had been my happy travelling companion throughout this book and she – I like to think it is a she – was with me to the end. When I got back to Wakefield Station I discovered I could catch a train that, in a mere four or five hours, would take me to Exeter or Plymouth. Then I could head down into Cornwall, have a cream tea with the cream on top and start all over again.

It was a tempting thought. But wiser counsels – and the fact that I didn't have a toothbrush with me – prevailed. I stuck to my original plan and got the train that would take me to King's Cross and home. Speeding southwards, though, I wondered about planning another trip in a couple of years' time. After all, when I had started my research, the Aberffraw Biscuit Co hadn't existed and the revivals of Coventry Godcakes and Grantham Gingerbread had been in their infancy. Wouldn't it be fun to go back and see how they all developed? I could find out if anyone in Brighton had latched on to Brighton Buttons and if anyone in Tavistock had realised that having invented the cream tea was something to make a fuss about. I could see if anyone had invented a new local product, like the Melrose Tart and the Norfolk Apple Bun, and if anyone in Aberdeen had discovered the secret of making a half-decent Buttery. I could even pluck up the courage to toss a Dorset Knob.

I'd reached this stage in my schemes when the refreshment trolley came juddering along. The man pushing it was decidedly down in the dumps: no one was buying anything from him, and he had to keep asking people to move their luggage so that he could squeeze past. It was only an hour or so since the scone at the Pontefract bowling green, but I bought a cup of tea and a Kit Kat anyway. It had been a friendly day, a friendly journey since my first foray to Kew all those months ago, and making this commonplace purchase seemed a friendly thing to do. Maybe next time I made this journey they'd be selling Goth Cake or Yorkshire Moggy Cake and this same gloomy man would have something to smile about. You never know.

ACKNOWLEDGEMENTS

It wouldn't have been possible to write this book without the generosity of the many bakers I interviewed. All the following gave their time (and their products) freely and enthusiastically, and I am most grateful to them:

Marion & Pete Symonds of the Portreath Bakery (www.portreathbakery.co.uk)
Laurence Swan of The Bath Bun (www.thebathbun.com)
Dale Ingrams of Sally Lunn's (www.sallylunns.co.uk)
Jo Roberts of Fabulous Welshcakes (www.fabulouswelshcakes.co.uk)
Jen Barrie & Jo Wordsworth of Cwmni Cacen Gri (cwmnicacengri.co.uk)
Dean & Emma Geldart of Tan Lan Bakery (www.tanlanbakery.co.uk)
Ian Edmonds & Diane McDougall of Real Lancashire Eccles Cakes (www.lancashireecclescakes.co.uk)
Gary Newman of Newmans of Radcliffe (www.newmansofradcliffe.co.uk)
John Slattery of Slattery Patissier and Chocolatier (www.slattery.co.uk)
John Barron of Romney's of Kendal (www.kendal.mintcake.co.uk)
Joanne & Andrew Hunter of The Grasmere Gingerbread Shop (www.grasmeregingerbread.co.uk)
Paul Carter of Bryson's of Keswick (www.brysonsofkeswick.co.uk)
Craig Murray of Alex. Dalgetty & Sons (www.alex-dalgetty.co.uk)
John & Linda Bell of the Aabalree Guest House, Dundee (aabalree.com)
Sandy Milne of Fisher & Donaldson (www.fisheranddonaldson.com)
James Stuart of Bells (www.bellsfoodgroup.co.uk)

Anthony Laing of Shortbread House of Edinburgh
(www.shortbreadhouse.com)
Lorna Bennett-Murdoch of Huffkins (www.huffkins.com)
Mo Joslin (www.farmhousekitchen.net)
Chris Howard, Jim Marshall & Clare Woods of Rose's
(www.rosesfinefoods.co.uk)
Jeff Vane of Vane's Bakery, 120 High St and 4 Church St, Dover
(no website)
Alison Wright of Fitzbillies (www.fitzbillies.com)
John Watt ('Grimsby') of Pye Baker of Norwich (pyebaker.co.uk)
Leigh Waite of The Heritage Cake Company
(www.theheritagecakecompany.co.uk)
Steve Prime of Esquires, Coventry
(esquirescoffee.co.uk/author/esquires-coventry)
Philip Brown of Brown's Original Banbury Cakes
(www.banburycakes.co.uk)
Alastair Hawken of Grantham Gingerbread
(granthamgingerbread.com)
Jo Botham of Botham's (www.botham.co.uk)
Steve Simpson of Thomas the Baker (www.thomasthebaker.co.uk)
Jemma Beagrie of the Old Original Bakewell Pudding Shop
(www.bakewellpuddingshop.co.uk)
Richard & Carolyn Young of the Original Farmers' Market
(thefarmersmarketshop.co.uk)

Pat Gould of Shire Foods of Norfolk (www.shirefoodsofnorfolk.co.uk) and Laura Crisp of Bettys (www.bettys.co.uk) also kindly sent me cake and information, and James Shepherd of Aberffraw Biscuit Co (www.aberffrawbiscuits.com) turned up in the nick of time.

In addition, I picked the brains of David Burnett, until recently publisher of Excellent Press, Ludlow; Alan Clark of Clark's Bakery,

Dundee; Jeremy Coote at the Pitt Rivers Museum in Oxford; Ivan Day, food historian extraordinaire; John Dunstan; Ian Jarvis of Pontefract; June Irani; Mared Wyn McAleavey, Curator Domestic Life at St Fagan's National History Museum, Cardiff; and Sian Thomas. I'm also grateful to Kerry Burn of www.onesuffolk.net; Sue Lawrence; Hilary Ransom of the WI; and Greg Stephenson of Cumbria Tourism for permission to use recipes; and to the many friendly and informative people I chatted to at food fairs and in markets, bakeries, delis and cafés as I ate my way around the country.

When you set off to write a book about cake you suddenly find you have *lots* of friends and relations eager to help with research. My thanks to all the following, who came up with ideas, stories, reference books and recipes; provided accommodation and chauffeuring facilities; helped with tastings and recipe testing; and offered enthusiasm, moral support and the occasional long overdue salad along the way. And my apologies to those whose wisdom and witticisms appear in the text as if they were my own: Ann; Anne & Derek; Betty; Brenda & Ken; Carol, John & Blod; Cec; Cherry-Anne & Roger; Elaine; Gill, Chris & Andrea; Jill; Jonathan; Julia & Kit; Julia & Peter; Linda & Andy; Liz; Lois; Mavis & Colin; Muna; Niki, Rod & Callum; Pat & John; Pom & Tim; Roger; Ros & Sam; Rosey & Raj; Sheena & Carl; Sheila & Andy; Sheila & Dave; Sue & Pat.

Once the book is written all sorts of other experts swing into action and in this context I have to thank Donna Wood, Susan Fleming, Joey Clarke, Janet Law, Tracey Butler, Tom Bromley, Jerry Goldie, Becca Thorne, David Wardle and Tory Lyne-Pirkis and Cecilia Keating of Midas PR. Gwenda Brocklehurst, Liz Haynes, Rebecca Needes, David Popey, James Tims, David Watchus and Katie Wilding were also inveigled in to test recipes. I'm grateful to them all.

Finally, my most profound thanks go to Helen and Rebecca, without whom…

BIBLIOGRAPHY

About Tavistock (Tavistock and District Local History Society, 2010)
Ayrton, Elisabeth *The Cookery of England* (André Deutsch, 1974)
Baren, Maurice *How It All Began in the Pantry* (Michael O'Mara, 2000)
Beeton, Isabella & Gerard Baker *Mrs Beeton's Puddings* (Weidenfeld & Nicolson, 2012)
Blythe, Ronald *Akenfield: Portrait of an English Village* (Allen Lane/ The Penguin Press, 1969)
Brears, Peter *A Taste of History: 10,000 years of food in Britain* (English Heritage, 1993)
Brears, Peter *Traditional Food in Shropshire* (Excellent Press, 2009)
Canning, Helen J *A Taste of Shropshire* (Excellent Press, 2012)
Chatterton, Lydia *Modern Cookery Illustrated* (Odhams Press, 1917)
The Country Side of Cooking (Spectator Publications, 1974)
David, Elizabeth *English Bread & Yeast Cookery* (Allen Lane, 1977)
Davidson, Alan *The Oxford Companion to Food* (2nd edition edited by Tom Jaine, Oxford University Press, 2006)
Duff, Julie *Cakes Regional & Traditional* (Grub Street, 2003)
Dunstan, John *Old Derbyshire Desserts* (Rams Head Books, 2008)
English Teatime Recipes (Salmon, 1998)
Fitzgibbon, Theodora *A Taste of Wales in Food and Pictures* (Pan, 1971)
Grigson, Jane *The Observer Guide to British Cookery* (Michael Joseph, 1984)
Hartley, Dorothy *Food in England* (Macdonald, 1954)
Jack, Ian *Pop Goes the Weasel* (Allen Lane, 2008)
Jekyll, Agnes *Kitchen Essays* (first published 1922; Persephone Books, 2001)
Jones, Julia, & Barbara Deer *Cattern Cakes and Lace* (Dorling Kindersley, 1987)
Joslin, Mo *Kentish Fare Recipes* (Maureen Joslin/Kentish Fare, no date)

Lawrence, Sue *On Baking* (Kyle Cathie, 1996)
MacBride, Stuart *Cold Granite* (HarperCollins, 2005)
Martin, Carolyn *Clotted Cream* (Tor Mark, 1999)
Mason, Laura, & Catherine Brown *The Taste of Britain* (Harper Press, 2006)
Mathie, Johanna *Favourite Scottish Recipes* (Salmon, 1996)
Mrs Beeton's Book of Household Management (Oxford World's Classics, 2000, abridged from the original 1861 text)
Norman, Jill *The Complete Book of Spices* (Dorling Kindersley, 1990)
Norwak, Mary *The 5 O'Clock Cookbook: a collection of family recipes for teatime* (Faber & Faber, 1960)
Pybus, Meg *Shropshire's Spicy Secret* (Keith & Meg Pybus, 1988)
Ray, Elizabeth (ed.) *The Best of Eliza Acton* (Penguin, 1974)
Rundell, Maria *A New System of Domestic Cookery* (first published 1806; Persephone Books, 2009)
Seymour, Jean *Lakeland Cookery* (English Lakes Counties Tourist Board, 1971)
White, Florence *Good Things in England* (first published 1932; Persephone Books, 1999)
The WI & Michael Smith *A Cook's Tour of Britain* (Willow Books, Collins, 1984)

Some of my information on Cumbrian Rum Butter came from egremont2day.com; on Simnel Cake from www.foodsofengland.co.uk; on Tottenham Cake from www.tottenhamquakers.org.uk and www.mehstg.com; and on Bakewell Puddings from bakewellonline.co.uk. The details of food sold at the Great Exhibition came from www.studygroup.org.uk. The websites www.bbc.co.uk/food, www.catholicculture.org, www.celtnet.org.uk, www.greenchronicle.com, londoneats.wordpress.com, www.lucycooks.co.uk, www.lynsted.com, www.nationalbakingweek.co.uk, www.spittoonextra.biz and www.visitwales.com were also useful sources.

INDEX